LOVE ALWAYS.
LOVE DAILY.

365 LOVE | Publishing

Copyright © 2012 by Torion Kent

All rights reserved.
No part of this book may be reproduced in any form or by any means without prior written consent of the publisher except brief quotes in reviews.

Cover Design by Svetlana Uscumlic
Illustrations by Lanous Wright, II

ISBN 978-0-9852475-0-8
Printed in the United States of America
First Edition, 2012

Published by 365 LOVE | Publishing
Promoting personal growth in love through creative expression

www.365lovedaily.com
notes@365lovedaily.com or
404-984-4071

To
LOVE
and those who desire to become
more like you

Acknowledgements

The motivation to complete this book is a result of God's love. It is His love that gave me the drive to write every word on every page. He surrounded me with wonderful people who supported and inspired me. He also gave me the resources needed to bring this work to completion. I am grateful for God's grace and mercy and for using me to share love with you and so many others. He receives the highest level of acknowledgement.

I would also like to express a deep sense of gratitude to:

David Kent, Jr., my husband and my best friend, for your unconditional love and support for all that I do. You continued to give me the extra motivation I needed to complete this work. Your unconditional love is a living example of what love is. You compliment me in a way that confirms its true meaning.

Jill Harden, my mother, for your love and my life, for reading my 365 Love messages every day, and for sharing your thoughts on all the notes, music and quotes. Some of our discussions were motivation for a number of messages in this work. I am thankful to you for sharing with me at a time when I was motivated to share with others.

Diamond Wright, my daughter, for using your voice to bring the 365 Love songs I wrote to life so that they can be shared with those who receive inspiration through music, and for continuing to spread love by sharing my 365 Love messages with others. "You are meant for greatness."

Lanous Wright, II, my son, for being a sounding board on the day I shared my 365 Love vision with you and for the grown up love you have inside of you. You continue to amaze me. God guides your hands to create art that astonishes others. I am grateful for your artistic contribution to this work. "You too are meant for greatness."

Evelyn King, my best friend, you are a frequent reminder of how love can and does bring positive change and how contagious it is. Our friendship and your personal evolution is a testimony that the love I have inside of me is being used as a vessel to make a difference to others. I applaud you for allowing love to take over your life so that you can experience the many blessings it has to offer.

Alison Jones, my best friend, for your giving spirit and loving heart. All that you do to show support and encouragement to me and so many others is a true blessing and true demonstration of love. I appreciate the many times you have looked out for me and my family, and the kind gestures you demonstrate to show how much you care on a regular basis.

Christopher Alexander, Kamisha Brown, Suzanne Downing-Jones Geraldine Elam, Ja'Cinta Fed, Alison Jones, Adele King, Trinise Luster, Gwenette Moore, Michael DeLance Thomas, Kimberly Williams and Tom Wilson, a special thanks to each of you for your time and your feedback. You made a difference in allowing me to make a difference to others. Thanks for your inspiration and confirmation that this book was a good thing to do.

365 Love Readers, for all of the e-mail and website comments in response to my daily messages. They are greatly appreciated. Your love for the love I share with you continues to inspire me to share love even more. I love you all.

Have you told someone you loved them today? I have.™

Introduction:
From My Heart to Yours

Today's NOTE

The year 2010 was a year of personal growth for me. I learned a lot more about people, life and love. I also spent a lot of time with family and friends and established new relationships. At that moment in time and still to this day, my home and my heart are filled with love.

I woke up on January 7, 2011 full of excitement. Love was heavy on my mind and I felt I had received a message that revealed part of my life's purpose. I thought about how much love I have inside of me and how much love I have to give. I thought about how much God wants us to love and how much He wants us to share love with others. I also thought about the lives I've touched just by sharing with others how much I love to love, and the many comments I received from family, friends and acquaintances to confirm this. I knew I was meant to share more love with others.

I immediately decided to spend a few minutes of my time each day spreading love– **from my heart to yours**. I named it 365 Love which represents love, all day, every day, all year round. I began by writing daily devotionals with an initial e-mail distribution listing consisting of family members and a few friends, asking that they pass the messages on to others. Over time, the distribution listing grew and grew.

The responses received from my readers inspired me to keep going, from simple responses just saying, "Thanks", to more detailed responses explaining how the 365 Love messages changed their day or their life. From there came the 365 Love website (www.365lovedaily.com) and gift products. I reviewed the content of all the songs I wrote and further evolved 365 Love to include song writing and music publishing. Then the idea of writing this book came. When love is involved, the blessings flow and flow. So, I know there is so much more in store. I can't wait to see what the future holds.

I am excited to share my personal thoughts on love **from my heart to yours.** I pray that the notes uplift you, the music embraces you, and the quotes inspire you. Most importantly, I pray that they support your personal growth in love. Love always. Love daily. 365 Love. ™

Have you told someone you loved them today? I have. ™

Love yesterday, today and future tomorrows, ™
Torion

Message in the MUSIC
Laura Izibor – **From My Heart to Yours**

Note the QUOTE!
"Love is as much of an object as an obsession, everybody wants it, everybody seeks it, but few ever achieve it, those who do will cherish it, be lost in it, and among all, never... never forget it." ---Curtis Judalet

Notes, Music and Quotes

People are inspired in different ways. **Notes, Music and Quotes** are used to deliver daily messages of love in three ways - Today's **Note**, Message in the **Music** and Note the **Quote**!

Today's NOTE

Today's Note is a personal message to inspire you to love. It may be presented in the form of questions to ask yourself or a personal experience. It may be a generic thought about love that everyone should and could experience. It may be a song or a poem. It may be a few simple comments. It is designed to make you think. It is an experience to relate to. It is a representation of love. **Today's Note** is purposely designed to be presented in different ways. The diverse delivery is intended to be interpreted in different ways, received in different ways, and reflected upon in different ways, but the ultimate goal is for everyone to grow in love.

Message in the MUSIC

Some of the most powerful messages and learning experiences are delivered through music. **Message in the Music** is a reinforcement of Today's Note through song. It includes a song title and the associated recording artist. It is suggested that you search the Internet for the song selection referenced so that you can listen to the words and the music. Web sites such as YouTube and Vevo allow you to hear the actual song and see a visual of the song through a music video or live performance. You can also search other Internet music sites such as Yahoo and Pandora if you want to just listen to the song. The wonderful world of music includes so many different genres and artists to choose from. The specific songs referenced in this book are based on the genres of music and recording artists I most frequently listen to. However, as you continue to read Today's Notes and listen to the selected song titles, I encourage you to begin thinking of your own favorite songs and/or other newly explored songs to find the **Message in the Music**.

Note the QUOTE!

Sometimes simple is good. Most often it is the little things my father gives me advice on that make the biggest difference. I recall a time I went to my father for advice on how to deal with people talking about me and telling lies. His response was, "People talked about Jesus." It was as simple as that. I knew what he meant without him having to say anything else and it made a difference, immediately. **Note the Quote!** is a daily quote that relates to Today's Note. It is an additional reinforcement of love, simply put.

Love Always. Love Daily. 365 Love.

Ten (10) Ways to Use This Book

This book is intended to be a resource to support your personal growth in love. It can be used in a variety of ways. Ten suggestions are listed below.

1. Read daily according to the **daily plan**.

2. Read **specific topics** of interest.

3. Read the entire book **at your own pace**.

4. Read the **quotes** for quick motivation to uplift, enlighten your spirits and share with others.

5. Search for and listen to the words and music of the selected song titles and/or find songs of your personal choice related to the topic and **reflect on the message in the music**.

6. **Highlight key points** and refer back to them at a later time.

7. Reflect on the messages and **put a plan in place** on how to use, practice and/or reinforce the concept on a consistent basis.

8. **Write down your own personal experiences** / reflections of love that relate to specific topics.

9. **Have discussions** with others about specific topics.

10. **Purchase additional copies** of the book as gifts for family, friends and coworkers to further promote personal growth in love.

Love Always. Love Daily. 365 Love.

Love Always. Love Daily. 365 Love.

Love Always. Love Daily. 365 Love.

January

"The most important thing in life is to learn how to give out love, and let it come in."

— Morrie Schwartz

Looking to Get There
January 1

Today's NOTE
I am on my way. I purchased my ticket, checked in my luggage, boarded, and I am off. I am ready to begin my journey and I'm **looking to get there**. I have prepared myself for this. It comes to me as no surprise, yet I am ready for any surprises that come along the journey. I am ready to learn. I am ready to grow because I know that this journey will give me so much more than I have at this moment, in this place, and at this time. My destination is a different place than I am now. I am excited for what is to come. I have a window seat so that I can see and enjoy the view along the way. And I am excited just **looking to get there**. And as I travel along my way, I plan to share everything I learn with you. I want you to use my experience as an appendix (or additional reference) to your roadmap. I want you to use it as a testimony to help you along the way when you are ready. I want you to know about the good places and the bad places. I want you to know about the good times and the bad times. I want to share, because I care. I am so excited. I'm **looking to get there**. Better yet, why don't you plan a journey too. It will be an exciting adventure. It doesn't matter which travel method you choose. It's totally up to you, just as long as you too are **looking to get there**. Destination is LOVE. Love always. Love daily. 365 Love. ™

Have you told someone you loved them today? I have. ™

Love yesterday, today and future tomorrows, ™
Torion

Message in the MUSIC
Clark Sisters - **Looking to Get There**

Note the QUOTE!
"Love wholeheartedly, be surprised, give thanks and praise - then you will discover the fullness of your life." --- David Steindl-Rast

---

Love Always. Love Daily. 365 Love.

It's Contagious and It Brings Change
January 2

Today's NOTE

Those who know me well know that my favorite word is "Love." I have tons of t-shirts with the word "Love" on them. I have a "Love" wall in my bedroom with different forms of the word in frames or ceramic tile. I have "Love" jewelry to include necklaces, earrings, bracelets and rings. I have "Love" posted as the screen saver on my home computer. I tell my family and close friends that I "Love" them all of the time. People I have frequent encounters with receive hugs from me with a friendly "Much Love" whisper in their ear. Both of my car tags have the word "Love" incorporated in them. I love "Love" songs and have customized play lists on my computer, iPod and iPhone especially for these types of songs. I "love."

God is Love and that in itself is powerful. Love is a true blessing. It is also a most incredible feeling. So, I believe in it, I live it and I breathe it. My thoughts are at most times positive and filled with it. I sat down and assessed how my love for this word and the feeling itself has spread to others and realized that **it's contagious and it brings change**.

I did not hear, "I Love You" much in my family during my childhood. However, as an adult I noticed that when I began to proactively say it more, my family in turn did the same. Initially, I was the one who was proactive in saying, "I Love You." Now, they are more proactive in saying it. Friends are more proactive in saying those words as part of our good-bye's after an outing, and during a visit or phone conversation. People who know me often tell me that they notice the word more. When they see a t-shirt or picture, they think about me because they know how much I love that word. When in actuality, without even realizing it, in thinking about how much I love the word, they are thinking about "Love" more often also. They read what an object/item has to say about love. They read a quote. They think about what they read and if it is really a good portrayal of the word "Love."

In sharing of myself and how I feel about "Love", it has spread to others, and to others... **It's contagious**. It's addictive. **It brings change**. It made them really think about the word. It was my goal to make anyone who read my car tags think about the word. One tag reads, "Love Is", and the other tag reads, "Love More." I received confirmation that the tags are meeting my intended purpose. A few people read them and initiated conversations with me about "Love." When someone reads a piece of clothing I wear, or a piece of jewelry I have on with the word "love" on it, it puts the thought in their mind if only for the moment. All of these are confirmations that love **is contagious and it brings change**. What are you doing to spread love? Love always. Love daily. 365 Love.™

Have you told someone you loved them today? I have.™
Love yesterday, today and future tomorrows,™
Torion

Love Always. Love Daily. 365 Love.

Message in the MUSIC
Jamie Foxx – **Love Brings Change**

Note the QUOTE!
"Love is just a word until someone comes along and gives it meaning." --- Unknown

The Glass is Always Half Full
January 3

Today's NOTE

When you think about the meaning of Love from a spiritual perspective, you can only think of good and with good is positivity. As you learn how to truly love, you also learn about being positive. What was dark is now light. What was sadness is now happiness. What was suffering is now healing. It's amazing how being filled with love can bring positivity to your way of thinking.

One of my favorite sayings is, "**The glass is always half full**. It's never half empty." Thinking positive becomes a choice. Take every experience, good and bad, and focus on the positive that came from it. Take a relationship that has ended and think about what good came from it. If I look at some of mine, I can list a few.

- I learned more about love.
- I learned to be thankful for the blessing of two beautiful children.
- I learned that a man "can" truly show love to a woman.
- I learned that love involves understanding.
- I learned to let go.
- I learned that I am a strong woman.
- I learned that a truly loving person can bring love out of others.
- I learned that love is contagious.
- I learned that love does not hurt, it listens and understands.
- I learned that everyone has a story.
- I learned that a person's past helps you understand who they are today and helps in determining how to relate to them and/or help them move forward.
- I learned......

What good things can you say you learned? When negative events take place in your life, try to focus more on the good that came from them. I assure you that it will make a difference in how you feel and how you are able to move forward. It will take weight off of your heart. It will bring you closer to love. It will help you grow in the love of yourself and others.

As Joel Osteen once said, "It may look like a setback, but it's really a set up for something better God has in store for you. Nothing happened to you, it happened for you." And always remember, the glass is not half empty, **the glass is always half full**. Love always. Love daily. 365 Love.™

Have you told someone you loved them today? I have.™

Love yesterday, today and future tomorrows,™
Torion

Message in the MUSIC
Mary J. Blige - Just Fine

Note the QUOTE!
"The most important thing in life is to learn how to give out love, and let it come in." ---Morrie Schwartz

Love Me for Me
January 4

Today's NOTE
Love **loves me for me**. It does not love me because I am someone else. It does not love me because it wants me to be someone else. It **loves me for me**. That's what love does. We are all uniquely different. You are you. I am me. We are who we are. Change comes from within. Love allows us to see the change we need to become more like love. Love uses others to show love, share love and give love. That love reflects on others who need love, and plants a seed. That seed is nourished and grows. Love does not force change. Love does not force love. It is natural and takes place when it is time. Your time is your time. My time is my time. When you love someone, love them for who they are today. Pray for who they will become tomorrow as they continue to grow in love. Realize that everyone is different and on their own personal journey. Love you for you. **Love me for me**. Love always. Love daily. 365 Love.™

Have you told someone you loved them today? I have.™

Love yesterday, today and future tomorrows,™
Torion

Message in the MUSIC
Christina Aguilera – Loving Me for Me

Note the QUOTE!
"The beginning of love is to let those we love be perfectly themselves, and not to twist them to fit our own image. Otherwise, we love only the reflection of ourselves we find in them."--- Thomas Merton

Look Like New
January 5

Today's NOTE

I know something that can make you **look like new**. There is no need for you to go to the store to buy additional makeup or new shoes and clothes. There is no need to go to the barber or hair salon to get your hair done. There is no need for a manicure, pedicure or new set of nails. No plastic surgery, tummy tucks or skin care is required. No need to buy a gym membership to work on your abs, arms and thighs. No dental work is required. Your "as is" vision will allow you to see things clearly. The newest super diet is not applicable. Because, all you need is love. When you know love and your actions demonstrate love, love will make you **look like new**. You will feel differently. You will see things differently. People will see you differently. You will have a different outlook on life. And that outlook will be one that is positive. Your light will shine naturally. With love, all of the other physical appearance things will fall into place effortlessly. You will realize that while they are a part of who you are, they are not the substance of who you are. You will be pleased with who you are and will gain new insight on a healthier, natural you, for you. Love always. Love daily. 365 Love.™

Have you told someone you loved them today? I have.™

Love yesterday, today and future tomorrows,™
Torion

Message in the MUSIC
Stephanie Mills - I Never Knew Love Like This Before

Note the QUOTE!
"We've taken an already great product and added a **new look**. We're confident it will appeal to a much wider audience." --- Tom Gorman

---

Love Always. Love Daily. 365 Love.

Message in the Music
January 6

Today's NOTE

I have always had a love for music. As a child, I would close the door to my bedroom and listen to my albums over and over again. I was particularly fond of "love" songs. I didn't realize this at the time, but I learned to love through listening to those songs. You could say that I got the "**message in the music**." Back in the day, there were lots of real singers. You could feel the emotion in their voices. You felt how much love they had for a person. The **message in the music** made you want the same love they had. You understood how they felt or what they were going through. It made you believe in love.

Do you remember these songs? Think about the words and how they made/make you feel.

OLD SCHOOL
- The Commodores – Just to Be Close to You / Still / Jesus is Love
- Luther Vandross – So Amazing / There's Nothing Better Than Love
- Whitney Houston – I Will Always Love You / You Give Good Love

NEW SCHOOL
- Music Soulchild – Love / Don't Change
- Brian McKnight – Still In Love With You / Back at One
- Mary J. Blige – Be Without You / Give Me You
- Michael Jackson – Lady in My Life / Heaven Can Wait
- Maxwell – Lifetime / This Woman's Work

There are so many love songs to choose from. What are some of your favorites? To this very day, I love buying full CDs just to see what undiscovered love songs I can find. I fall asleep listing to "love" songs. I make play list after play list of love songs - general love songs, wedding love songs, love songs about men, love songs about women, love songs for intimate moments, love songs about how to love, love songs about moving on, love songs about..... I also create special playlists for family and friends.

Just think about it. Someone took the time to create the right combination of musical notes and put those specific lyrics down on paper, because they thought about love and wanted to share it with others through song. They put their **message in the music**. They wanted others to know how they felt about "love" – that wonderful word, that beautiful feeling, that emotion that lifts and brightens your day. I want to share it too. The next time you hear a love song, take the time to really listen and reflect on the **message in the music**. Love always. Love daily. 365 Love.™

Have you told someone you loved them today? I have.™

Love Always. Love Daily. 365 Love.

Love yesterday, today and future tomorrows, ™
Torion

Message in the MUSIC
Kelly Rowland – This is Love

Note the QUOTE!
"You don't love someone for their looks, or their clothes, or for their fancy car, but because they sing a song only you can hear." --- Unknown

The Best in Me
January 7

Today's NOTE

Love brings out **the best in me.** It allows me to give. It allows me to live. It allows me to grow. It allows me to know. It allows me to share. It allows me to care. It allows me to learn. It allows me to earn.

When you are in love, you find yourself doing things that you may have never done before. You sometimes find yourself giving more of yourself than you ever have. There is a spirit in you that makes you want to give. If you think about the five love languages – acts of service, quality time, gifts, physical touch, and words of affirmation – you find yourself giving more of each of these. It comes naturally and the best of each love language comes out of you. As I grew in love and as a woman over these years, I noticed how different I was as I experienced a "new" love. **The best in me** came out each time. I gave of myself in ways that even surprised me. When another person loved me deeply in return, unselfishly, manly, openly, honestly, willingly, caringly, spiritually, devotedly…..,it brought out even more of **the best in me**.

I had the pleasure of meeting some wonderful men over the past three years prior to writing this book. Each of them showed me a different kind of love that brought out **the best in me** and I learned from each experience. I feel that I brought out the best in them as well.

- I brought out a regular smile, when this was something that was not often done
- I brought frequent positivity in their lives (the glass is always half full)
- I brought family fellowship
- I brought a new way of communicating – openly and lovingly, without arguments
- I brought love, love, love ….through the use of the five love languages, spiritual affirmation, and more

While I may not have the same relationship with those men today, I learned from each of them and they helped me grow. I am blessed to have had them enter my life to confirm a man's love for a woman and allow me to show a unique kind of love to and for a man. I am thankful to them for sharing themselves with me and helping to bring out **the best in me**. It made me that much better, that much stronger, that much wiser, that much more knowledgeable, and that much more of a great woman.

Love uplifts and supports. It is patient and kind. It magnifies and inspires. It listens and learns. All of these things and more help bring out the best in a person. They bring out **the best in me**. Instead of focusing on the negative, helping a person see the positive in every situation brings out their best.

Love Always. Love Daily. 365 Love.

Listening to their ideas and encouraging them to move forward with them brings out their best. Recognizing the things they do well and reminding them of that on a regular basis brings out the best in them. Telling them you love them on a daily and frequent basis brings out the best in them. When everything around them seems to be going wrong, reminding them of what is going right brings out the best in them. When they feel their world is crumbling, reminding them that God loves them and so do you, brings out the best in them. LOVE brings out the best in them. Love brings out **the best in me**. Love brings out the best in you too. Love always. Love daily. 365 Love.™

Have you told someone you loved them today? I have.™

Love yesterday, today and future tomorrows,™
Torion

Message in the MUSIC
Marvin Sapp – **The Best in Me**

Note the QUOTE!
"I love you not because of who you are, but because of who I am when I am with you." ---Roy Croft

Love Always. Love Daily. 365 Love.

The Voice Within
January 8

Today's NOTE

Love includes trust. That includes trusting yourself. Trusting yourself is a part of loving yourself. When you love yourself, you learn to listen to **the voice within**. You know what you know and you follow through with what you know. What you don't know, you find out more about in an effort to make the best decision possible. You have to trust **the voice within** when it comes to love. You have to love yourself enough to listen, act, and react. **The voice within** is guided by love and is built on strong faith. **The voice within** knows what is right and wrong. **The voice within** knows what is good and bad. **The voice within** can tell you what to do and what not to do. And when you truly love and love yourself, **the voice within** will guide you in the right direction. It will provide positive guidance. It will help you make the best decisions. And those decisions will always be aligned with love. You have to trust it. You have to listen to it. You have to react to it. You have to act on it. Love always. Love daily. 365 Love.™

Have you told someone you loved them today? I have.™

Love yesterday, today and future tomorrows,™
Torion

Message in the MUSIC

Christina Aguilera - **The Voice Within**

Note the QUOTE!

"If you have an opportunity to use your voice, you should use it." --- Samuel Jackson

---

Love Always. Love Daily. 365 Love.

Stairway to Heaven
January 9

Today's NOTE
Are you preparing to climb the stairway? What stairway you ask? The **stairway to heaven**. The **stairway** is always present, but is not always being used. This is a special **stairway**. It doesn't matter what age you are or what your physical condition is. There are no limitations on who can or cannot climb based on their abilities. All you have to do in order to climb the **stairway to heaven**, is choose to do so. You must choose love. Love puts you on a path to climb the **stairway to heaven**. It will not be an easy task to get to the top. You will get started and tumble back down a few steps from time to time. You may get stuck on a step. You may get tired and feel you cannot reach the top. You may feel the steps are too small or too large. But you can still choose to get back up, continue and move forward on the **stairway to heaven**. It is the best direction to go in. It is a great journey to climb. And when your journey is complete, the top you will reach. Are you ready to start climbing? Have you already begun your journey? If you haven't started already, it's not too late to begin. Start now. Continue now. Don't ever give up. Keep climbing **the stairway to heaven**. Love always. Love daily. 365 Love.™

Have you told someone you loved them today? I have.™

Love yesterday, today and future tomorrows,™
Torion

Message in the MUSIC
O'Jays - **Stairway to Heaven**

Note the QUOTE!
"There is only one path **to heaven**. On Earth, we call it love." --- Karen Goldman

---

Love Always. Love Daily. 365 Love.

What Matters Most
January 10

Today's NOTE

I love to read motivational books. This includes, but is not limited to, those about leadership, love of self and others, and spiritual guidance. They serve as reminders of things I already know and aide in personal growth. They also assist in helping me to understand myself and others. When I read these types of books, I like to highlight specific thoughts that I may want to further reflect on, come back to as a reminder at a later time, or share with others. I like to think of them as the "ah-ha" comments.

My mother gave me a book titled, *The Purpose Driven Life by Rick Warren*. In summary, the book helps you to understand why you are here and God's plan for you. It's a 40 day spiritual journey to help you discover God's purpose in life for you. I held on to the book for years, but never read it until 2007. This book kept coming up as I met new people. One day, an old friend was visiting, saw the book on my bookshelf, and mentioned how good it was. At that moment, I felt God was sending me a message that it was time for me to move forward with reading this book. It came up too many times, too often, from "different" people. I finally read it and immediately began to share it with others. I bought copies to give as birthday gifts and for other occasions. I realized that when it was originally given to me, I was not prepared for what it had to offer. It was meant for me to read the book at that particular moment in my life.

Because I love to love, Chapter 16 was one of my favorites – **What Matters Most**. The chapter begins – "Life is all about love. Because God is love, the most important lesson he wants you to learn on earth is how to love. It is in loving that we are most like him, so love is the foundation of every command he has given us." Additional topics in this specific chapter include – The Best Use of Life is Love, The Best Expression of Love is Time, and The Best Time to Love is Now.

I have shared this specific chapter with family and friends and asked that they really think about its content.

- Do you love as much as you could?
- Do you spend quality time with those that matter?
- Do you think about love and have a desire to truly love now? Or is it when it is convenient?

Love truly is **what matters most**. Think about how you feel when you know that you are in love. It is a phenomenal feeling. Go beyond the love of another person and think about how you feel when you think about how much you love God and how much you know He loves you. Think about how you feel when you know that you are loved by your family members and close friends. Think about when a child expresses his or her love to you with something simple. Think about the love of a pet. Nothing else matters at that particular moment. No worries, no pain, no hurt. Nothing else matters. The feeling is so overwhelmingly good, that it is a confirmation of **what matters most** at that time. We can learn to love all the time and have that feeling all the time. God wants that for us. I want it for us too. Want it for yourself. Love always. Love daily. 365 Love.™

Have you told someone you loved them today? I have.™

Love yesterday, today and future tomorrows,™
Torion

Message in the MUSIC
Janet Jackson – Doesn't Really Matter

Note the QUOTE!
"Love means living the way God commanded us to live. As you have heard from the beginning, his command is this: Live a life of love." --- 2 John 1:6

Do You Know?
January 11

Today's NOTE
There is so much that love provides, yet at the same time, there is so much that is not realized.

Do You Know?
Do you know that love loves you?
Do you know that love is in you?
Do you know that love is for you?
Do you know that love gives?
Do you know that love lives?
Do you know that love gives time?
Do you know that love saves lives?
Do you know that love is kind?
Do you know that love is divine?
Do you know that love shares?
Do you know that love cares?
Do you know that love is always on time?
Do you know that loves shines?
Do you know that love brings forth each day?
Do you know that love makes a way?
Do you know that love plants seeds?
Do you know that love provides everything you need?
Do you know?
© 2011

Love always. Love daily. 365 Love.™

Have you told someone you loved them today? I have. ™

Love yesterday, today and future tomorrows,™
Torion

Message in the MUSIC
Michelle Williams - **Do You Know**?

Note the QUOTE!
"All, everything I understand, I understand because I love." --- Leo Tolstoy

---

Love Always. Love Daily. 365 Love.

I Love Your Smile
January 12

Today's NOTE

A friend forwarded me a song in response to a previous song used for the *Message in the Music*. The song was titled, "**I Love Your Smile**" by Shanice. She informed me that it was one of her favorite songs and the message in the music made her think about love. It also reminded her of my smile. The song is simple and expresses love through thoughts of a person's smile. Little did she know, it was one of my favorite songs from the past as well.

I love to smile. It just makes me feel good inside. There's no better way to start your day off than by spreading love with a simple smile. It does not take much effort and it does not cost a thing. Think about how you feel when you smile. Think about how you feel when you:

- see others smile at you
- wake up and smile at your loved one to say, "good morning"
- smile as you're saying, "hello"
- see a smile on a child's face
- smile because you see an old friend or loved one

Have you ever realized that when another person smiles at you, it often times makes you smile back? You do it without even realizing it.

I frequently get comments from people saying that I smile all of the time, or "**I love your smile**." Some may compliment me that it is a good thing. Others may ask me, "Why?" My response is, "It just makes me feel good." I sometimes respond, "Why not?" or "I want to pass it on and make others smile too." Their response is typically a big smile in return. And that's the response I am looking for. **I love your smile** too. A person looks so much happier with a smile. It brings life into the room. It makes for a much happier face. For that moment, you feel good. It brightens the day. It uplifts and adds joy to the moment. Keep doing it and you feel good all the time. It works for me. Try it for you. Are you smiling just thinking about the love that comes from a smile? I am. Love always. Love daily. 365 Love.™

Have you told someone you loved them today? I have. ™

Love yesterday, today and future tomorrows,™
Torion

Message in the MUSIC
Shanice – **I Love Your Smile**

Note the QUOTE!
"Always remember to be happy, because you never know who's falling in love with your smile." --- Unknown

Better Than Gold
January 13

Today's NOTE
Love is **better than gold**. You may feel that its monetary value cannot match up against the price of gold, but I beg to differ with you. Love has a much greater value than gold or any other precious metal. It can be shared limitlessly. It does not spread thin. It cannot be crushed or lost. It keeps on giving. It can be found anywhere and everywhere. It shines all over with its own unique glow. And the beholder magnifies it even more. You can always see it. And those who have it gain more love when they give it and share it. Love is **better than gold** anytime, any day. Its value is in the hearts of those who have faith and believe. Love always. Love daily. 365 Love.™

Have you told someone you loved them today? I have.™

Love yesterday, today and future tomorrows,™
Torion

Message in the MUSIC
Yolanda Adams - **Better Than Gold**

Note the QUOTE!
"We don't love to be loved in return. We love to love." --- Leo Buscaglia

Beauty
January 14

Today's NOTE
Have you ever noticed how much more beautiful a person is when you're in love with them? That's because there is **beauty** in love. I was discussing the song "**Beauty**" by Dru Hill with a friend.

> *"Walks by me every day. Her and LOVE are the same.*
> *The woman has stolen my heart and **Beauty** is her name."*

And if you know the rest of the song, you're aware of how much in love with **Beauty** this man is. He sees **beauty** in her smile. He sees **beauty** in the way she talks. He sees **beauty** in how she walks. He notices the simple things about her that make her beautiful and because of her **beauty**, he is willing to give of himself to fill her heart with love.

They say that **beauty** is in the eyes of the beholder. Well, love brings out **beauty** too. Not just the love of another, but a loving person represents **beauty** too. Think about people you know who are kind hearted, uplifting, nice, peaceful, caring, and giving. You see the **beauty** in them as a whole. All of these words are used to describe love. And that **beauty** does not necessarily describe their outer appearance. It describes their inner spirit, their character. And when you see them, you think of love and **beauty**. Who do you know in your circle of friends or family members that can be best described as **"Beauty?"** Love always. Love daily. 365 Love.™

Have you told someone you loved them today? I have.™

Love yesterday, today and future tomorrows,™
Torion

Message in the MUSIC
Dru Hill – **Beauty**

Note the QUOTE!
"You don't love a woman because she is beautiful, but she is beautiful because you love her." --- Unknown

It Listens
January 15

Today's NOTE
Communication is an important part of love. It involves being able to express oneself to others. **It** also **listens**. It hears, it understands and **it listens**. This includes listening to yourself and listening to others.

I've listened to friends and loved one's talk about frustrations in their relationships. The relationship may have been with a friend, family member, coworker, boss, etc. Quite a bit of that frustration stemmed from lack of or ineffective communication. Some people think that because they tell a person how they feel, they are communicating. They don't understand the response they may or may not receive as a result of it, but in the process, they didn't really **listen** to themselves. Some feel that because they hear what is said, they are communicating, but in the process, they did not really **listen**. When you love you must first be able to **listen** to yourself. You must also be able to **listen** to others. With listening comes understanding. It's not what you say, it's how you say it. It's not about just participating in the conversation, it's about truly listening.

How well you **listen** to yourself and others determines the outcome of the communication effort. When you love, you think about what you say and how you say it. You **listen** to yourself. When you love, you hear what the other person is saying and you **listen** to them.

Words can have both a positive and a negative impact. They can heal a wound or cut like a knife and create one. They can bring tears of joy or tears of pain. They can bring understanding or bring about anger. They can encourage more open communication or cause a shut down that prevents a person from saying anything at all. They can make you happy or frighten you. They can make you **listen** or bring about deaf ears. They can make the difference in holding on to the love of your life or losing them completely.

The next time you communicate with someone and you really want them to hear, you really want them to **listen**, think about what you are saying and how you are saying it. **Listen** to yourself first. That's what love does. **It listens**. The next time someone wants to talk to you, make sure you are listening. Don't interrupt; don't talk over them, open your heart and your ears to understand. That's what love does. **It listens**.

If communication is broken in your relationship, look at yourself first and think about how you communicate. Did your communication cause a shut down in the other person? Were you kind or cut throat? Did you **listen** to yourself first? Are they open to talking to you or do they no longer communicate? Did you truly **listen** when the other person expressed themselves to you? Were you receiving of the information with understanding or did you just get angry? It all makes a difference.

Love Always. Love Daily. 365 Love.

As a final note.... Don't lose out on love because you fail to **listen** to yourself and others. Love **listens**. Love always. Love daily. 365 Love.™

Have you told someone you loved them today? I have.™

Love yesterday, today and future tomorrows,™
Torion

Message in the MUSIC
Beyonce – **Listen**

Note the QUOTE!
"Listening is an attitude of the heart, a genuine desire to be with another which both attracts and heals." --- J. Isham

The Potter's Story
January 16

Today's NOTE

The Potter's Story is a familiar one to me. I've heard it a number of times, in a number of different, but similar ways. For those who are not familiar with this story, it goes something like this...

There was once this big glob of not so attractive clay that nobody wanted. One day, a man came along and scooped up the clay. He took it home and began to shape and mold it. The clay wanted the man to stop, because it hurt so badly, but the man replied, "Not yet." Next, the man put the clay in the oven. It was extremely hot in there. The clay wanted to get out of the oven really badly. The man replied, "Not yet." When the clay was taken out of the oven, it was placed on the counter to cool off and rest. Just when the clay thought it was over, the man picked it up and began to paint it. The paint was sticky and wet. It was not a pleasant feeling at all. The clay wanted it to stop, but the man replied, "Not yet." Next, the clay was put in the oven at an even hotter temperature than before. The clay wondered why it was being put though so much and felt that it could not take it anymore. It was just fine being that big glob of clay. It wanted to get out, but the man replied, "Not yet." Finally, the man took the clay out of the oven to let it cool. Later, the man picked up a mirror and allowed the clay to see itself. It was now a beautiful piece of pottery. It was ready to fulfill its purpose.

I would typically relate the story to God's love for us and his desire to keep working on us until we are shaped to fulfill the purpose he has for us. I would also relate it to how we go through trials and tribulations so that we can become better as a person. Today, I reflected on the story a little differently. Today, I was able to see how love can help us see things in others that they themselves do not. Through love, we live out **The Potter's Story** in our own special way. Through love, we motivate, inspire, guide, share, encourage, uplift, and praise to help others reach their fullest potential. When we love, with love, and through love we become a positive influence, we bring out the best in others; we begin to open our eyes and are able to see what can be. That's what love can do. And when we love, we do it too.

Do you have a **Potter's Story** to tell? Have you been **the Potter** for someone? Has someone been **the Potter** for you? Remember that God uses us and others to fulfill a purpose. Love is good. God is good. God is love. Enough said. Love always. Love daily. 365 Love.™

Have you told someone you loved them today? I have.™

Love yesterday, today and future tomorrows,™
Torion

Message in the MUSIC
Mario – Do Right

Note the QUOTE!
"Let no one ever come to you without leaving better and happier. Be the living expression of God's kindness: kindness in your face, kindness in your eyes, and kindness in your smile." --- Mother Teresa

I Have a Dream
January 17

Today's NOTE
As the world celebrated Dr. Martin Luther King, Jr. day this week, I reflected upon the famous **"I Have a Dream"** speech. I thought about its purpose and the character of the deliverer of this profound message. I thought about the people who gave of themselves for a just cause during the civil rights era. I thought about where we have come from and where we are today. I thought about history. Most importantly, I thought about love.

The **"I Have a Dream"** speech touched the heart of millions at that specific moment and on that specific day. It still does today. It stemmed from a desire to be treated as civil human beings. The desire to be allowed the rights and freedoms granted to us by God. It was spoken out of love for fellow man. All of the events that lead up to Dr. King making that speech were based on a willingness to "give" of oneself for a greater cause. That's love. It was a natural desire to "give" unselfishly and charitably. That's love. It was a combined effort of people loving each other enough to take a stand and do something about it. They were acting as Potters for so many of us. That's love.

As a little girl, **I had a dream** to be happy when I grew up. That's it. Simple as that. I stuck with it and continued to reach for it. Love brings happiness and I have found that. I continue to grow in it and it continues to fill my life with joy. Through love, we earn the right to create our own **"I Have Dream"** speech. On this day, I challenge you to make a conscience choice to love. Make a choice to be love, to share love, to give love, to want love, and to desire love. Love always. Love daily. 365 Love.™

Have you told someone you loved them today? I have.™

Love yesterday, today and future tomorrows,™
Torion

Message in the MUSIC
Brandy – One Voice

Note the QUOTE!
"Love is that condition in which the happiness of another person is essential to your own." --- Robert A. Heinlein

---

Love Always. Love Daily. 365 Love.

There Could Never Be Another You
January 18

Today's NOTE

You were created as a unique individual. There is no one else like you. Your hair, your eyes, your ears, your nose.... **There could never be another you**. You have unique qualities in you. This includes qualities you are aware of and those you are not. Your smile, your character, your talents, your looks, your body, your athletic ability, your work ethic, your creativity, etc. are uniquely yours and yours alone. Others love the unique qualities in you. You should love those qualities too. **There could never be another you**.

Each of us has something special to share with others. We are placed in the position to share our life experiences with others for a purpose. God uses us to fulfill that purpose for ourselves and others. You are uniquely special and your unique qualities have, can and will make a difference to someone.... yesterday, today, and/or in future tomorrows. **There could never be another you**.

Whenever you begin to think about what you are not, change that frame of thought and begin to think about what you are. **There could never be another you**. Whenever you begin to think about what you cannot do, change that frame of thought and begin to think about what you can do. **There could never be another you**. Whenever you begin to think that no one loves you, change that frame of thought and begin to think about who you love. **There could never be another you**. Whenever you hold your head down in disappointment, change that frame of thought and lift your head up with a desire to learn and move forward. **There could never be another you**. Because you are uniquely you, I love you and others love you too. Love always. Love daily. 365 Love.™

Have you told someone you loved them today? I have.™

Love yesterday, today and future tomorrows,™
Torion

Message in the MUSIC
Brian McKnight – **Another You**

Note the QUOTE!
"To the world you may be just one person, but to one person you may be the world." ---Brandy Snyder

---

Love Always. Love Daily. 365 Love.

Understanding
January 19

Today's NOTE

Part of loving others is to have **understanding**. This includes **understanding** where a person came from, why they are who they are, where they are today, and where they are going. **Understanding** also involves meeting the other person half way. There is sometimes a level of compromise involved. So often, people express themselves, but fail to listen and respond with **understanding**. Love listens and understands. When you take the time to truly understand, you grow in love. Love and **understanding** do not always require that you remain in the same space, the same place or the same situation. They allow you to continue as is, move forward and/or move on. In doing so, it brings about peace in your heart. Love and u**nderstanding** also bring about positive change in yourself and others.

When you are involved in any relationship with a friend, family member, boyfriend/girlfriend, spouse, associate, etc., use love to help you understand and make the best of all situations. When there is love and **understanding**, it becomes a win-win situation for all involved. Use it with love and in an effort to grow in love.

Before you continue your day, respond to these questions:

- When you listen to others, do you take the time to reflect and truly understand them?
- Do you think about what is really being said?
- Do you control your natural desire to react immediately or become defensive?
- Do you love with **understanding**?
- In **understanding**, did you change a behavior to better the situation?

Have you taken the time to love, listen and understand someone today? Love always. Love daily. 365 Love.™

Have you told someone you loved them today? I have.™

Love yesterday, today and future tomorrows,™
Torion

Message in the MUSIC
Xscape – **Understanding**

Note the QUOTE!
"Inside the heart of each and every one of us there is a longing to be understood by someone who really cares. When a person is understood, he or she can put up with almost anything in the world." --- Ed Hird

The Potential of Every Man
January 20

Today's NOTE
I love all of the good things about men. I love all the positive things about men. Regardless of previous experiences and lessons learned, I will never give up on them. When you love, you have faith. And with faith comes more love. Because I love, I never allow anyone to make me give up on it. And neither should you. There are good men (and women). And they have qualities that make you want to love them, be loved by them and stay in love with them. For everything they are and are not, I see great potential in them.

The Potential of Every Man (POEM)

The POTENTIAL OF EVERY MAN
Goes beyond what you may say or do
Being a child of God alone
Speaks countless words of the greatness in you
Your strength, your courage
Your ability to love and romance
Explore the mind of a woman to make her want to dance
In her thoughts of the POTENTIAL OF EVERY MAN

Your intellect, your skills that have been untapped
Your growth of knowledge
Gained from the present and the past
And just the thought of all the things you can do
Helps define the beauty of the potential in you

And when I think of your potential
I get a feeling of warmness inside
My mind, my body, my inner thighs
A tap into my soul at the thought of your inner strength
A sense of peace, serenity, and bliss
Creative, yes indeed you are
Boldness brighter than a mid night's star
Your real trueness helps me to better understand
More about my thoughts on the POTENTIAL OF EVERY MAN

You can create great things within the touch of your hands
Teach a young boy how to become a real man
Your inspiration, vision, depth and insight

Love Always. Love Daily. 365 Love.

Your faithfulness, your love of life
Your spirituality and fear of God
Your uniqueness is great, not fake or odd
Nice, that's you
And the greatness of the potential in you

You have the ability to do great things
And God will protect you with His angel's wings
He has a definite plan for you
Knowing all of who you are and what you are meant to do
He will unleash what has been destined as your life's plan
Because He knows your true destiny
And the full **POTENTIAL** **OF** **EVERY** **MAN**

© 2007

Love always. Love daily. 365 Love.™

Have you told someone you loved them today? I have.™

Love yesterday, today and future tomorrows,™
Torion

Message in the MUSIC
Angie Stone – **Brotha**

Note the QUOTE!
"These three things continue forever: faith, hope, and love. And the greatest of these is love." --- I Corinthians 13:13

Love Always. Love Daily. 365 Love.

Act On It
January 21

Today's NOTE

I've shared many different views on love. I've presented questions to make you think about how you love, how others love, and how to grow in love. Now it's time to think of ways to **act on** love. **Act on** love today. **Act on it**, right here and right now! As the old saying goes, "Actions speak louder than words."

Love is the ultimate "**it**" that we should all learn to **act on**. To **act on** love you should.....

- Love it
- Embrace it
- Choose it
- Want it
- Believe in it
- Desire it
- Pray for it
- Relate to it
- Understand it
- Receive it
- Don't be afraid of it

- Care for it
- Don't let go of it
- Hold on to it
- Share it
- Spread it
- Smell it
- Need it
- Dream it
- Receive it
- Be it
- Think it

- Use it
- Don't abuse it
- Talk about it
- Tell it
- Listen to it
- Touch it
- Feel it
- Hug it
- Breathe it
- See it
- Love to love it

When you **act on** love, you put things in motion to become a better you and bring out the best in others. It brings you closer to peace and happiness. It brings you closer to God's desire for all, to love and love others. Love always. Love daily. 365 Love.™

Have you told someone you loved them today? I have.™

Love yesterday, today and future tomorrows,™
Torion

Message in the MUSIC
Musiq Soulchild – **Today**

Note the QUOTE!
"Don't ask God to guide your footsteps if you are not willing to move your feet." -- Unknown

---

Love Always. Love Daily. 365 Love.

Always
January 22

Today's NOTE

It's so easy to get caught up in the negative. When you look at the news, there is a stronger focus on negative things going on in the world than positive things going on in the world. A fire, a crime and a wreck are examples of not so positive things. I don't ever recall listening to the news and hearing 100% positive. Then you can look at life events that take place in everyday households.... A child gets in trouble with the law, a divorce, a family member dies, someone loses their job, a relationship has turned for the worst ..... I could go on and on. While these things give an initial appearance of being negative, are they really? When you are strong in faith and love, you see these situations differently. Remember, the glass is **always** half full. It's never half empty. When you are filled with love, you begin to think more positive about things. It's **always** easier for you to let go. It's **always** easier for you to move on. It's **always** easier for you to believe that things are going to be OK, regardless.

Love is a choice. You can make a conscious decision to choose it every day. Never let a negative situation make you give up on love. **Always** choose it. God is love and **always** know that God is in control. He will never give up on you and He will **always** love you. He has a plan for each of us and these everyday events are a part of his plan. Through love you believe, and through belief the impossible can happen.

Never let a negative situation remain a negative. **Always** think about love and find the positive in it. **Always** find a lesson learned from it. **Always** look for what love brought out of it. **Always** think about how love can change it. **Always** think about how love can make you grow and become a better person as a result of it. **Always** think about love. **Always**... Love always. Love daily. 365 Love.™

Have you told someone you loved them today? I have.™

Love yesterday, today and future tomorrows,™
Torion

Message in the MUSIC
Kirk Franklin – **Always**

Note the QUOTE!
"It's not the magnitude of our actions, but the amount of love that is put into them that matters." --- Mother Teresa

E.N.S.
January 23

Today's NOTE

I often hear people express the desire to give up on love when they encounter one bad relationship after another. I've heard comments about "never" loving another again, "never" opening the heart to let someone in and "never" trusting another person. I've also heard, "I don't need anybody" in my life. Each of these could include relationships with family, friends or romantic companions.

Well, I am here to tell you that **Everybody Needs Somebody (E.N.S.)**. God put us on this earth to love. He specifically created Eve so that Adam would not be alone. He does not want any of us to be alone.... **Everybody Needs Somebody (E.N.S.)**. Love brings us closer to others. Love allows us to share hopes and dreams. Love lifts us up when we are down. Love helps us to encourage others. Love takes care of basic needs and because of it, **Everybody Needs Somebody (E.N.S.)**.

People come in our lives for a reason, a season or a lifetime. The key here is that they "come into our lives." **Everybody Needs Somebody (E.N.S.)** to love. **Everybody Needs Somebody (E.N.S.)** to experience life's challenges to become stronger individuals. **Everybody Needs Somebody (E.N.S.)** to make a difference in who they are, and what they are destined to be. **Everybody Needs Somebody (E.N.S.)** to learn from and to teach. **Everybody Needs Somebody (E.N.S.)**.

Never close yourself off to the thought of loving others. That's not what God wants us to do. He is love, His greatest gift is love, and His purpose for us is to love. We are to love Him, ourselves and others. Love is not just something we want, it's something we need. In order to grow in it, and experience it, everybody needs it..... **Everybody Needs Somebody (E.N.S.)**. Love always. Love daily. 365 Love.™

Have you told someone you loved them today? I have.™

Love yesterday, today and future tomorrows,™
Torion

Message in the MUSIC
Keite – **Everybody Needs Somebody**

Note the QUOTE!
"We are all born for love... it is the principle existence and it's only end." --- Benjamin Disraeli

The Greatest Gift
January 24

Today's NOTE

The greatest gift you can give or receive is love. Just think about it for a moment. The gift of love is everlasting. There is no price tag that you can put on it. You can't throw it away or lose it. It's just there. And it follows you wherever you go when you have it in you or receive it from others.

When you reflect on some of the happiest moments in your life.....quality time, a special gift, a kind word of affirmation, physical touch, and/or an act of service...you find that those moments existed because of love. Hence, the five love languages are components of some of **the greatest gifts** one can provide. Most people think of a gift as a material item. However, through love, gifts can stretch beyond the imagination.

- When your child gives you a card that s/he made in school. They put their all into it and deliver it to you with a "huge" smile of their face. They put their love into it. Wow! That's **the greatest gift.**

- When your family member or friend just gives you a call out of the blue to let you know that you were thought of. That's love.... **the greatest gift.**

- When you are having financial difficulties, and all of a sudden a check comes in the mail, or a friend is able to lend a helping hand. That's love....**the greatest gift.**

- When you are having a bad day, and out of the blue, someone does something nice for you. They share a smile, they provide you with words of encouragement, they stop by to give you a hug, or they invite you to lunch or some other special place. They lift your spirits without even knowing it. That's love....**the greatest gift.**

- When you look up into the sky and see the sun shining. The air is fresh and the day is simply beautiful. That's God's natural gift to us. That's love...**the greatest gift.**

The greatest gift is not always in what we can see or touch. It is pure love. Today and every day I encourage you to love. If there is no other gift you have to give, you should always know that when you choose to love, and share love with others, you are able to give **the greatest gift** anyone could ever receive. Love always. Love daily. 365 Love.™

Have you told someone you loved them today? I have.™

Love yesterday, today and future tomorrows,™

Love Always. Love Daily. 365 Love.

Torion

Message in the MUSIC
Tamica Scott – **The Greatest Gift**

Note the QUOTE!
"These three things continue forever: faith, hope, and love. And the greatest of these is love." --- I Corinthians 13:13

God Must Love You
January 25

Today's NOTE
Look at you. You are one magnificent being. You have a specialness in you like no other. You a filled with an inner quality that makes you, you. Where ever you are right now, whatever you are doing right now, and whatever you are going though right now, know that **God must love you.** He has to. Look at all that you have and all that you have become. Think about what is forthcoming and what you have gone through and overcome. **God must love you.**

You have, what you have, because that is what you are meant to have at this moment, and at this time. God doesn't always give you what you want, but I can guarantee you that He gives you what you need, when you need it most. It's all in His time. God is good to you, all the time and every time. **God must love you.**

There is not much to see when you look down. However, when you look up, you see that there is so much more around you. Don't compare yourself to the Jones'. There is always someone that will have more than you. There is also someone that will have less than you. The important thing to note is that "you have" what you have, so **God must love you.** Love always. Love daily. 365 Love.™

Have you told someone you loved them today? I have.™

Love yesterday, today and future tomorrows,™
Torion

Message in the MUSIC
Baby Face – **God Must Love You**

Note the QUOTE!
"What we are is God's gift to us. What we become is our gift to God." --- Eleanor Powell

The Little Things You Do
January 26

Today's NOTE

I had the honor of being asked to perform at the 25th Wedding Anniversary celebration for some old friends of mine (Kojak and Tee). This couple roller skates almost every weekend and has been doing so since I began roller skating in the 9th grade at Jellibeans. That's been over 25 years. So, I guess I've known them as long as they've been married.

Tee recalled that I used to dance with a group called "Guess?" They planned to invite several Jellibeans and Sparkles skating friends, but wanted to have it focused more on old school. Tee asked me almost every weekend for over a year about dancing at their special event. She wanted to be able to show family and friends a taste of what dancing was like "back in the day."

Well, that day came on Saturday, January 24, 2011. The dance group included me and 4 guys I used to dance with. We all arrived together. When Tee and Kojak saw everybody, they were so excited to see that I was able to get all of the guys together for their event. We danced and the crowd went wild. Tee and Kojak especially loved it.

The next day, they gave me a call and expressed their sincere appreciation for dancing at their event. They were both overly grateful and went on, and on, and on giving us thanks. They mentioned once again, that we made their day. After I hung up the phone, I called all of the guys and shared the comments from Kojak and Tee. I then reflected on how something so little to us brought so much joy to them. Sometimes you don't realize how much **the little things you do** have a great impact on others. To think that something I love to do so much, being shared with another, could bring so much joy and excitement. It was just **a little thing** that was done out of love, that made a positive difference in their day. In return, **a little thing** as simple as "Thank You" made a difference to me.

- My girlfriend had to be taken to the emergency room last week and I spent the night with her there. She was thankful as well….**the little things**. It was something done out of love. It was the giving of some of my time because I cared.

- I sent a text message to another friend to encourage her in an effort to lift her spirits. The timing was perfect….**the little things**. For that moment, it took her mind away from her troubles and made a difference. It was done out of love.

- I woke up this morning. I can breathe, I can hear, I can see, I can walk, I can talk, I have my sanity, I can love, and I am loved ….. God has truly blessed me… **the little things.**

Love Always. Love Daily. 365 Love.

The little things you do let others know that you love. **The little things** that you may not really think about and may take for granted every day lets you know that you are loved. It does not always require something of great magnitude. A little bit of love can make a world of difference to another. Continue to love with **the little things you do**. Love always. Love daily. 365 Love.™

Have you told someone you loved them today? I have.™

Love yesterday, today and future tomorrows,™
Torion

Message in the MUSIC
New Edition – Thank You

Note the QUOTE!
"Do not think that love in order to be genuine has to be extraordinary. What we need is to love without getting tired. Be faithful in small things because it is in them that our strength lies." --- Mother Teresa

---

Recognize It
January 27

Today's NOTE

Yesterday I spoke about how the little things you do, show that we love and how much you love. The little things also let you know that you are loved when provided by others. The key is to **recognize it.** Love comes to you in many ways. Through a message, through an event, through a stranger passing by, through a celebration, through a song, through a sermon…. God sends you love through other people and other things. People demonstrate their love through even the most little things. The key is to **recognize it.**

There may be times when you spend time focusing on what you don't have or can't do. However, when you think about what you do have and what you can do, it is an unconscious recognition of love. Taking care of yourself is love. **Recognize it**. Showing appreciation for what you have is love. **Recognize it**. Being there for another person is love. **Recognize it**. Someone lending you a helping hand is love. **Recognize it**. Sometimes having to hear another person say "no" is love. **Recognize it**. Sometimes things taken away or removed from us for a better purpose or cause is love. **Recognize it**. A smile received from another is love. **Recognize it.**

Love does not always come in ways you expect to receive it in or in ways you demonstrate. Everyone has their own unique way of showing it. The key is to **recognize it.** Because a person does not love like you, does not mean that they do not love you. Look for the little things that demonstrate love and be able to **recognize it.**

As you go through your day, how often do you really sit down and take the time to **recognize** love?   Do you recognize it…

- When you're at work?
- When you're in traffic?
- When you're at home?
- When you're out with family or friends?
- When you're sitting alone having some quiet time?

Take time out to reflect on love and **recognize it** each day. Grow in it. Show your appreciation for it. Acknowledge it. Give thanks for it. You will find yourself becoming more positive and feeling better about love and life as a whole. Love always. Love always. Love daily. 365 Love.™

Have you told someone you loved them today? I have.™

Love yesterday, today and future tomorrows,™
Torion

Message in the MUSIC
Musiq Soulchild – Love

Note the QUOTE!
"It's so easy, to think about Love, to talk about Love, to wish for Love. But, it's not always easy to recognize Love, even when we hold it in our hands." --- Jaka

---

My All
January 28

Today's NOTE

I was scrolling through some of my favorite romantic love songs today. One of the songs that stood out to me was, **My All** by Mariah Carey. It's a beautiful love song. The music and the words are so eloquently put together and express the desire to be with someone because of your love for them.

I stopped to think about how much a person is willing to give of themselves when they are in love. When you are truly in love, you want to give your **all**. I reflect upon moments in my life when I have loved. I gave **my all**. I was giving and caring. I was communicative, I was open, I was honest. I was understanding. I listened. I loved. I gave **my all**. I surprised myself at times realizing that I gave more of myself than I realized I was capable of giving. Unconsciously and naturally, I gave **my all**. Sometimes it was recognized, and other times it was not, but knowing deep inside that I gave **my all** was good for me.

We all want to be loved. You may have moments in your life when you don't think so. That moment may even be now, but deep inside everyone wants to be loved. Know that it is possible. Know that there is someone out there for everyone. Know that it will come in time. God will bring someone in your life when it is time. Not on your time, but His time. Until then, continue to pray for love, practice love and grow in love. You will know deep inside that you are ready and willing to give your **all**. To give of yourself in love.

For those of you who currently have a romantic loved one in your life, show your appreciation for them. Be good to them. Be good to yourself in the process. Communicate and listen. Be understanding. Love. Give your **all**. Love always. Love daily. 365 Love.™

Have you told someone you loved them today? I have.™

Love yesterday, today and future tomorrows,™
Torion

Love Always. Love Daily. 365 Love.

Message in the MUSIC
Mariah Carey – **My All**

Note the QUOTE!
"I believe that two people are connected at the heart, and it doesn't matter what you do , or who you are or where you live; there are no boundaries or barriers if two people are destined to be together." -- Julia Roberts

Can You See It?
January 29

Today's NOTE

I was in the beauty salon one day and noticed a tattoo on the arm of one of the barbers.

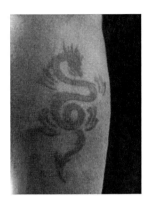

I told him that I really liked his tattoo as it was my favorite word. The barber looked at me as if he was confused by my statement. I then told him that LOVE was my favorite word. He looked at the tattoo and looked at me again, confused. I moved my fingers across the tattoo and showed him how I saw the word LOVE. **Can you see it?** Look closely.

- The tail forms the "L."
- The first loop moving up from the tail is the "O."
- The dip following that is the "V"
- The spikes on top of the dragon's head represent the "E."

He agreed in amazement that it indeed looked like the word LOVE and told me that no one had ever told him that before. He had that tattoo on his arm for several years. It was just a dragon to him, but to me it was LOVE. Others overheard the conversation and looked at the tattoo again to notice what they had never noticed before.

This situation reminded me of *The Seven Habits of Highly Effective People* by Steven Covey. In this particular book, there is a picture of a woman. Depending on how you look at the picture, you see an old hag or a beautiful young lady. Covey uses it to convey how the influences in our lives have made a silent, unconscious impact on us and shape our frame of reference and our paradigms (relationship of items to one another). It then moves on to talk about the power of a paradigm shift.... The "Aha!" experience... When you finally "see" it/things differently.

In both of these cases, someone had to point out the "more positive" component for others to **see it**. Once that was done, the "Aha!" experience took place. In both cases, I thought of how powerful love is. When we love, we see the positive side of things more often. We see in others what someone else may not. We see the good. We are more optimistic. Our eyes are opened. And what makes it even better is that we have the ability to share it with others. To help them see it. See

Love Always. Love Daily. 365 Love.

Love. We are able to help others begin the paradigm shift to love. We help them experience the "Aha!" moment. The dragon vs. the word LOVE is just one example. The old hag vs. the beautiful woman is another. Positive vs. negative (or good vs. bad). **Can you see it?** Can you? If so, share it with others so that we can all continue to know and grow in love. Love always. Love daily. 365 Love.™

Have you told someone you loved them today? I have.™

Love yesterday, today and future tomorrows,™
Torion

Message in the MUSIC
Eric Benet – **I Know**

Note the QUOTE!
"Love isn't finding a perfect person. It's seeing an imperfect person perfectly." -- Sam Keen

Love Is
January 30

Today's NOTE
One of my car tags reads, "**Love Is**." I chose this wording to draw attention to it as people drove through the streets. And, as they read it, it would make them think about love and fill in the blank....**Love is** _____.

I was at the gas station one day when a gentleman passed by and said, "Hello, **Love is**." I looked puzzled for a moment, as I had temporarily forgotten that the wording was displayed on my car tag. After I replied with a friendly, "Hello", he in turn replied, "I thought God was Love." I responded with a BIG smile, "He is. The intent was to make you think about it. And you did, right?" He agreed. Then on my way I went. Once again, mission accomplished. While this particular gentleman spoke up, I am sure there were a number of others who read my tag on that day, in that same location, and thought about what **Love is**.

First and foremost, God is Love. Then we can go even further in an effort to use every positive word that we know of to further describe love. It can go on infinitely. My choice of words may seem simplistic, but others may come up with choice words that make it seem complicated. Yet, it is still love. It's my words. It's their words. What about yours? What choice words would you use to describe what **love is**? Fill in the blank for yourself. **Love is** _____.

You may come up with one word, a few words, a sentence, a paragraph, or pages. The key is that you come up with something. The goal is to always keep love in your thoughts. Keep it in your prayers. Keep it in your heart. Make it a daily practice. Know what **love is**. Love always. Love daily. 365 Love.™

Have you told someone you loved them today? I have.™

Love yesterday, today and future tomorrows,™
Torion

Message in the MUSIC
Tonex – **God is Love**

Note the QUOTE!
"And so we know and rely on the love God has for us. God is love. Whoever lives in love lives in God, and God in him." --- I John 4:16

Love Always. Love Daily. 365 Love.

I Smile
January 31

Today's NOTE

I know I've written about the power of a **smile** before. However, I heard one of the most exciting songs on the radio this morning while I was on my way to work - **I Smile** by Kirk Franklin. It is so awesome. The song had me bouncing around in my car and **smiling** my heart out. When I got home from work, I immediately searched for the song. I had to have it. I had to hear it again. I searched iTunes. No luck. I searched Yahoo Music. No luck. I searched You Tube. There it was! As I sit here and write, I've listened to the song over, and over, and over. I just couldn't resist the temptation of writing about the power of a **smile**, again.

Those who know me, know that I love to **smile**. I mean I REALLY love to **smile**. It's a habit for me. It makes me feel good inside. And it is oh so true that regardless of how I am feeling, when **I smile**, it just does something to me. It does something positive and wonderful. It's contagious too. When **I smile**, I get lots of **smiles** in return. Hopefully, me just talking about **smiling** is making you **smile** too (hint, hint).

It's as if the song writer went inside my head and captured my thoughts on how I feel about smiling. I'm just bubbling inside with excitement right now as I continue to listen to this song. Plus, I like the tempo. It's a quicker, picker, upper. The song talks about how things may be gloomy at times, or may have been gloomy for a while, but knowing that God is doing his work, is the reason why **I smile**. Knowing that I am loved is **why I smile**. It speaks of a heavenly power from up above and how it brings about a desire to **smile**. It also talks about how you look so much better when you **smile**. I tell this to people "all of the time." Like I said, it's as if the song writer was in my head. And the hook,..... the hook and bridge make you just want to get up, start chanting, and **smile, smile, smile, smile**.

I just had to use this as an opportunity to share the song, "**I Smile**" with others. I had to use this as an opportunity to spread more love. I had to use this as an opportunity to make you **smile**. Love always. Love daily. 365 Love.™

Have you told someone you loved them today? I have.™

Love yesterday, today and future tomorrows,™
Torion

Message in the MUSIC
Kirk Franklin – **I Smile**

Note the QUOTE!
"If I could reach up and hold a star for every time you've made me smile, the entire evening sky would be in the palm of my hand." --- Unknown

Love Always. Love Daily. 365 Love.

Love Always. Love Daily. 365 Love.

February

"I love those who love me, and those who seek me find me."
— Proverbs 8:17

Back to the Basics
February 1

Today's NOTE

Love can be easy. And at the same time, it can be difficult. When you put all of the possible situations and lie experiences you can think of together, the overall outcome takes you **back to the basics,** love. You can put individual words together to form sentences that describe love. It is still love. Those sentences can be put together to form paragraphs that further describe love. It's still **back to the basics**, love. Those paragraphs can form pages. Those pages can form books. Those books can form libraries. In summary, it's still best described with one word, love.

Think about it for a moment and relate it **back to the basics** of math. You first learned about numbers at home, at the nursery, or in elementary school. The numbers 1 - 10 are **the basics** for helping you to get to 11 - 100, and so on. They build off of one another. You then learned about basic math problems using addition (+), subtraction (-), division (/) and multiplication (x), **the basics**. As you moved through higher levels of education, every math subject possible built off of these same **basic** numbers and mathematical concepts -- geometry, algebra, calculus, physics, chemistry, statistics, etc. Almost any career you can think of depends on knowledge of this same **basic** information -- a doctor, a carpenter, a contractor, a fireman, an accountant, a cashier, an engineer, an architect, a banker, etc. No matter how advanced the mathematical concept and no matter how complex the career, they all require going **back to the basics** to get the job done. **The basics** are the foundation.

When you build a house, the foundation is the basis for its stability. If the foundation is not right, neither will the house be. It may be OK short term, but as time passes, it becomes unstable. The foundation is a part of **the basics** of building a good, quality house.

These same concepts apply to love. Regardless of how complicated love gets, how big or small it is or may appear to be, it all goes **back to the basics** - God. God is love. Through Him all things are possible. Through Him, you are loved and can find love. Whatever kind of love you are looking for, no matter how big or small, He will help you get there. **The basics** are the foundation, the building blocks to help you grow in love. To find love. To be more like love. Never forget the importance of starting with **the basics**. Love always. Love daily. 365 Love.™

Have you told someone you loved them today? I have.™

Love yesterday, today and future tomorrows,™
Torion

Message in the MUSIC
BeBe and CeCe Winans – Close to You

Note the QUOTE!
"I love those who love me, and those who seek me find me." --- Proverbs 8:17

Love Always. Love Daily. 365 Love.

Give Yourself to Love
February 2

Today's NOTE
God is Love.

I met with a friend to help with a project he was working on. In between business talk, we reflected on some of my 365 Love messages and some of the ministry work he has done. We also talked about how much we have grown over the years and how when you **give yourself to love**, so many doors open for you. Following this meeting, I checked my e-mail and received a poem written by one of my best friends with a similar theme. The poem referenced going through life doing right and wrong, forgetting about and/or neglecting love, but yearning for love. The end result was one that required **giving yourself to love**.

When **you give yourself to love**, you open up a whole new world for yourself. You find constant peace and joy in your life. You find that your days are brighter. You find a sense of happiness that at times is indescribable. When you **give yourself to love** you always have a friend. You are never alone. You know that things are going to be OK. You just know. When you **give yourself to love** you don't worry. You appreciate and rejoice. Your head is always lifted high. You are whole. You have everything you need. You have a sense of security.

Give yourself to love. Don't be afraid of it. Don't be afraid to embrace it. Don't be afraid to hold on to it. Don't be afraid to share it. Don't be afraid to **give yourself to love**. Love always. Love daily. 365 Love.™

Have you told someone you loved them today? I have.™

Love yesterday, today and future tomorrows,™
Torion

Message in the MUSIC
Brandy – **Give Me You**

Note the QUOTE!
"Love can touch us one time and last for a lifetime, and never let go till we're gone." --- Titanic Theme, My Heart Will Go On

---

Singing Your Song
February 3

Today's NOTE
An important part of growing in love and finding love is loving yourself. You love yourself enough to have a song. Your own song. And regardless of the challenges presented to you in life, you love yourself enough to continue **singing your song**.

Loving yourself means not allowing someone to keep you from **singing your song**. When you love yourself, no one can force you to change who you are for them. Loving yourself means assessing yourself first and changing those things that you know need to be changed to make you a better person in love. You change you for a better you. Loving yourself means that no one can make you feel insecure about yourself. You are strong enough in love to have confidence in who you are. Loving yourself means that when you look in the mirror each day, you feel good about who you are, where you are and where you are going. You love that you are loved. You love what God has created you as you are and what you are destined to become. Loving yourself means that you are able to let go of people and things that you know are not good for you. It sometimes means saying "no" to what you want (the things that prevent you from **singing your song**) and saying "yes" to what you truly need (the things that allow you to keep **singing your song**).

Loving yourself means you are fully aware that you have your own song. You wrote it. It is yours and yours alone. No one else has it. No one else can take it. No one else can make it. No one can repeat it or duplicate it. So, love hard, love long, love deep, and love strong. Never stop. Always keep on **singing your song**. Love always. Love daily. 365 Love.™

Have you told someone you loved them today? I have.™

Love yesterday, today and future tomorrows,™
Torion

Message in the MUSIC
Christina Aguilera – Keep on Singin' My Song

Note the QUOTE!
"Since love grows within you, so beauty grows. For love is the beauty of the soul."
--- St. Augustine

Think About It
February 4

Today's NOTE

I love being loved. I **think about it** (love) all of the time. Just the thought of it makes me tingle inside. I wake up and go to sleep almost every day listening to love songs...romantic, spiritual, or brotherly love songs. Seeing a couple holding hands makes me **think about it**. A beautiful, sunny day makes me **think about it**. Going to church on Sunday listening to a powerful sermon makes me **think about it**. Arriving home safely each day makes me **think about it**. Having someone to talk to and/or think about me each day makes me **think about it**. And, there are so many other things that make me **think about it**.

When I **think about it**, there is a magnificent feeling that comes over me. One that makes me feel that anything is possible. I **think about** how blessed I am. I **think about** family and friends that love me. I **think about** how far I have come. This includes the things I have gone through (good and bad) to help me get to where I am today. I **think about** love and loving others. The romantic love is a bonus (smile). I **think about** spending quality time with someone special. A good man who is understanding, loving, spiritual and kind. I **think about** how much God loves me. I **think about** my son and my daughter, and how blessed I am to have given birth to them and see them grow into beautiful young adults. I **think about** everyone who has crossed paths in my life for a reason, a season, or a lifetime. I **think about** love. What makes you **think about it**? Love always. Love daily. 365 Love.™

Have you told someone you loved them today? I have.™

Love yesterday, today and future tomorrows,™
Torion

Message in the MUSIC
Luther Vandross – **Think About You**

Note the QUOTE!
"If I had a flower for every time I thought of you, I could walk in my garden forever." --- Alfred Lord Tennyson

Love Always. Love Daily. 365 Love.

No Worries, Everything's Cool
February 5

Today's NOTE
Love presents **no worries**. Because with it, **everything's cool**. I was listening to music by Anthony Hamilton and thought about the words of his song, Cool. The music video is good also. Basically, he makes the best of every circumstance. Regardless of what happens or what he does or does not have, **everything's cool**. Because he loves, because of positive thinking, something good can result from all situations. Because he loves, there are **no worries, everything's cool**.

This is so true. I think about how I feel about love. A situation may present itself that has a temporary hold on me. However, I have become strong in love and faith. So, I think about God's love and how every situation is under His control. I think about love and begin to think positively --the glass is always half full, it's never half empty. I immediately change my frame of thinking and tell myself, "**No worries, everything's cool**." And it is so. When I was studying in preparation for my Project Management Professional (PMP) exam, every day of the week prior to my exam, I was presented with a work or family situation that could have had me stressed and unfocused if I allowed it to. I immediately let go and put things in His hands, said special prayers and told myself, "**No worries, everything's cool**." I passed the exam that Friday, and by the end of the week, there were **no worries. Everything** was actually **cool**.

Think "love" daily. Think 365 love. When you find yourself feeling low, lift your spirits and think about love. Think about everything that it is. Tell yourself, "**No worries, everything's cool**." Believe it, pray about it, and speak it into existence. Love always. Love daily. 365 Love. ™

Have you told someone you loved them today? I have. ™

Love yesterday, today and future tomorrows, ™
Torion

Message in the MUSIC
Anthony Hamilton – **Cool**

Note the QUOTE!
"Love asks me no questions, and gives me endless support." --- William Shakespeare

---

My Life

Love Always. Love Daily. 365 Love.

February 6

Today's NOTE

Everyone has a story. Everyone has their own experiences. Everyone has their own life. When I look at **my life**, I can say that I have truly evolved as a person, as a woman and in love. **My life** is what I choose to make it. It is my choice. No one can control it, no one can dictate it. God has a plan for it. It is up to me to figure out what His plan is and move forward with it. **My life** is full of my experiences. What I was, I was. What I am, I am. This is **my life**. In deciding how I want to live, I choose to love. I choose to make it the best that it can be. I choose to share. I choose to care. I choose to grow. I choose. This is **my life**. I choose peace. I choose happiness. I choose to be happy. I choose. This is **my life**. You have yours. What do you choose? Choose to love. Love always. Love daily. 365 Love.™

Have you told someone you loved them today? I have.™

Love yesterday, today and future tomorrows,™
Torion

Message in the MUSIC
Mary J. Blige – **My Life**

Note the QUOTE!
"Love conquers all things." ---- Virgil

So Amazing
February 7

Today's NOTE
Today represents one month since the start of 365 Love (in 2011). It is **so amazing**. Not only have I continued to spread love to others, but in doing so, I have now realized how much I truly enjoy writing about it. I find myself engulfed in it. I find that I am passionate about it. When you are passionate about something, you are so into it. You commit to it. You continually work to improve upon it. You enjoy every aspect of it. It is **so amazing**.

I have received a lot of positive feedback from 365 Love. People have shared their stories about how 365 Love has been **so amazing** to them…. how it has touched their lives…. how it has made a difference in them …. how it has made them think about love more often. My e-mail distribution listing has almost doubled from family and friends sharing with their friends, and their friends, and so on. That's **so amazing**. I have received letters in the mail, reply e-mails, notes of encouragement, personal phone calls, other shared love experiences, and more. I have heard about how others received love and shared love. That's what love does. That's what love is… **so amazing**. Love always. Love daily. 365 Love.™

Have you told someone you loved them today? I have.™

Love yesterday, today and future tomorrows,™
Torion

Message in the MUSIC
Luther Vandross – **So Amazing**

Note the QUOTE!
"God is love. He didn't need us. But he wanted us. And that is the most **amazing** thing." --- Rick Warren

365 Love Poem
February 8

Today's NOTE
One of my best friends, Evelyn T. King, writes poetry on a regular basis. She surprised me by sending me a poem she wrote especially for **365 Love**. In celebration of one month of **365 Love**, she created a piece to include references of all the topics I wrote about to date. She let me know how I unknowingly served as a life coach for her through my discussions about how I handle certain life events in addition to my **365 Love** notes. She has watched me grow as I have watched her. This is just another demonstration of how love is contagious. It is an example of how **365 Love** makes a difference. Love always. Love daily. 365 Love.™

Have you told someone you loved them today? I have.™

Love yesterday, today and future tomorrows,™
Torion

Message in the MUSIC
Natalie Cole – I've Got Love on My Mind

Note the QUOTE!
"At the touch of love, everyone becomes a poet." ---- Plato

A Song for You
February 9

Today's NOTE

I love music so I choose to share it daily as a part of 365 Love. There is something about music and a good song that brings emotions to life. I can always find love in it. Sometimes we can get a message we need to hear from music, from **a song**. After all, **a song** was created because someone dumped their thoughts and added music and a melody to it.

Today, I have **a song for you**. It is **a song** about love. It is **a song** of love. It is love. I choose to give it to you from me. Take this **song for you**. Use it. Embrace it and share it. Pass it on to someone else. Spread it around. Dedicate the **song for you** to someone else. Let it make a difference. Let it bring a smile. Let it brighten someone's day. Let it comfort and heal. Let it be love. Love always. Love daily. 365 Love.™

Have you told someone you loved them today? I have.™

Love yesterday, today and future tomorrows,™
Torion

Message in the MUSIC
Donny Hathaway – **A Song for You**

Note the QUOTE!
"Words make you think a thought. Music makes you feel a feeling. A song makes you feel a thought." --- E. Y. Harburg

The Point of it All
February 10

Today's NOTE

365 Love is intended to touch lives and promote personal growth in love through love. That's its purpose, love. That is **the point of it all**. Love is a reality that we should all come to face. It is what is meant to be. Everything we have and all that we are is because of love. Our purpose is to love. That is **the point of it all**.

Take a moment to think about love. Love is not negative, it is positive. Love is not bad, it is good. Throw away all of the negative situations you have "attempted" to associate with love, for they do not represent love. Think about the positive. Think about positive things that have come from negative situations. Think about all that is good.

- What does love mean to you?
- How does love make you feel?
- What makes you feel loved?
- Do you love yourself?
- In loving yourself, how do you treat yourself?
- In loving yourself, how do you allow others to treat you?
- How do you show others you love them?
- How often do you think about love?

If you truly thought about all that is good, if you truly thought about love, a smile should be on your face right now (smile). **That's the point of it all**. Now think about how you could feel if you thought about these things on a daily basis. Now think again about how you could feel if you thought about love on a daily basis. There is no way you cannot feel good about love. That's **the point of it all**. The more you think about it, the more you act on it. The more you act on it, the more you see positive change in your life. The more your life changes because of love, the more you grow in love. And that's **the point of it all**. Love always. Love daily. 365 Love.™

Have you told someone you loved them today? I have.™

Love yesterday, today and future tomorrows,™
Torion

Message in the MUSIC
Anthony Hamilton – **The Point of it All**

Note the QUOTE!
"You know you're in love when you can't fall asleep because reality is finally better than your dreams." --- Dr. Seuss

Love Always. Love Daily. 365 Love.

The Abnorm? Or the Norm?
February 11

Today's NOTE

I was reflecting on a discussion I had with an old friend several years ago as part of a reading exercise we were working on together. We asked each other the question, "What do you think others would remember most about you when you are gone?" I gave her my response. In turn, she gave me hers. She responded that she thinks others would remember me for Love. She went on to say that I am a very loving person and that is no longer the norm. She mentioned that it was sad to say that the norm is not so loving and that true love has become **the abnorm**. While I was flattered by the response, I was also saddened. **Abnorm**al is something that is not common. It is something that is strange. It is something that most people do not do. It is different. Is love truly **the abnorm**? Is this what love has become?

I thought about my divorce and how so many people wanted me to "take him to the cleaners", or "do this to him", or "do that to him." My response was, "Why?", or "I don't want that", or "I don't need that." I felt that if I did all the things people were suggesting, it would only be done out of vengeance, not because it was something right or something I truly needed or wanted. God said, "Vengeance is mine." So, I left everything in His hands and made the process simple and easy. This example was used by my friend as one of the justifications to support the "loving person" in me as well. What are your thoughts?

- Is love now **the abnorm** vs. **the norm**?
- Is love **the abnorm** for you and how you love personally?
- Is love **the norm** for you and how you love personally?

Some may feel that love is **the norm**. Others may feel it is **the abnorm**. If you feel that it is **the abnorm**, 365 Love is here to support a change in that. It is here to support a change in you. Love will no longer be **the abnorm** in your life. Love will become **the norm**. 365 Love is here to provide you with daily doses of love to transform **the abnorm** to **the norm**. It's here to promote growth in love. It's here to guide you on your own personal journey in love. It's here to be a constant reminder of love... spiritual love, brotherly love, romantic love and family love .... love through notes, music and quotes. It's here to enforce how much you can and should love yourself. It's here to enforce how much you should and can love others. It's here to remind you that love is **the norm**. God wants us to love - to love him, to love ourselves, and to love others. He wants love to be **the norm**. Love is **the norm**. Love always. Love daily. 365 Love.™

Have you told someone you loved them today? I have.™

Love yesterday, today and future tomorrows,™
Torion

Message in the MUSIC
Marvin Sapp – Don't Count Me Out

Note the QUOTE!
"All, everything that I understand, I understand only because I love." --- Leo Tolstoy

Tonight
February 12

Today's NOTE
Tonight is a good night to love. There's something about the calmness in the air and the stars in the sky. There's something about the mood that brings a twinkle in your eye. There's something about tonight that feels just right. So, that makes **tonight** a good night to love. **Tonight** is a good night to show someone how much you care. It's a night to forgive. It is a night to move forward. **Tonight** is a night to open your heart to receive love. It's a night to release all of your fears and worries. It's a night destined to be better than any other night. **Tonight** is "the" night to choose love.

Why **tonight**? Why not? Why put off something for another night when it can be done **tonight?** Why not give it a try? **Tonight** is not just any night. It's a special night. **Tonight** is the night you decide to love. **Tonight** is the night you decide to love more. **Tonight** is the night you decide to give into something you have desired and/or resisted. **Tonight** is the night you listen to your heart because you know what's in your head is perfectly aligned with it. Give in to love **tonight**. Love always. Love daily. 365 Love.™

Have you told someone you loved them today? I have.™

Love yesterday, today and future tomorrows,™
Torion

Message in the MUSIC
Yolanda Adams – **Tonight**

Note the QUOTE!
"Dear friends, let us love one another for love comes from God. Everyone who loves has been born of God and knows God. Whoever does not love does not know God, because God is love." --- I John 4: 7 – 8

The Four Loves
February 13

Today's NOTE

We see, hear and/ or think about love on a daily basis. Even if it is just by listening to the radio, watching a TV commercial or looking at a billboard while driving down the street, we encounter love. We know it as many different things and share it in many different ways. We are touched daily by **the four loves**.

- *Storge* - Affection; the love of a family member or a child to parent relationship
- *Phileo* - Friendship; brotherly love
- *Eros* - Romance; sexual in nature involving the love of a man or woman
- *Agape* - Unconditional; charity; the unselfish love of others; unconditional; self-sacrificing

It's hard to resist being touched by one or more of **the four loves**. We love when we participate in family gatherings and raise our children. We love when we appreciate and care for our friends. We love when we give in to the affection of a romantic relationship. We love when we give our time to help others. We love. No matter how hard a person may try to deny love, it's hard not to give in to at least one of **the four loves**. That's what makes love so loving (smile). It surrounds us. You can't run away from it. It keeps coming at you. So why not embrace it? Embrace **the four loves**. They all happen in their own time and in their own space, but they do happen. Love happens. **The four loves** happen to and for anyone and everyone. Including me. Including you. Including her. Including him. Love conquers all. Love is all we need. That's love. **The four loves**. Love always. Love daily. 365 Love.™

Have you told someone you loved them today? I have.™

Love yesterday, today and future tomorrows,™
Torion

Message in the MUSIC
Ne-Yo – Stop This World

Note the QUOTE!
"Love is of all passions the strongest, for it attacks simultaneously the head, the heart, and the senses." --- Lao Tzu

---

Love Always. Love Daily. 365 Love.

So Good
February 14

Today's NOTE

I feel oh, **so good** today. It is "love" day. While I personally choose to love on a daily basis, because today is considered "love" day, I am overflowing with it. Today is **so good**, because for some, they put an extra effort into showing others that they love today. This is a step closer to love for some. For others, it is just another day. I am excited to see mothers, daughters, husbands, boyfriends, girlfriends, bosses, school children, grandmothers, brothers, sisters and just people in general spread love. Companies put extra effort into producing products with my favorite word on it - love. It's everywhere. It's hard to walk into most stores without seeing something representative of love. It is **so good**. When some may never choose to share love on any other day of the year, they drop their guards, put all things aside and decide to love today, on "love" day. Sometimes, they decide to love just because. Other times, they decide to love because they truly do love. That is **so good**.

- Wouldn't it be **so good** if everyone could keep this going all of the time?
- Wouldn't it be **so good** if people who do not practice it often would choose this particular love day to start something new?
- Wouldn't it be **so good** if they would choose this day to begin their journey of choosing to love daily? 365 Love daily?

Wow, that would be **so good**. That would be so amazing. That would be love, growth in love. Love always. Love daily. 365 Love.™

Have you told someone you loved them today? I have. ™

Love yesterday, today and future tomorrows, ™
Torion

Message in the MUSIC
Melinda Watts – **So Good**

Note the QUOTE!
"We were given two hands to hold, two legs to walk, two eyes to see, two ears to listen. But why only one heart? Because the other was given to someone else for us to find." --- Unknown

---

Love Calls

Love Always. Love Daily. 365 Love.

February 15

Today's NOTE

We are meant to love. God loves us and wants us to love others. Some try to fight love or resist love. Some don't really know love, but when **love calls**, there is nowhere to hide. When **love calls**, you know it. You can't help it. You can't resist it. No matter how hard you try, when **love calls**, it takes over. Sometimes love is saying "no." Sometimes love has to be "tough." But, when **love calls**, regardless of how we have to respond to it for the better purpose, it is what it is. **Love calls** through a friend. **Love calls** through family. **Love calls** through others lending a helping hand. **Love calls** through intimacy. **Love calls** in many different ways. Can you remember a time when **love called**? Have you made a **love call** lately? Love always. Love daily. 365 Love.™

Have you told someone you loved them today? I have.™

Love yesterday, today and future tomorrows,™
Torion

Message in the MUSIC

Kem – **Love Calls**

Note the QUOTE!

"One word frees us of all the weight and pain in life. That word is love." --- Sophocles

Don't Lose It
February 16

Today's NOTE
Think about something you really, really love to do.

- How much do you appreciate it?
- How much effort do you put into learning more about it?
- How much time do you invest in it?

Now think about a material item you love. It could be a collectible item, an antique, a photo, a piece of jewelry, a car, etc.

- How well do you take care of it?
- How valuable is it to you?
- If you love it, you **don't** want to **lose it**, correct?

The way you think about that material item or hobby / activity is the way you should feel about love. You should appreciate it. You should have a passion for it. You should put your all into it. You should dedicate time to it. You should do more with love and to grow in love so that you **don't lose it**.

So often, we don't think about love in this way. We don't think about the act of practicing love. We don't think about holding on to it, or doing the right things necessary so that we **don't lose it**. We don't think about studying love. When you really love to do something, you research it. You participate in it often. You associate with others who do similar things. You talk about it. You might even earn a degree in it. Why not do the same for love? If you want it, put more into getting to know about it and never stop learning. Never stop growing.

When you love, you treat others with respect. You listen. You give. You understand. You are positive. You are patient. You are kind. You do all these things and others to hold on to it so that you **don't lose it**. Think about growing in love daily. Make it a part of your every day ritual. Love yourself and others. Don't forget about it and **don't lose it**. Love always. Love daily. 365 Love.™

Have you told someone you loved them today? I have.™

Love yesterday, today and future tomorrows,™
Torion

Message in the MUSIC
Anthony Hamilton – Her Heart

Note the QUOTE!
"Men always want to be a woman's first love. Women have a more subtle instinct. What they like is to be a man's last romance." --- Oscar Wilde

It's Never Too Late
February 17

Today's NOTE

I sometimes pull out old books I have read to reflect on some of the key points I highlighted. *The Love Dare* by Steven and Alex Kendrick is a 40 day challenge for couples to practice unconditional love. I pulled this particular book out to reflect and noted a sticker on the cover referencing the book being based on the movie, *Fireproof*. I bought the movie more than three months prior, but never watched it. So, I popped it in the DVD and completed my review. The movie was very touching. And while referencing the love dare, the main point I got from the movie was that **it's never too late** to love.

While the book and movie focus on relationships, the point presented is applicable to love in general. It can relate to how we love ourselves in addition to how we love others. Just when you think you've had enough.... just when you think you can love no longer.... just when you are ready to give up......just when you begin to think that you don't want to love again......there is hope. As long as you have faith, clear your heart and focus on the true meaning of love, **it's never too late** to love.

Love is a choice. You can make a conscious choice to love today and every day. Regardless of your decision to start, today, tomorrow, the day after that or the day after that, **it's never too late**. **It's never too late** to develop and strengthen your faith. **It's never too late** to start over again. **It's never too late** to begin to love. **It's never too late** to grow in love. Lift your head up, pray, think positive, treat people right, do the right things, think and act unselfishly, and choose to love. **It's never too late**. Love always. Love daily. 365 Love.™

Have you told someone you loved them today? I have.™

Love yesterday, today and future tomorrows,™
Torion

Message in the MUSIC
Deitrick Haddon – Baby, You're a Star

Note the QUOTE!
"Love bears all things, believes all things, hopes all things, endures all things. Love never fails." --- 1 Corinthians 13:7 - 8

Jesus is Love

Love Always. Love Daily. 365 Love.

February 18

Today's NOTE

Today's note is simple and to the point. God is love. **Jesus is love**. That in itself is enough express love on any given day. Knowing that **Jesus is love**, is knowing that you are love. It is knowing that you have love inside of you and that you have love to give. You are the recipient of love on a daily basis. You are meant to love. Continue to love others as Jesus loves you. There is no need to say more. Love always. Love daily. 365 Love.™

Have you told someone you loved them today? I have.™

Love yesterday, today and future tomorrows,™
Torion

Message in the MUSIC

Commodores – **Jesus is Love**

Note the QUOTE!

"For God so loved the world that he gave his only begotten son." --- John 3:16

Love Always. Love Daily. 365 Love.

Can't Let Go
February 19

Today's NOTE

I grew up listening to music, trying my best to do the right things and being good to people. I was attached to all of the family shows and fell in love with the positive relationships on those shows. My journey for love as a youth was based on occasional church, internal instinct, peer awareness, observation, television and love songs.

I had my first real boyfriend in the 11th grade. I experienced love to include the good and the bad. Overall, it was a positive "1st love" experience (2 years) that set the path to my evolution in love and relationships. I only experienced a few more relationships with men before I met my ex-husband in college. I experienced the ups and downs of a long term relationship. We were together for 18 years before we divorced. As a result, I became stronger and wiser. I assess things differently now which makes it easier to recognize and let go of things that are not good to me and for me. I am the same person in character, but different in other ways.

Everything before college was simple. You met guys in school or other common high school social places. There were no big expectations. Everybody lived primarily with their mother and/or father. So, I had never really experienced dating as an adult. And this new experience in the "real world of dating" was definitely different. I dated few men after the divorce. Regardless of how the relationships ended, I looked at each one as the glass being half full, never half empty. I took them as a lessons learned, held my head up, and moved on.

At no time did I let anyone stop me from having faith in love. I heard a countless number of men and women claim to give up on love. They allowed the actions of others to drain their desire to love. Not me, **I can't let go** of love. I **can't let go** of the desire to love. I **can't let go** of the desire to be loved. Never. I love love too much. I have faith and know that God wants us to love. So, I keep it in the forefront of my thoughts. God put Eve on this earth so that Adam would not be lonely. That was the purpose. While bad people may enter our lives from time to time or cross our paths, there are good people out there too. There is not just one me, or you. So, when it comes to love, I **can't let go.** No matter what anyone says, no matter what anyone does, I **can't let go** of love. A relationship will come in time. When you love, love God, love yourself and love others, everything else falls into place. Plus the feeling of love is such a joy, I would not, will not, do not, and **cannot let go** of it.

Continue to work on loving yourself and growing in love. Everything else will come in time. Keep your faith. Pray. Do the right things. Treat people right. Check yourself first to make sure you are good for yourself and then others. When you are not good for you, how can you be good for someone else? Don't ever let go of love. Hold on to it and have faith in it. God is love. He will never let go of

Love Always. Love Daily. 365 Love.

His love for you. So, you **can't let go** of love either. Love always. Love daily. 365 Love.™

Have you told someone you loved them today? I have.™

Love yesterday, today and future tomorrows,™
Torion

Message in the MUSIC
Anthony Hamilton – **Can't Let Go**

Note the QUOTE!
"It's been said that you only truly fall in love once, but I don't believe it. Every time I see you, I fall in love all over again." --- Unknown

I Got You
February 20

Today's NOTE

Love shows support. It's the brotherly, friendship, phileo love that says, "**I got you.**" It's the romantic, eros love that says, **"I got you."** It's the affectionate, family, storge love that says, "**I got you.**" It's the charitable, unconditional, unselfish, agape love that says, **"I got you."** Love says, **"I got you."** When you love, you are there through thick and thin. You make the tough decisions to help others get through or make it through. You reach down to help lift someone up. You lend a helping hand. It's an "**I got you**" mentality. You forget something important...**I got you.** You're under the weather and feeling down...**I got you.** You're sick and shut in...**I got you. I got you** because I love you. **I got you** because God wants us to love and love one another. **I got you** because of who you are and my desire to show love to you and for you.

- How often do you demonstrate your love for another by displaying that **"I got you"** mentality?
- How often to you tell a loved one, **"I got you!"**?

Love always. Love daily. 365 Love.™

Have you told someone you loved them today? I have.™

Love yesterday, today and future tomorrows,™
Torion

Message in the MUSIC
Whitney Houston – **I Got You**

Note the QUOTE!
"There is no remedy for love but to love more." --- Henry David Thoreau

Never Too Much
February 21

Today's NOTE
Love makes the world go around. It's in everything you do. And when you love, you feel there's **never too much** love to give or receive. You wake each day giving love, effortlessly. God's love for us is **never too much**. The love of a parent or best friend is **never too much**. The love of a significant other is **never too much**. Keep loving, because when it comes to love it is **never too much**. Love always. Love daily. 365 Love. ™

Have you told someone you loved them today? I have. ™

Love yesterday, today and future tomorrows, ™
Torion

Message in the MUSIC
Luther Vandross – **Never Too Much**

Note the QUOTE!
"Being deeply loved by someone gives you strength, while loving someone deeply gives you courage." --- Lao Tzu

Strawberry Letter
February 22

Today's NOTE

I often listen to the Steve Harvey show on the radio in the morning on the way to work. There is a section on the show called, **"Strawberry Letter"** where advice is given on love and relationships. On this particular day, a lady wrote a letter asking for advice on what to do about an abusive relationship she was involved in.

The writer was married for over 15 years. Her husband was a business man, a church man, a lover man, and a jerk at home. He was well respected in their city and was a deacon in the church. He was both physically and mentally abusive to his wife (the writer). The writer mentioned that she wanted to leave, but was afraid for her life. She also asked if God would forgive her and her children if she left.

This particular letter made me reflect on a relationship I had with a 28 year old man when I was just 18 years old. I knew the man for a few years prior and he was the "sweetest" thing. Everyone loved him. He was so nice. The beginning of the relationship was wonderful. We never argued. We never had a disagreement. We always had fun and enjoyed each other's company. The more involved we became, the more possessive and controlling he became. I originally thought it was cute. I was fascinated that this older man was so "into" me.

One day, we ran into an old boyfriend of mine who was back in town on military leave. We said, "hello" to one another in passing and that was it. The fact that the old boyfriend was present in the same place as we were, ignited this "new" personality. I later found out that my 28 year old boyfriend had a crush on me when I was younger, long before he ever expressed a romantic interest in me, and never liked seeing me with the old boyfriend back in the day. After a brief conversation on the way home, he punched me in the face. I literally saw stars. I never saw it coming. Never had a clue. This guy who loved me, caressed me, was so nice to me, punched me. God was watching over me that night, though. A police pulled up behind us in the car shortly after it happened. See, I was driving, so I immediately put on brakes in the middle of the road after he punched me. The cops took him away. However, two days later he came back crying and apologizing. He told me how much he loved me and how he lost control. I took him back (WRONG!). The next event was a whole punched in my wall. The next was shaking me by holding my wrists causing me to punch myself in the lips. Next, he locked me out of my own apartment. I then reflected upon a family member being in an physically abusive relationship. She was beat so bad that she had to learn how to speak, read and write all over again. No more. I refused to be in that situation. I refused to be a victim. I broke my lease and moved immediately. I was not about to be a victim of mental or physical abuse. I was 18 years old, in college, and on my way to bigger and better things. I was then able to let go and move on.

Love Always. Love Daily. 365 Love.

A 3 month, short term relationship I had in 2011 made me reflect on the one from when I was 18 years old. While no physical violence was involved, the thought of a person being so nice and loving, and then having a split personality that was mean and full of anger was similar in nature to me. The sudden burst of jealousy and control. To see the look in their eyes as anger took control of them over matters that would normally require basic communication to resolve. To hear the tone in their voice and their choice of words as anger took over. The instances became more frequent as time passed. They were warning signs that I had to take action on. Warning signs are just that, they warn you of the dangers ahead. I had to follow my gut and make note of the warning signs. I had to let go and move on. No matter how good, great and wonderful things were going on one end, the warning signs took precedence.

This was NOT love. Love does not hurt. Love is not abusive. Love is not negative. God does not have a desire for anyone to harm us physically, verbally or mentally. It is not healthy. It is not Godly. It is not love. God does not want us to remain in those types of situations. We have to move on. We have to let go and let God. For that type of relationship is not in God's plan for us. God wants us to love one another. Violence does not represent love. Anger does not represent love. Vengeance does not represent love. When you love yourself first, it's easy to let go of something that you know is not good. As for the lady in the **Strawberry Letter**, that is not love. So, I would say the same to her. Love is patient. Love is kind. Love listens. Love understands. Love is not a part of this **Strawberry letter**. Love always. Love daily. 365 Love.™

Have you told someone you loved them today? I have.™

Love yesterday, today and future tomorrows,™
Torion

Message in the MUSIC
Mary J. Blige – Ain't Really Love

Note the QUOTE!
"Love is patient, love is kind. It does not envy, it does not boast, it is not proud. It is not rude, it is not self-seeking, it is not easily angered, it keeps no record of wrongs. Love does not delight in evil but rejoices with the truth. It always protects, always trusts, always hopes, always perseveres." --- 1 Corinthians 13

Soulmates
February 23

Today's NOTE

I love movies. One of my favorite love stories is *What Dreams May Come* featuring Robin Williams and Cuba Gooding, Jr. It's the story of two people who are connected to one another by love as **soulmates**. A tragedy enters their relationship with the death of their children and then the husband shortly after. The husband is caught between two worlds because of his love for his wife. He watches her grieve over the loss of her family and attempts to connect with her to console and protect. The true demonstration of their love for one another is shown in yet another life changing event that reconnects them as **soulmates**. (OK, I have to leave it at this in case you haven't seen the movie and want to see it for yourself (smile)).

- Do you believe in **soulmates**?
- Do you believe in the concept of there being one person out there specifically meant to love you?
- Have you ever met someone that you were so connected with, that you felt there could be a possibility of you being **soulmates**?

There are different views on **soulmates**. This can be for a friend, family member, or romantic relationship. All are similar in that two separate individuals are connected as if they are one. One in union. One in compatibility. One in love. And it's all natural.

When I think about the concept of a **soulmate**, regardless of the context, I think about love. Love for another that is understanding. Love for another that is unconditional. Love for another that is honest. Love for another that compliments. Love for another that gives. Love for another that is charitable. Love. What are your thoughts? Love always. Love daily. 365 Love.™

Have you told someone you loved them today? I have.™

Love yesterday, today and future tomorrows,™
Torion

Message in the MUSIC
Chrisette Michele – Is This the Way Love Feels

Note the QUOTE!
"Love is composed of a single soul inhabiting two bodies." --- Aristotle

---

Love Always. Love Daily. 365 Love.

First Love
February 24

Today's NOTE
Do you ever stop to think about your first love?

Most people would normally think of a **first love** from a romantic relationship perspective. The time you had with a boyfriend/girlfriend as a teen or young adult is probably the most memorable. Mine was very positive and lasted for 2 years. Then college and life stepped in. Others may have different or similar stories to tell, both positive and not so positive. But when asked about the **first "love"**, the relationship at some point was good.

Now, think about where you are in your life today and what is important to you. Think about how you have matured mentally and spiritually. Think about everything you know about love. Think about all that is good. Now take a moment to think about that question again. Was the response the same?

God is Love. He is the alpha and the omega. He is the first and the last. So, in response to answering that question again, I would say that He is my **first love**. He provides a place where the greatest love of all is found. He provides the kind of love that can be delivered by no other. He is the friend of friends. He is the father of fathers. He is the love of all loves. Wow! How incredible is that? Think about the greatness in Him and all that His love can do and does. A true **first love** that provides an experience so magnificent that it is hard to describe with just a few words. Now think about "that" **first love** daily. Use those thoughts to guide you through your day. Use that love to make a difference to someone else's day. Use it to help you grow in love. Love always. Love daily. 365 Love.™

Have you told someone you loved them today? I have.™

Love yesterday, today and future tomorrows,™
Torion

Message in the MUSIC
Kirk Franklin – **First Love**

Note the QUOTE!
"You know you truly love someone when every day you meet is like the first time you fall in love." --- Unknown

---

In Spoken Word

Love Always. Love Daily. 365 Love.

February 25

Today's NOTE

I received an email from a reader sharing comments about how she enjoyed reading 365 Love. She also thought I might be interested in a **spoken word** piece titled *Love* by the artist, Se7en the Poet. I Googled the name and the title of the piece and reviewed a wide range of search results. I was first able to find and listen to a snippet on iTunes. I then found the Facebook site for the artist, but no spoken word. I refined my search again and was able to find the actual website for the artist. He happens to have a video section on the site where you can hear his **spoken word** piece titled, *Love*. I later found it posted on YouTube.

I happen to love spoken word. Floetry, Jill Scott, and The Floacist are some of my favorite recording artists. While they primarily include singing in their recorded pieces, there is spoken word also. I also like to attend poetry events. The specific **spoken word** piece by Se7en fully describes love in a number of different ways. He talks of his love for love. He talks of things that make him feel love. He talks of spreading love and how it would be with and without love. I loved it so much that I thought he was in my head, at one time or another, reading my thoughts. I was like, "Yeah, that's it. I agree." I loved the piece so much that I wanted to use this 365 Love to share it with you. I couldn't have said it better myself. The musical background adds a special touch.

A special thanks goes out to Heather S. for sharing this **spoken word** piece with me so that I could share it with you, and hopefully you with others. It's another example of how love is contagious. Keep sharing love. Keep growing in love. Love always. Love daily. 365 Love.™

Have you told someone you loved them today? I have.™

Love yesterday, today and future tomorrows,™
Torion

Message in the MUSIC
Se7en the Poet – Love

Note the QUOTE!
"Love is but the discovery of ourselves in others, and the delight in the recognition." --- Alexander Smith

---

I Feel Good
February 26

Love Always. Love Daily. 365 Love.

Today's NOTE

I woke up, turned on some good music and started my day off with some serious dancing. That's right, at 7 AM, I started the day off dancing. And I still got it if I may say so myself (smile). It felt good. It felt real good. And it was all good. Then off to work I went. **Feeling good**.

Today, as like most days, **I feel good**. Right now, at this moment, I still **feel good**. **I feel good** because I love and am loved in return. **I feel good** because I love myself. I am God's creation. I am special. I am unique. I am like no other. And for that, **I feel good**. **I feel good** because I know that God loves me. **I feel good** knowing that I have family and friends that I love and they in turn love me. **I feel good** knowing that yesterday is in the past, today is a brand new day, and tomorrow always brings something new and opportunities to give, gain and reach for something better. **I feel good** because I control my destiny. **I feel good** knowing that I always have a choice and that the choice is mine and mine alone.

There's something about love that is always good. It is a good feeling. There is nothing you can say or do, that is truthful about love, that does not represent a good feeling. Find some joy in the day that makes you **feel good**. Reflect on something that brings a smile to your face and makes you **feel good**. Give love that makes you and someone else **feel good**. Love always. Love daily. 365 Love.™

Have you told someone you loved them today? I have. ™

Love yesterday, today and future tomorrows, ™
Torion

Message in the MUSIC
Tone, Toni, Tony – **Feels Good**

Note the QUOTE!
"Since love grows within you, so beauty grows. For love is the beauty of the soul."
--- St. Augustine

Lovely Day

February 27

Today's NOTE

Today is a **lovely day**. It's a new day. It's a day that has been given to you, me and others. It's a day to do something new. It's another day that allows you the opportunity to show, learn, know and grow in love. It's a great day, a beautiful day, a blessed day, a **lovely day**.

We wake each day and take things that are naturally provided to us for granted. For most of us, we can feel the things we touch such as the softness of another person's hands. We can breathe in the freshness of the air. We can smell the pleasant scents of dinner cooking in the kitchen. And when it's time to eat, it tastes, oh, so good. We can see the sun shining during the day and the beauty of the stars and the moon in the midnight sky. We can hear the sweet sounds of birds chirping in a nearby tree or the musical instruments playing jazz on the radio. We can walk in the park and enjoy the beauty of the day. We can talk to family, friends and loved ones on the phone. All of this and so much more is what makes today and every day a **lovely day**.

- Do you ever take the time to give thanks for all of "these" things?

I can assure you that there is someone, somewhere that does not have one or more of these same natural opportunities. Imagine what it would be like without any one of them. Sometimes we spend so much time thinking about what we don't have. We neglect to think about and appreciate what we do have. And then be thankful for each day that we have them. These things help make each day a **lovely day**. These every day, simple things make each day a **lovely day**. Embrace the love that comes from these natural things and give praise, love and thanks for each and every **lovely day**. Love always. Love daily. 365 Love.™

Have you told someone you loved them today? I have.™

Love yesterday, today and future tomorrows,™
Torion

Message in the MUSIC

Kirk Franklin – Gonna Be a **Lovely Day**

Note the QUOTE!

"The greatest honor we can give God is to live gladly because of the knowledge of his love." --- Julian of Norwich

---

Love Always. Love Daily. 365 Love.

Believe
February 28

Today's NOTE

Yesterday's church sermon was powerful as always. I am always revived and motivated to move forward with the week after starting it off by attending church. The chorus to one of the songs performed by the choir was "I **believe**...It's already done." As soon as I heard it, tears began to roll from my eyes, because I truly **believe** that. It was so powerful and personal at the same time. I **believe** it because of my personal experiences. Specifically, about my belief in love. God is love and God is good. **Believe** in God and know that it is already done. **Believe** in love and know that it is already done. Whatever you are going through, **believe** and it is already done. It's already taken care of. Know that it may not be today or tomorrow, but when you truly **believe** and have faith, you just know that it is already done.

These past few years have been filled with personal growth for me. I know it, feel it and can truly testify to it. I have a stronger faith in love. I am happy all of the time. I can smile each day knowing that regardless of what I am faced with, love will take care of it. I am not stressed about anything or any situation. I feel good about life all because I truly **believe**. I **believe** in the power of love. I **believe** in God's love. I **believe** that it's all in His hands. I **believe** that whatever comes before me, I can release it to Him and it's already done. It's taken care of. My renewed belief and faith have made a difference in my life.

The glass is always half full, never half empty. Any issue presented to me, may catch me off guard for the moment. But know that the moment is a brief one. I quickly remind myself of my belief in the power of His love, pray about it, do what I feel I can to act on it, and know that it is taken care of. It's already done. Love will take care of me and any situation. I am never presented with any situation that God does not prepare me to handle. I **believe** that. I am never presented with any situation that does not have a purpose behind it. That purpose can be to mold me or for me to mold someone else. I **believe** that.

I was talking to my mother yesterday. She was looking at a program where they were talking to people who recently lost their homes due to foreclosure. Out of all the people who provided comments, only one person mentioned how excited she was to see what God had in store for her. My mom mentioned that she never thought about it that way, until she heard the lady speak. My response would have been similar, because there is a purpose in why she lost the house. It is a material item. While we all want a house, car and so many other material items that are a common part of everyday life, we are not meant to have everything right now. We are not meant to have that specific thing right now. She demonstrated how much she **believe**s in love....His love.

I **believe** in love and the power it has to do great things. I **believe** in the power love has to heal. I **believe** in the power love has to do the impossible. I **believe**

Love Always. Love Daily. 365 Love.

in the power love has to change people and situations. The feedback I receive from my 365 Love readers is a confirmation of that. I **believe** in love. Spread love. Share love. Show love. Love always. Love daily. 365 Love.™

Have you told someone you loved them today? I have.™

Love yesterday, today and future tomorrows,™
Torion

Message in the MUSIC
James Fortune – **I Believe**

Note the QUOTE!
"Love wholeheartedly, be surprised, give thanks and praise, then you will discover the fullness of your life." --- David Steindi-Rast

Love Always. Love Daily. 365 Love.

Love Always. Love Daily. 365 Love.

March

"The best and most beautiful things in the world cannot be seen or even touched, they must be felt with the heart."
— Helen Keller

Right in the Middle
March 1

Today's NOTE
My mom shared a song with me a few days ago. I took the time to really listen to it yesterday. It's titled, "**Right in the Middle**" by Luther Vandross. The title didn't really phase me when she first told me about it, but when I finally listened to the song, it really did have a good message in it. It references a number of things that are opposite...bad vs. good, pain vs. joy, etc. The point of it all is to note that there are good things **right in the middle**. Things can be fine **right in the middle**. While things are not always perfect, don't miss out by focusing on the potential for something bad to happen or by lingering on the past. The present is **right in the middle** of the past and the future. Today is **right in the middle** of yesterday and tomorrow. You can choose to love today, **right in the middle**, which can lead to a more positive future. What was done before you reached the middle (today) is done. Learn from it and move forward. Focus on the love in everything. Focus on the good aspects of everything. Focus on the present and what the future has yet to bring. Choose to begin to make a difference and to love now, today, while you are **right in the middle**. Love always. Love daily. 365 Love.™

Have you told someone you loved them today? I have.™

Love yesterday, today and future tomorrows,™
Torion

Message in the MUSIC
Luther Vandross – **Right in the Middle**

Note the QUOTE!
"The best and most beautiful things in the world cannot be seen or even touched, they must be felt with the heart." --- Helen Keller

While You Were Sleeping
March 2

Today's NOTE

I was at my mother's house last week and noticed a caption for the name of a movie she was watching at the bottom of the TV screen - **While You Were Sleeping**. I've never seen this movie before, but immediately thought about a poem I wrote with the exact same title. I thought about that poem today and decided to share it with you.

Often times, you think about things going on here and now, or while you are awake, but loves comes to you even while you are sleeping. People pray for you while you are sleeping. Family and/or loved ones do things for you while you are sleeping. Think about your mother's love as you were growing up. She watched over you **while you were sleeping**. She placed the covers on you **while you were sleeping**. If you were sick, she checked your temperature **while you were sleeping**. She made sure you were breathing OK **while you were sleeping**. Great things and the littlest of things were done for you out of love by someone, somewhere **while you were sleeping**. God was watching over you **while you were sleeping**. He does it every day.

While You Were Sleeping

While you were sleeping
I said a prayer
Because I love you
And Because I care
I prayed you would be safe from harm
And wake to be held again in my arms
That you are blessed with God's amazing grace
That you wake to see my smiling face
That angels would whisper in your ear
To let you know that I am here
That your dreams be filled with happiness, not fear
That you wake wanting and desiring to have me near
For thankfulness in guiding you through
The love of family and friends, and the goodness in you
For continued days filled with happiness
and lessons learned from past sorrows
For the past, the present, and future tomorrows
And all of this, filled with purpose and meaning
Was done for you
While you were sleeping

© 2010

Love always. Love daily. 365 Love.™

Love Always. Love Daily. 365 Love.

Have you told someone you loved them today? I have.™

Love yesterday, today and future tomorrows,™
Torion

Message in the MUSIC
Lyfe Jennings – Must Be Nice

Note the QUOTE!
" The life and love we create is the life and love we live." --- Leo Buscaglia

---

Still in Love
March 3

Today's NOTE

I am **still in love**. Regardless of what has been and is presented to me, I am **still in love**. The devil does not want to see us happy. When peace, love and joy are in place, he pokes his head in there and tries to stir things up a bit. He tries to disrupt things, but when you are strong in faith, and you love, that's hard for him to do. It's hard for him to do it to me, because I am **still in love**.

As I have continued my 365 Love journey by sharing love with others and continuing to grow in love personally, the devil has made a number of attempts to change my mood, change my demeanor, and challenge my faith. He has not succeeded, because I am **still in love**. When he couldn't achieve this through me personally, he began to work on those that are close and dear to me. Well, you know what? I love too much for him to be successful with that. I still have faith. I still believe. I still know that God will handle it. I am **still in love**.

The minute he makes an effort to step in to destroy, I use my faith in love to conquer the situation. Everything happens for a reason and there is a reason everything happens. I will always be presented with situations that test my faith and my love. When I have faith in love, I can make it through those situations. There is a continued smile on my face and the glass is always half full. I am **still in love**. And with that, I know that the impossible is possible. I know that today and tomorrow are brighter days. I know that things are going to be alright. I am good knowing that where I am today is where I am meant to be and that tomorrow always presents new opportunities for something greater. The same can happen for you. Keep your head up. Keep your faith. Keep your love. Let go of any situation that is not good and release it to love. Release it to God. God is love and love changes things. This I know. You have to have faith and let it. Love always. Love daily. 365 Love.™

Have you told someone you loved them today? I have. ™

Love yesterday, today and future tomorrows,™
Torion

Message in the MUSIC
Brian McKnight – **Still in Love**

Note the QUOTE!
" Don't hold on to anger, hurt or pain. They steal your energy and keep you from love." --- Leo Buscaglia

Women
March 4

Today's NOTE

Women are natural nurturers. We are born and raised to love. As little girls, we are given baby dolls to play with. We take care of them as if they are our own children. We tend to be more sensitive to things. We take care of the "boo - boo's" when our children fall and hurt themselves. We may tolerate more because we love. We may hang in there longer because we love. We may do a little more because we love. We are able to take care of, deal with, and handle certain things because we love and of how we love. We are gentle. We are comforters. We are fragile. We love.

We all are born with no worries. And for the most part, we are naturally happy. As young children, we smiled, laughed, played and enjoyed the simple things in life all of the time. The door knob was interesting. The hair on our mother's head was intriguing. A plastic bottle top was fun to play with. Simple things. Wouldn't it be nice to have consistent happiness in our lives similar to what we had in our early childhood? We loved during our youth when we didn't even realize what love was. As we grew older, events took place in our lives to change how we feel about it. Those events changed our views about love. We allowed things and people to take away, hide, or disrupt how we love. It is now hard for some of us to remember love, embrace love, practice love, and/or hold on to love.

Love is the key to happiness. It's the key to joy. It's the key to peace. It's the key to finding and fulfilling your purpose in life. I am challenging all **women** (and men) to hold on to love. If you've lost it, find it. If you've let it go, get it back. If you've dropped it, pick it back up. If you've forgotten it, remember it. If you're afraid of it, don't be. If you've broken it, fix it. If you've buried it, dig it up. If you're sleeping on it, wake it up. If you're tired of it, tough it out and deal with it. Continue to love. Grow in love. Love always. Love daily. 365 Love.™

Have you told someone you loved them today? I have.™

Love yesterday, today and future tomorrows,™
Torion

Message in the MUSIC
Various Artists – Four **Women**

Note the QUOTE!
" **Women** wish to be loved not because they are pretty, or good, or well bred, or graceful, or intelligent, but because they are themselves."--- Henri Frederic Amiel

Devotion
March 5

Today's NOTE

When you have a high interest in doing something, you are **devoted** to it. You spend time on it and with it. You study it. You research it. You may stay up all night with it. You spend money on it. You constantly think about it. You talk to others about it. You hang around people who know about it. You brag about it. Do you do the same when you have a high interest in love? Why not spend that same amount of energy on love?

Devotion is defined as committed love; deep love and commitment; great dedication and loyalty; strong enthusiasm and admiration for somebody or something; fervent religious or spiritual feeling. As you can see, the definition itself includes love. However, most of us don't really think about being devoted to love; not just the love of one another, but the actual act of love itself.

To grow in love, you need to have that same amount of **devotion.**

- **Devotion** to spending time loving
- **Devotion** to studying love
- **Devotion** to thinking about love
- **Devotion** to demonstrating love
- **Devotion** to giving
- **Devotion** to treating others with love and respect
- **Devotion** to being good to yourself and loving yourself
- **Devotion** to doing the right things
- **Devotion** to forgiving others
- **Devotion** to love

Love always. Love daily. 365 Love.™

Have you told someone you loved them today? I have.™

Love yesterday, today and future tomorrows,™
Torion

Message in the MUSIC
Earth Wind and Fire – **Devotion**

Note the QUOTE!
" Love is the master key that opens the gates of happiness." --- Oliver Wendell Holmes

Always and Forever
March 6

Today's NOTE

Love is eternal. It's been around for a long time and it's not going anywhere. It's going to be here **always and forever**. No matter where you go or what you do, love is around you and will remain around you....**always and forever**. You see, for every positive, there is a negative. But love is so positive that it can change how you feel about the negative. Because when you love, a negative situation is no longer negative. It's a lesson learned. It's a testimony to give. It's the storm that is molding you into what you are destined to become. It's the test of your faith. It's the thought of the glass being half full vs. half empty. Love is the ultimate. It outshines and overcomes anything and everything **always and forever**.

- Think of any personal experience you've had (positive or negative).
- Now think about love.
- Remember --- God is love. God is good. Love is good.
- Think about all that love is and what love really means.

If you truly have faith in what love is, you believe in all that it can do. You believe and know that love conquers all, **always and forever**. You know that if you put anything in God's hands, it is taken care of **always and forever**. Embrace love. Share love. Give love. Love always. Love daily. 365 Love.™

Have you told someone you loved them today? I have.™

Love yesterday, today and future tomorrows,™
Torion

Message in the MUSIC
Luther Vandross – **Always and Forever**

Note the QUOTE!
" We are all born for love. It's the principle existence and it's only end." --- Benjamin Disraeli

Side Effects
March 7

Today's NOTE
I was reviewing my notes from a previous church sermon on **side effects**. The pastor talked about how everything has a **side effect**. He used commercial advertisements about new drugs and the associated **side effects** as an example. He tied everything together and moved forward with the sermon by discussing the **side effects** of having faith.

I thought about this some more today. Love definitely has its **side effects**. When you smile at someone, there is often a smile in return. When you help a person or give to a person, there is typically a display of gratitude. When you help someone grow, there is a **side effect** of them becoming a better person. That's love and some of its **side effects**. Love spreads. It's contagious. It grows. Love seeps through the tiniest of cracks and causes magnificent things to happen. Love shines. And the ultimate **side effect** of all of this love is more love. Love always. Love daily. 365 Love.™

Have you told someone you loved them today? I have.™

Love yesterday, today and future tomorrows,™
Torion

Message in the MUSIC
Kelly Price – Can't Run Away

Note the QUOTE!
"When you smiled you had my undivided attention. When you laughed you had my urge to laugh with you. When you cried, you had my urge to hold you. When you said you loved me, you had my heart forever." --- Unknown

Family
March 8

Today's NOTE

My **family** got together this past weekend to celebrate my youngest brother's birthday. We laughed, talked, ate, watched movies, played games, and more. We were **family**. A **family** that put everything aside to get together in celebration of my brother. We were there out of love for him and one another.

Early that morning, an unexpected event took place which prevented my brother from showing up. We decided to get together anyway to celebrate. My mom, all of my siblings and their spouses / significant others, friends and the children were there. Even my first cousins and their **families** were there. As **family**, we shared love with one another. The blessing of the food included a special prayer for my brother and our **family**. Regardless of what was going on in each of our individual lives, whether we were worried about something, mad at someone, or hurting inside, all of that was put aside because we were there together as **family**. We love each other. We realize that while we want everyone to be the best they can be, we are not perfect. We are each on our own journey to find our purpose in life. We are each unique individuals. We are each still growing in love and are at different levels of evolvement at this time. But when it all boils down to it, **family** is **family**. We are **family**. We love our **family**. We love.

I sat back for a minute and looked across the room to see how much fun everyone was having. I smiled inside and out. It was a good feeling to see love fill the room. It was my **family**. It was **family** love. God is good all of the time. Love always. Love daily. 365 Love.™

Have you told someone you loved them today? I have.™

Love yesterday, today and future tomorrows,™
Torion

Message in the MUSIC
Sister Sledge – We are **Family**

Note the QUOTE!
"Whatever they grow up to be, they are still our children, and the one most important of all the things we can give to them is unconditional love. Not a love that depends on anything at all except that they are our children." -- Rosaleen Dickson

It Does Not Hurt
March 9

Today's NOTE

I often hear people say that love hurts. Earl Hardy has plenty of clothing marketing this thought and so many people buy into it. There are also clothing items and tattoos with hearts showing daggers going through them. All are marketing negative thoughts of love. It's interesting to me how people choose to purchase items with negative thoughts on them and actually wear and promote them. Some people purchase these items because they actually feel it is true. Others don't really take the time to think about the message at all. They are considered "hot" items to buy. So, they purchase them because they're fashionable or what everyone else is wearing.

I think about the message of any item I purchase with wording or symbols displayed on it...especially when it has a reference to love. I disagree with the belief that love hurts. **Love does not hurt.** When you love, you may hurt because of the action of another, but the act of love itself does not hurt. A person who truly loves you will not intentionally hurt you. A person doing wrong to you is not demonstrating love. A wrong act is not a representation of love. But so often, people associate someone they love treating them wrong to the thought that love hurts. **Love does not hurt.** Love is good. Used as a noun or a verb, love is good. It's all good, all of the time and nothing less. There is nothing hurtful about something or someone that is truly good. There is nothing hurtful about love. So, with these thoughts in mind, the wording on the Earl Hardy clothing should really say, "bad things hurt." But we know that's not about to happen, right?

The next time you choose to purchase an item that references love, think about this message. Think about the thought behind it. Think about what it is promoting. Think about what you want to promote. Think about whether it is encouraging and supporting growth in love. Look to promote positive thoughts about love. Love is contagious. So, choose a positive message of love. Know that there is nothing but good in it and be proud of that. I choose to purchase items displaying and advertising love, because love is good and **love does not hurt.** I choose to keep adding to my collection of love shirts. I choose to continue adding to my collection of love jewelry. I choose to continue adding pictures to my love wall. **Love does not hurt.** I choose to love. Love always. Love daily. 365 Love. ™

Have you told someone you loved them today? I have. ™

Love yesterday, today and future tomorrows, ™
Torion

Message in the MUSIC
Smokie Norful – It's All About You

Note the QUOTE!
"True love is eternal, infinite, and always like itself. It is equal and pure, without violent demonstrations. It is seen with white hairs and is always young at heart." --- Honore de Balzac

Happy Feelings
March 10

Today's NOTE
I am happy all of the time. I am happy because I know and feel love. I am happy because I choose to love. I am happy because I know that each day I love, I surround myself with love, I act on love, I receive love, and I am growing in love. And love is a **happy feeling**.

When I think about love and ....
- my son and daughter --- **happy feelings**
- my family ---- **happy feelings**
- my friends --- **happy feelings**
- my job -- **happy feelings**
- my health --- **happy feelings**
- my sanity --- **happy feelings**
- my ability to choose --- **happy feelings**
- my ability to love ---- **happy feelings**
- the beauty of the day --- **happy feelings**
- the opportunities the day brings --- **happy feelings**
- and so many other things --- **happy feelings**

There are so many good things that I appreciate in life. There are so many good things going on in my life. There are so many things, people and situations to love. All give me **happy feelings**. I am happy. I love. Love always. Love daily. 365 Love.™

Have you told someone you loved them today? I have.™

Love yesterday, today and future tomorrows,™
Torion

Message in the MUSIC
Maze featuring Frankie Beverly – **Happy Feelings**

Note the QUOTE!
"There is no remedy for love, but to love more." --- Henry David Thoreau

Love Never Fails
March 11

Today's NOTE

I went to the Kem concert yesterday. Opening acts included Lidisi and Musiq Soulchild. It is so true that **love never fails**. There was so much love and positivity in the room that you could not help but feel good about love.

Lidisi is a relatively new artist to me. She opened the show. Apparently, she has been around for a while. However, I am only recently becoming aware of her. I loved her voice, her choice of songs and her spirit. She was very humble and had a great sense of humor, if I may say so myself. She performed solo, with just an acoustic guitar player and one background vocalist. Simply beautiful. Her ending remarks were positive. "When you look in the mirror, look at yourself good. Love yourself. Because if you don't love yourself. How are you going to love someone else?" **Love never fails**.

Musiq Soulchild hit the stage with his numerous love ballads and upbeat friendship songs. You know them --- Love, Don't Change, Teach Me, So Beautiful, BUDDY.... My goodness. Love, love, love, love, love! I have a great admiration for Musiq's creativity in the songs he writes and his choice of words about love. There is positivity and promotion of love from beginning to end through song. And you can tell when he is up on stage that he LOVES to sing. He is passionate about it. I loved it. Once again, **love never fails**.

Then came Kem. He was so smooth walking up on that stage in his brown suit with that slim body of his. He brought us one love song after another....Share My Life, If It's Love, Why Should You Stay, You're on My Mind, Love Calls...and on, and on, and on. I was in heaven. Definitely my type of music. My type of motivation. My type of love through music and song. Kem spent some extra time singing his song, **Love Never Fails**. He opened with the story behind why he wrote the song. I listened to it closely. He referenced a past relationship he had with a woman who was good to him, but he was too stupid to realize it. He took lessoned learned from the relationship and noted how the end result taught him how to love. Because of his relationship with her, he realized all that was good and was able to treat the next person better. While he may have regretted it, he was thankful for it. Again, **Love never fails**. Even though he was no longer in that relationship, love succeeded. He learned about love and how to love. He shared his story through this song. **Love never fails**. He ended his show giving thanks to God for His blessings. He shared that there is nothing he can do or has accomplished without Him. He incorporated crowd participation as he quoted, "God is good...All the time. All the time....God is good." Humble and appreciative, giving glory and honor to God. Totally awesome. That's love. **Love never fails**. Love always. Love daily. 365 Love.™

Have you told someone you loved them today? I have.™

Love Always. Love Daily. 365 Love.

Love yesterday, today and future tomorrows,™
Torion

Message in the MUSIC
Kem – **Love Never Fails**

Note the QUOTE!
"Love is but the discovery of ourselves in others, and the delight in the recognition." --- Alexander Smith

Make it Count
March 12

Today's NOTE
Tomorrow is never promised to us. So, we have to make the best of today and every day. We have to make every day count. Why not spend that time demonstrating love? Why not spend that time being good to yourself and others? Why not spend that time enjoying life and living it to the fullest? Why not spend that time making good choices? Why not spend that time making the best of what you have? Why not **make it count**? Love makes the difference. With love, you can **make it count.** Love always. Love daily. 365 Love.™

Have you told someone you loved them today? I have.™

Love yesterday, today and future tomorrows,™
Torion

Message in the MUSIC
Chrisette Michele – Love is You

Note the QUOTE!
"Love is not a matter of counting the days, but making the days count." --- Jayme

Here I Stand
March 13

Today's NOTE
God is good all of the time. All of the time, God is good. I joined a new church today. I was and I am still so excited about having a new church family.

For the past 3 years, I frequently talked about my desire to find a new church home, but had yet to act on it. I would watch church on TV and/or read my Bible, but no new church home. In January, shortly after I began 365 Love, I was invited to church by a close, special and dear friend. I have been attending church every Sunday since then. For the past few weeks, I was planning to join, but for different reasons, I did not. Today was going to be my day. Well, anything that could have happened in an effort to deter me from going to church did --- the time change, woke up late, a personal illness, my car was booted (in my own parking garage --go figure). All of that just made me want to go to church even more. I truly felt that something was trying to deter me from going. As I grow spiritually through love, situations keep presenting to challenge my faith in love, all that it is, and all it can do. But for every bump, all I could think of was that there was a reason for everything. I would figure it out now (or later) and move on. It was a test of my faith. It was a test of how much I love. It was a test of how much I believe in love, and I most definitely believe.

As I paid the money to the boot service man (or whatever his official title is), he explained that my car was booted because I did not have a parking sticker on it and reminded me of the notices sent by the apartment complex. I received one about a month ago, but did not address it at the time. I told him that I was not upset with him. He was just doing his job. I then told him I was going to church and I was going to have a wonderful day. I said it with a smile on my face and wished him a "good day" once the transaction was complete. As he was leaving, he stopped his car beside me, rolled down the window and told me not to let the situation get me down. I should go to church and give praise and honor to God. He felt that something good was going to happen to me and for me, and he said it with conviction. Well, something good did happen to me. I joined the church.

I thanked God for allowing me to have the funds to get the boot off my car immediately. I thanked God for the fact that the boot service man was still there (the car had just been booted right before I was leaving for church). I am sure that the boot service man typically encounters angry people when he boots their car. Because I was nice about the situation, he was able to share a positive message with me. I thanked God for his message.

As I was searching for songs to include with 365 Love today, I listened closely to the words of **Here I Stand** by Usher. It is one of many of my favorite love songs. The chorus goes like this -
>*No matter how far I go.*
>*And no matter how long it takes.*

Love Always. Love Daily. 365 Love.

No one or nothing can change.
*Forever yours **here I stand.***

Listening to this song today, I thought about love in a different way - not about a romantic love, but of a spiritual love. I thought about how much God loves. I thought about how much he loves me. I thought about how much he loves us. Regardless of what happened today, God said, "**Here I stand**. There is nothing that can happen to you that I did not give you the strength and the resources to handle." I had the strength to get out of bed this morning. I had the money to pay for removal of the car boot. I had a car to boot. I had gas to make it to church. I had clean clothes to wear to church. I thought about how each obstacle was presented to me today and how much I have grown in love. I thought about my choice to love. Love kept me calm. Love kept me positive. Love got me to church this morning. Love made me think of the glass being half full (not half empty). Love made my day joyful. Love gave me the inspiration to share this story with you. Now that's love. Love is good. Love says, "**Here I stand**." Love always. Love daily. 365 Love.™

Have you told someone you loved them today? I have.™

Love yesterday, today and future tomorrows,™
Torion

Message in the MUSIC
Usher - **Here I Stand**

Note the QUOTE!
"The life of love we create is the life of love we live." --- Leo Buscaglia

Love Always. Love Daily. 365 Love.

Something Special
March 14

Today's NOTE

Love is **something special**. Especially the love of a child. My sister in-law sent me a text message today noting how proud she was of my little niece. She is 7 months old and just began to crawl forward (instead of backwards). How exciting is that? And my brother adores his child. Just talking about how she looks and what she does daily fills his heart with excitement. You can feel his love for my niece even when talking to him on the phone.

Love is **something special**. I gave my grandmother a digital photo frame recently. She is 95 years old and has never seen one before. She typically does not like to get out of the house much, so she misses out on a lot of family events. I put 100s of photos of family events she has missed for the past few years on a jump drive for the frame. She was so amazed. Everyone got a kick out of her comments as she kept trying to figure out how the digital photo frame worked. It was too funny. It was even funnier to hear her comments about the photos.

Love is **something special**. My son sent me a text message last week to say that he loved me and I was the greatest, hardest working mother in the world; and he hoped I knew how much he really appreciated me. It put a huge smile on my face and made my day that much better.

Love is **something special**. My daughter sings and had her first one-hour solo performance at Underground Atlanta this past weekend. I was so proud of her. The crowd actively participated in her performance by dancing and cheering. She got lots of tips as well. Family was there to support her performance. To our surprise, her old group members showed up and reunited on stage for one song. One member was 8 months pregnant and still got on stage to sing and do the dance routine.

Love is **something special**. A friend was in need of a favor over the weekend. I was able to help out. It made a difference in their day. In addition, I felt good knowing that I was able to help.

Love is **something special**. My mom calls me daily. One of her favorite things to say is, "I was just checking to see if your eyes, toes, and fingers (or some other body parts) were still working." Other times she calls to talk longer periods of time or just to see how I am doing.

Love is **something special**. I frequently tell my staff members that I appreciate them. I cannot accomplish all that I can without their support. We are all on the same team and we are in this together. So, their efforts do not go unappreciated. It's nice to get text messages, phone calls and visits from them to let me know that they appreciate me as well. Sometimes, it's just a simple, "Thank You" that makes the difference (both ways).

Love Always. Love Daily. 365 Love.

Love is **something special**. Somewhere, there is someone who feels that they have the weight of the world in their shoulders. A kind note from a friend, a phone call, a surprise card or letter in the mail will make all the difference in the world. Just a little thing, that is the right thing, on the right day, at the right time.

Love is **something special**. Love always. Love daily. 365 Love.™

Have you told someone you loved them today? I have. ™

Love yesterday, today and future tomorrows,™
Torion

Message in the MUSIC
Usher – **Something Special**

Note the QUOTE!
"Love is something eternal. The aspect may change, but not the essence." --- Vincent Van Gogh

It Keeps on Spreading
March 15

Today's NOTE

I was listening to a radio interview with the gospel recording group Mary Mary this morning. They spoke of how their music has changed over the years and the feedback they receive about it. Some have criticized their music because some of it has "rhythm" to it. Others appreciate how it uplifts and motivates them and/or someone they love. The radio show host reminded listeners of a popular quote - *"The definition of insanity is doing the same thing, the same way, and expecting different results."* So, in order to get different results, there needs to be a change. Love changes things. And love touches us in different ways. The way we love, how we love, and receive love is different for different situations and for different people. Regardless, it's love. And when we love, **it keeps on spreading.**

Mary Mary was asked to describe how they felt knowing that their music was being played in night clubs. Specifically, the song, "God in Me," was referenced. Their response was that they control the content of their music, but they can't control where their music is played. They will always give praise to God, because that is who they are and where their faith resides. But it's nice to know that their music is being played in other, non-traditional gospel music places, because that means its spreading. And **it keeps on spreading**. So, if their music can spread to night clubs or "dark places" where gospel music is not traditionally played, that means the message is being heard. I agree with their comments. That means a seed is being planted so that "love" can grow. And from there **it keeps on spreading**. That is what love does. That is what love can do. You can take it anywhere. You can share it with anyone. And **it keeps on spreading.** Love always. Love daily. 365 Love.™

Have you told someone you loved them today? I have.™

Love yesterday, today and future tomorrows,™
Torion

Message in the MUSIC
Mary Mary – God in Me

Note the QUOTE!
"Neither a lofty degree of intelligence nor imagination nor both together go to the making of genius. Love, love, love, that is the soul of genius." ---- Wolfgang Amadeus Mozart

Quote from Einstein

Love Always. Love Daily. 365 Love.

March 16

Today's NOTE

Albert Einstein is known as the father of modern physics and won a Nobel Prize for his general Theory of Relativity. A coworker shared one of Einstein's quotes with me today.

"A human being is a part of the whole that we call the universe, a part limited in time and space. He experiences himself, his thoughts and feelings, as something separated from the rest; a kind of optical illusion of consciousness. This illusion is a prison for us, restricting us to our personal desires and to affection for only the few people nearest us. Our task must be to free ourselves from this prison by widening our circle of compassion to embrace all living beings..."

I thought about this quote and how it can relate to love. Specifically, I thought about how we should work to evolve in love...the love of God, the love of self, and the love of others.

- The first is covered with your personal faith and spiritual beliefs. Some people are raised on Christian beliefs. Others have to find their way as they experience life.

- Next, it is important to love yourself. I have referenced this in a number of previous 365 Love notes and I will continue to emphasize this over and over again. You have to love yourself before you can truly love someone else.

- Following, we tend to automatically love our family and close friends. That is something that typically comes natural for most. Others may have to put some extra work into it.

- Loving others goes beyond family and friends. The ultimate, agape love, is charitable love. It is giving of yourself and your time unconditionally and unselfishly to help others. This includes those that may not be near to us or dear to us. It's the part of love that touches on the last part of Einstein's quote. It covers the compassion for <u>all</u> living beings.

So, without even using the word "love" per se, even Einstein realized the importance of and need for everyone to grow in love. That's just a little something to think about from another person's perspective. Love always. Love daily. 365 Love.™

Have you told someone you loved them today? I have.™

Love yesterday, today and future tomorrows,™
Torion

Message in the MUSIC
Jennifer Hudson - Giving Myself

Note the QUOTE!
"In real love you want the other person's good. In romantic love you want the other person." --- Margaret Anderson

So Beautiful
March 17

Today's NOTE
Stop for a moment and take a good look in the mirror. What do you see? Look real hard. Do you see love? Look at yourself again. Look at all of your features. Wow! You are **so beautiful**. Look at your eyes and how deep they are or how they sparkle in the light. Look at your lips and how nice they are when you smile. Look at your nose and how shapely it is on you. It fits so perfectly in the middle of your face. Look at your cheeks and how they look when you smile. Look at your hair and how it adds to your facial features. Look at how you wear it to further define who you are. Look at your body. It is shaped perfectly just for you. You love yourself and that's what makes you **so beautiful**. There is someone out there that agrees with me. There is someone out there that agrees with you, because you are **so beautiful**. Now, that's love. Love always. Love daily. 365 Love.™

Have you told someone you loved them today? I have.™

Love yesterday, today and future tomorrows,™
Torion

Message in the MUSIC
Musiq Soulchild - **So Beautiful**

Note the QUOTE!
"Since love grows within you, so beauty grows. For love is the beauty of the soul."
--- St. Augustine

It Makes it Alright
March 18

Today's NOTE
Love makes it alright. It can be a great way to start and end your day in the best possible way. You wake up. You go to work or school. You pass people in your car or on the bus. You have interactions with your boss, co-workers and customers. You later go to a social event, the mall, church or a restaurant. You go home. You get the bills from the mailbox. You interact with your loved ones - significant other, children, parents, siblings and/or roommate. You watch TV - a movie, series or the news. Throughout the day, you interact with others directly and indirectly. Regardless of whether those interactions are positive or negative, with love it **makes it alright**. Regardless of whether your interactions resulted in good news or bad news, love **makes it alright**. You can't control what others do or say, but you can control how you respond to their actions. Love prepares you to deal with those everyday situations. You have a choice. Choose to love. Love helps you say the right words the right way. Love helps you do the right things at the right time. Love helps you pray for those that may not have been so pleasant to you during the day, but you still want to help them deal with whatever they are going through. Love helps you with patience and understanding. Love helps you listen and hear with compassion. Love helps you deal with situations for a positive outcome. Love **makes it alright**. Love always. Love daily. 365 Love.™

Have you told someone you loved them today? I have.™

Love yesterday, today and future tomorrows,™
Torion

Message in the MUSIC
Marvin Sapp - He Has His Hands On You

Note the QUOTE!
"Love is a gift from God, and as we obey His laws and genuinely learn to serve others, we develop God's love in our lives. Love of God is the means of unlocking divine powers which help us to live worthily and to overcome the world." --- David B. Haight

Prayer
March 19

Today's NOTE

Prayer is powerful. It changes things. It is a demonstration of unconditional love. One of my readers (Judith C.) previously shared with me a 2011 **prayer** calendar for the month of March. Each day of the month notes a specific scripture and a specific topic for you to pray about. The scripture for today was Colossians 3: 12 - 17. The **prayer** topic for the day was to *"Pray for families in crisis."*

As I watched the news of the recent earthquake in Japan, this specific **prayer** resonated with me. This natural disaster caused thousands among thousands of people to lose family and loved ones. While you may not have been personally impacted by this event, these were human lives. The people who lost their lives in the earthquake had families. Someone loved them and they loved in return. They were mothers, fathers, sons, daughters, cousins, aunts, uncles, grandmothers, grandfathers, nieces and nephews, and grandchildren. I ask that each of you extend a special **prayer** on their behalf. Pray for their families. Pray for families in crisis. And while you may or may not be aware of other families in crises around the world, in your country, in your city, in your neighborhood, or within your own distant and immediate families, I'd like to ask that you extend a personal **prayer** for those families as well. That's love. That's agape love. That's unselfish love. That's charitable love. **Prayer** is love. Love always. Love daily. 365 Love.™

Have you told someone you loved them today? I have.™

Love yesterday, today and future tomorrows,™
Torion

P.S. Special thanks to Judith C. for sharing her prayer calendar with me so that I could share the power of love through prayer with others.

Message in the MUSIC
Deitrick Haddon – My **Prayer**

Note the QUOTE!
"God allows us to experience the low points of life in order to teach us lessons we could not learn in any other way. The way we learn those lessons is not to deny the feelings but to find the meanings underlying them." --- Stanly Lindquist

---

Love Always. Love Daily. 365 Love.

Positive Thoughts
March 20

Today's NOTE

I had the privilege of being invited to a poetry event last night - "Winter Word and Wine Down." It was hosted by a local Atlanta poet, Tina ATL, and included an evening of **positive thoughts** through poetry and song. The overall ambiance was nice - dim lighting; candle lit tables; wine, fruit, cheese and crackers. It was very romantic.

The evening started with the DJ playing some old school music. He played good, clean, old school music. Guests mingled while enjoying the food and wine. Once the show began, it was on! The poets were phenomenal. And the musical artists toped it off with their original songs. I am always in awe of the words a person chooses to describe their thoughts through spoken word and song. The evening was filled with **positive thoughts**. **Positive thoughts** of love. **Positive thoughts** of love for women and men. **Positive thoughts** of love for people. **Positive thoughts** for the appreciation of everyday things and moments. Every male poet had a special piece about their love for women. They shared titles like - *I Love You, I Appreciate You, Woman, I Apologize in Advance*, and *The One That Got Away*. The women in turn were a little more risqué, but spoke or sang positively as well, *Square, Fine Time for a Glass of Wine, You Don't Know What You're Getting Yourself Into, Unity,* and *My Funny Valentine*. **Positive thoughts** from positive people in a positive environment. **Positive thoughts** of love.

The poets had a way of acting out their words and walked through the crowd as they expressed themselves. It amazes me how they remember so many words. The passion in their voices make you feel what they are saying. They bring you into their reality; their reality of love. The singers were so smooth and eloquent. Most had jazzy sounds that reminded me of artists like Jill Scott, India Aire, Chrisette Michele, Lyfe Jennings and Maxwell. Their voices were in alignment with the overall theme and ambiance of the evening. There were no strangers in the place; just people enjoying each other, enjoying the occasion, enjoying **positive thoughts** - thoughts of love.

The evening ended with the MC thanking all of the participants and the guests. Again, **positive thoughts** from positive people, for positive people. Once the evening was over, you could not help but be filled with **positive thoughts** of love. You wanted to feel love. You wanted to share love. You wanted to be love. You wanted to grow in love. You wanted to see more of love. It's yet another confirmation that love is contagious. I commend all of the artists who share love through spoken word and song. That's love. Love always. Love daily. 365 Love.™

Have you told someone you loved them today? I have.™
Love yesterday, today and future tomorrows,™
Torion

Love Always. Love Daily. 365 Love.

Message in the MUSIC
New Edition - Still in Love with You

Note the QUOTE!
" Your words are my food. Your breath is my wine. You are everything to me." --- Sarah Bernhardt

Give Thanks
March 21

Today's NOTE

So often, we take people and every day things for granted. A simple "thank you" makes all the difference in the world. Do you **give thanks** for the simple things in life? Do you **give thanks** for simple deeds done by others? Do you **give thanks** to people for being who they are in your life? Do you **give thanks** for love? Love gives thanks. It shows appreciation and humbleness for what you have and what you have yet to receive. Giving thanks is a way of giving back in its simplest form. Thanks (or Thank You) is the one or two word phrase that can make a difference in a person feeling good (out of appreciation for the response) or feeling indifferent (for lack of receipt of the response). It doesn't take much time or energy to do. It doesn't have a cost associated with it. It is brief and to the point. It can be expected or come as a total surprise. Yet, it often makes an impactful difference.

There is so much to be thankful for. As you continue to grow in love, practice giving thanks. **Give thanks** today and every day...

- for waking up
- for being able to see the sun shine
- for family and friends
- for someone lending a helping hand
- to your parents for bringing you into this world
- to your employer for allowing you the opportunity to have /maintain a job
- to your friend for being there for you
- to your children for bringing joy into your life
- for all that you have and all that is yet to come
- for lessons learned
- for being alive
- for your health
- for people who have entered your life for a reason, a season and for a lifetime
- for lessons learned
- for_____ (fill in the blank....and keep going)

Love always. Love daily. 365 Love.™

Have you told someone you loved them today? I have.™

Love yesterday, today and future tomorrows,™
Torion

Message in the MUSIC
Smokie Norful – Still Say, **Thank You**

Note the QUOTE!
"Make it a habit to tell people thank you. To express your appreciation, sincerely and without the expectation of anything in return. Truly appreciate those around you, and you'll soon find many others around you. Truly appreciate life, and you'll find that you have more of it." --- Ralph Marston

Walk
March 22

Today's NOTE

Today's prayer, as noted on my March 2011 prayer calendar, is to "Pray to **walk** in love" . The definition of ***walk*** is to move or travel. It is also defined as putting one foot in front of the other at a moderate pace. So, today's prayer can be restated as a prayer to move forward in love, or a prayer to take one step at a time to move forward in love, or a prayer to move forward in love in moderation.

Sometimes, we have to take small steps in order to progress or grow. We have to take our time. We have to **walk**. As the old saying goes, "you have to crawl before you **walk**" or "you have to **walk** before you run." Each is a progressive step before the other can take place. To grow in love, we have to practice it on a consistent basis. We have to pray for our personal progression in this area. We have to pray to **walk** in a positive direction of love. Pray to love yourself, pray to love family and friends, pray to love charitably, and pray to love romantically.

Think about this and where you are in your life with love. For some, it may come easy and seems effortless to accomplish. For others, it is a true journey. It all depends on where you are and where you are coming from. Know that it is progressive and is a realistic goal. Know that you can take your time and **walk** in love. Know that your **walk** will move you that much closer love. Begin or continue to **walk** your journey in love today. Love always. Love daily. 365 Love.™

Have you told someone you loved them today? I have.™

Love yesterday, today and future tomorrows,™
Torion

Message in the MUSIC
Mary Mary – **Walkin'**

Note the QUOTE!
"Love worketh no ill to his neighbor; therefore love is the fulfilling of the law." --- Romans 13:10

Love Always. Love Daily. 365 Love.

It Motivates You
March 23

Today's NOTE
What **motivates you**?

I have 50 staff members (5 direct reports and 45 indirect reports). This month, I scheduled one-on-one meetings with each and every staff member. It was an opportunity for me to have personal face time with everyone and to hear their thoughts on things going well and opportunities for improvement. It was also an opportunity for me to get to know them better. One of the questions asked during my meeting was "What **motivates you**?" I further explained the question to reference motivation that drives them to do a good job, a great job, or an exceptional job. I did not really anticipate what type of response I would receive from the many diverse personalities and nationalities. But to my surprise, all of the responses received to date can be summed up as one word…love.

Self-love
- "I am self motivated"
- "Just knowing that I did a good job"
- "Knowing that I put my best into it to accomplish a goal"

Brotherly Love
- "I want to make sure I do my part to make it easy for my team mates"
- "I want to make sure that my bosses can accomplish what needs to be done by me doing a good job"

Family Love
- "My family"
- "I do it for my mother and father. They worked hard for me and I want to make them proud knowing that I can work just as hard"

Charitable / Unconditional Love
- "I enjoy knowing that I have satisfied the customer and helped them to do their jobs better"
- "Being able to help others"
- "I appreciate having the opportunity to work for such a great organization"

I anticipated that one response may have been "money" or "promotion opportunities." I am about 90% done with my staff meetings and have yet to receive either of those responses. All were 100% positive responses. It was a pleasure hearing the comments and how passionate some of the staff members were about their response. I heard stories about family and friends. I also found out more about childhood experiences. It allowed everyone to share with me how much they love. Now that's love. Love always. Love daily. 365 Love.™

Have you told someone you loved them today? I have. ™

Love Always. Love Daily. 365 Love.

Love yesterday, today and future tomorrows,™
Torion

Message in the MUSIC
Mariah Carey / Whitney Houston – When You Believe

Note the QUOTE!
"In dreams and in love there are no impossibilities." --- Sarah Bernhardt

Love Always. Love Daily. 365 Love.

Your Own Path
March 24

Today's NOTE

We all have a purpose in life. We live each day, traveling the **path** to get us there. We go through life's experiences, the ups and the down, to mold us for what we are meant to be. Throughout the journey, we experience all aspects of love. We are happy because of love and we are sometime sad because we love. Some have given up on it and then found it again. We all have our own **path** to travel and that is a part of it.

I was at a college graduation several years back and recall a story presented by the guest speaker. He noted that we all have a destination in life, and God has mapped out individual **path**s to get us there. He related this to the use of a navigational system. Once you put the destination in, it gives you specific directions on how to get there. If the directions tell you to turn left and instead you turn right, the navigational system will re-map the directions to get you to your final destination. It may take longer, but for every wrong turn you make, the system will re-map directions to get you there. That's what God does for us. That's what love does. When we believe in it, it continues to put us on the **path** to fulfill our purpose.

Sometimes the route to take is clearly in front of us as is with the use of a navigational system. We know the right way and the wrong way. Sometimes it may not be as evident, but eventually reveals itself to us. However, we make personal choices. We choose to do what we know is right or take chances and do what we know is not. Regardless, when we are ready to grow in love and in life, our **path** is re-mapped for us and we begin moving in a new direction towards fulfilling our purpose. Whatever that purpose is, it includes love. And with love, that sometimes means having to let someone go (like a child, family member, friend, or romantic love)...having to let a situation go...having to move on...loving yourself first. When you can let go of someone or something that is not good for you, you are growing in love.

What **path** are you on? Are you making choices that you know are not good for you? Are you making conscious choices that are taking you off your **path** of growth / progress? Are you making choices that you feel good about to move forward in love and life? Think about it. Your **path** is set. It is predetermined. The choices you make determine how long it takes you to get there. Choose the **path** of love. Love always. Love daily. 365 Love.™

Have you told someone you loved them today? I have. ™

Love yesterday, today and future tomorrows,™
Torion

Message in the MUSIC
Luther Vandross - For You to Love

Note the QUOTE!
"It's so easy to think about love, to talk about love, to wish for love. But it's not always easy to recognize love, even when we hold it in our hands." --- Jaka

Love Always. Love Daily. 365 Love.

Journal of Gratitude
March 25

Today's NOTE

Each day, I think of how love was part of a conversation, situation, or resource I experienced. I was talking to one of my staff members about their personal interests the other day and he mentioned a *Journal of Gratitude* that he writes in daily. He got the idea from a speaker he heard some time ago and has been writing in it ever since. He frequently goes back and reads some of his past entries and it constantly motivates and inspires him. It's like self-motivation. I found the **Journal of Gratitude** to be an interesting concept. It reminded me of 365 Love - daily notes, music and quotes about love. The **Journal of Gratitude** consists of writing daily notes about being grateful.

Gratitude is an emotion that occurs after people receive help, depending on how they interpret the situation. It is also thankfulness, appreciation or gratefulness. Love is gratitude. Love is thankfulness. Love is appreciation. Love is gratefulness. So, the **Journal of Gratitude** is yet another way to express love through gratitude. I have found that the more I write about love and read about it, the more I see it and feel it on a daily basis. When I reflect on what I have written, it makes me feel it even more. I would imagine that the same would take place for the **Journal of Gratitude**. Why not try it? What do you have to be grateful for? Your health? Your job? Your sight? You family? Create your own personal **Journal of Gratitude**. Think of something to be grateful for daily and write it down. Go back on a weekly basis to reflect on what you have written before. Find something EVERY day. When you begin the process, I assure you that it will help you become a more positive thinker. It will help you begin looking at love and life in a different way. It will make you feel better about different situations. It will help you grow in love. Love always. Love daily. 365 Love.™

Have you told someone you loved them today? I have.™

Love yesterday, today and future tomorrows,™
Torion

Message in the MUSIC
Boyz II Men – Thank You

Note the QUOTE!
"True love begins when nothing is looked for in return." --- Antoine De Saint-Exupery

---

Love Always. Love Daily. 365 Love.

You Can Always Find It in a Song
March 26

Today's NOTE

I was searching for songs to go along with the 365 Love note yesterday. Brian McKnight is one of my favorite artists, so naturally I was going to look through his extensive catalogue of songs. His song writing ability is so awesome, and his choice of words used to compose his love songs is incredible. His voice is an added bonus. Even though he is primarily an R&B artist, he always includes at least one gospel song on his CD to give honor and praises. I listened to lots of music to find the right song that would map closely to the message for the day. In the process, I came across a song performed by Brian McKnight that I never heard before. It's titled, "Everything You Touch is a Song," and was originally recorded by the Winans. I found the title and the words to the song to be so nice. While I did not use this song for a previous 365 Love note, it is the basis for today's.

It made me think about my love for music and tie-in to love through song.

- Have you ever listened to someone speak and began to think about a song related to the topic or phase included in their words?
- Have you ever listened to a song and thought about how closely it relates to a situation you previously or recently experienced?
- Have you ever listened to a song that actually helped you make a change in your life?
- Have you ever listened to someone talk about something and said to yourself, "That could be a song?"

I do it all of the time. Somehow, love is always there. You can always **find it in a song** whether you are looking for it or not. You will find it. It will find you. It will touch you. That's love.

I may be in church listening to a new song that touches my heart and brings tears to my eyes. The tears may be of joy or sorrow, because I can relate so well to it through a personal experience or my awareness of the experience of another. I may be listening to the radio and hear a new song that just makes me want to get out of the car and dance. It may also cause me to reflect on my life. Or it may just bring a smile to my face, because it is a confirmation of something good. That's love. And again, you can always **find it in a song**. Just listen. Listen closely. Listen to love. Hear and see how love spreads through song. That's the power of a song. That's the power of love. Love always. Love daily. 365 Love.™

Have you told someone you loved them today? I have.™

Love yesterday, today and future tomorrows,™
Torion

Message in the MUSIC
Brian McKnight - Everything You Touch is a Song

Note the QUOTE!
"Music is love in search of a word." --- Sidonie Gabrielle

It's a Process
March 27

Today's NOTE
I am currently reading *The 21 Most Powerful Minutes in a Leader's Day* by John C. Maxwell. It's a leadership development book designed to be read in small, daily portions. Week 3 begins the chapter on The Law of **Process** --- Leadership develops daily, not in a day.

The same applies with love. It's a **process**. It takes time. It takes experience. It develops daily, not in a day. You have to practice love to grow in love. You have to learn more about love to grow in love. That doesn't mean that it's easy. It doesn't mean that there will not be mistakes. In order to become good at anything, you have to work on it.

Think about a new job. You have to learn how to do the job before you become good at it. You repeat what you were originally taught and how it was taught to you. You may then come up with your own **process** to make it work more efficiently for you. As new scenarios are introduced in your job, you take what you know and refine existing **process**es or create new **process**es to get the job done. Over time, you know your job like the back of your hand. You may even be considered a "subject matter expert." You can train others to do the job. You can resolve problems based on your experiences in the job, but you had to get the experience first. It was a **process**; a learning **process**. It developed daily, not in a day.

Learning to love the right way, God's way, takes time. For some it's a shorter period than for others, but it's a **process** for everyone. It's a daily **process**. You just have to keep at it. Keep practicing it. Repeat it. Revise it. Use lessons learned to become better at it. Love always. Love daily. 365 Love.™

Have you told someone you loved them today? I have.™

Love yesterday, today and future tomorrows,™
Torion

Message in the MUSIC
Earth, Wind & Fire – All About Love

Note the QUOTE!
"One word frees us of all the weight and pain in life. That word is love." --- Sophocles

The Ability to Move Forward
March 28

Today's NOTE

So often we are held back by frequently reflecting on our past or what we wish we could be. We look at our personal faults. We loathe on material things we wish we had. We hold on to what others have done to us to cause hurt and pain. We don't let go.

Love provides **the ability to move forward**. Faith and belief in love, helps us to appreciate who we are and what we have. Love helps us to let go and let God. Love helps us to think about the good in what is vs. the bad in what was and what is not. Love helps us to separate ourselves from negative people and negative things. It brings us closer to everything positive. Love opens our eyes to see things differently. It helps us to see good when otherwise we may not have. It helps us appreciate. It helps us to be humble. It helps us realize when it is time to move on. It helps us take the steps necessary to move in a more positive direction mentally, physically and spiritually. Love helps us to see those qualities in us that are good and keep them in the forefront of our minds. Love helps us see the qualities in us that are a work in progress and improve upon them. Love helps us to feel good about what we have accomplished and helps us put actions in place to progress. Love allows us the ability to say "hello" to something new and "goodbye" to something old. Love helps us to build upon good things and become even better. Love helps us to take negative experiences as lessons learned to improve on ourselves and our actions. It helps us to forgive others and ourselves.

Love is an enormous power. It changes things. It can make the impossible, possible. We have to open our hearts to receive it. We have to believe in it. It provides **the ability to move forward**. Love always. Love daily. 365 Love.™

Have you told someone you loved them today? I have.™

Love yesterday, today and future tomorrows,™
Torion

Message in the MUSIC
Chrisette Michelle – Blame It On Me

Note the QUOTE!
"It's not any fix we're in that causes us to suffer. Rather, it's the stuff we invent about our situation that creates the struggle. It's not who we think we are, but what we're not that makes us lose our way." --- Susan L. Taylor

Feel Good
March 29

Today's NOTE

Even though my head is stuffy, my nose is runny, and my throat is sore from the ailment of a bad cold, I **feel good** today. I feel really, really good today. I **feel good** inside and out. I feel like having fun. I feel like dancing. I feel like singing. I feel like kicking off my shoes and resting my feet. I feel like shouting with joy. I feel like smiling. I feel like doing whatever I want to do. I feel like giving praises. I feel like laughing . I feel like crying happy tears. I feel like doing something new and different. I feel like doing something I love to do. I feel like playing hop scotch and "1-2-3 red light." I feel like eating some of grand mama's good soul food. I feel like swimming at the park. I feel like playing "hide and go seek." I feel like watching the sun set. I feel like hanging out with a good friend. I feel like some "me" time. I feel like going for a long ride. I feel like watching a good movie. I feel like roller skating. I feel like reading a good book. I feel like writing a song. I feel like being adventurous. I feel listening to some good music. I feel like having a romantic evening. I feel like holding hands. I feel like being the recipient of a passionate kiss. I feel like hugging a good friend. I feel like catching some lightening bugs in a jar. I feel like getting my hair and nails done. I feel like shopping. I feel like a good massage. I feel like doing so many other "**feel good**" things. Just thinking about all of the possibilities makes me **feel good**. I just **feel good**. I feel real good. That's love. That's **feel good** love. Love always. Love daily. 365 Love.™

Have you told someone you loved them today? I have.™

Love yesterday, today and future tomorrows,™
Torion

Message in the MUSIC
TLC - Good Love

Note the QUOTE!
"To love is to receive a glimpse of heaven." --- Karen Sunde

Meet the Browns
March 30

Today's NOTE

I don't watch TV much, but I have a few shows that I am addicted to and watch regularly. **Meet the Browns** is one of them. It is so funny to me, especially Mr. Brown himself. If I ever need a good laugh, I can count on **Meet the Browns** to get the job done for me. Two of the main characters on the show are actually married - Mr. Brown and Cora Simmons (father and daughter on the show) are Mr. and Mrs. David and Tamela Mann (in real life).

I was listening to a radio interview with David and Tamela today. I was particularly interested in their responses to questions about their relationship on and off the set. They have been married for over 20 years. They met through a common friend and wound up singing together as members of Kirk Franklin and the Family's first multi-platinum gospel album. They mentioned that the main thing that keeps their marriage alive is that they actually like each other. I was interested in finding our more about the couple, so I searched the internet and found their website at www.tillymannmusic.com. I loved the fact that a married couple, who loved one another, decided to have a website together to promote their collective and individual works (as one). This was a true representation of commitment to one another, support for one another, and their unity with one another. While they each have their own identities, they made a collective decision to partner in marriage and in their work efforts. Wow! That is so awesome to me. I was so excited reviewing the website and how well it was put together. The site includes interview and performance clips by the couple. It also includes individual and collective projects supported by the couple.

A portion of Tamela's bio reads as follows:
What kept the marriage strong then—as it does now—is laughter, and more importantly, the ability to laugh at life and persevere through the good and bad. "David is always there for me and makes me laugh," she says. "It's hard to be upset with him because he cracks me up. He makes me the maddest and happiest of any person I have ever met!"

Now that's love. That is a prime example of how a couple can work together and be happy together. They are both grounded in faith and love the Lord. They laugh together and pray together. The key word is "together." We often hear of drama regarding couples. It is such a pleasure to hear the "good" stories. These stories help strengthen my belief in love. It lets me know that it is possible and that it exists. I love to read about them and share them with others. Things may not always come easy, but it is so much easier when you love. When you know how to love and believe in love. When both persons in a relationship know that the goal is to work together, not as individuals. It's a "we vs. me" mentality that keeps it going. That's what love is. That's what love needs. That's how love gives. That's how love maintains. So as you look for examples of good relationships to learn from, I encourage you to go **Meet the Browns**.

Love Always. Love Daily. 365 Love.

I am in the process of developing my own "love" story. This story reminds me in some ways of my own. I guess that's one of the reasons I became so attached to it. And it keeps getting better and better as each day passes. I look forward to being able to share it with you one day. Maybe sooner than you think (smile). And it is all because two people love. Love always. Love daily. 365 Love.™

Have you told someone you loved them today? I have.™

Love yesterday, today and future tomorrows,™

Torion

Message in the MUSIC
Tamela Mann – Speak Lord

Note the QUOTE!
"And if it all falls apart, I will know deep in my heart, the only dream that mattered had come true. In this life, I was loved by you." --- Colin Raye

Love Always. Love Daily. 365 Love.

Maslow's Hierarchy of Needs
March 31

Today's NOTE

Maslow's Hierarchy of Needs was a topic covered in my previous studies in management, psychology and project management. It is a psychology theory, proposed by Abraham Maslow, describing the stages of growth in humans. It is often represented in the form of a pyramid, to include the fundamental needs at the bottom and the need for Self-actualization at the top. The needs at the bottom must be met before you can reach the top.

- <u>Physiological Needs</u> are the basic requirements for human survival. If these requirements are not met, the body cannot function.
- <u>Safety Needs</u> take precedence when the physical needs are relatively satisfied. They include personal and financial security, health and well-being, and safety against accidents/illness.
- <u>Belongingness and Love Needs</u> are based on relationships such as friendship, intimacy and family.
- <u>Esteem Needs</u> include the desire to be accepted and valued by others including the need to be respected and to have self-esteem and self-respect.
- <u>Self-actualization</u> involves a person achieving their full potential and realizing that potential. Maslow describes this as this as the desire to become more and more what one is, and to become everything that one is capable of becoming.

In order to reach a clear understanding of the self-actualization level of need, one must achieve and master the previous needs. Most people fail to reach the top portion of **Maslow's hierarchy of needs**, often struggling with the bottom level needs. Love is a key and important part of getting there.

Love Always. Love Daily. 365 Love.

People need to feel a sense of belonging and acceptance, whether it comes from social groups (athletic teams or the office/work) or small groups (family and mentors). They need to love and be loved by others. They need romantic, brotherly, charitable, or family love. In the absence of these elements, many people become susceptible to loneliness, social anxiety, and depression.

According to **Maslow's** theory, fulfilling the need for love (belonging) can often overcome the physiological and security needs - the bottom two levels. I believe this to be the case in reality as well. You have to get past these levels to move forward to the last two levels.

Love is the basis for satisfying all needs, including **Maslow's Hierarchy of Needs**. Knowing love, giving love, and believing in love helps you take care of basic, safety and belongingness needs. With personal growth in love comes loving yourself and all that you are and yet to be. With that comes a level of love that addresses esteem. Once the esteem need is accomplished, we can move on to the top level, self-actualization. We all have a purpose in life. We are on a journey to find that specific purpose and fulfill it. God has that plan for us and God is love. Love will get us there. It takes care of all of our needs. It is the key. Love is the foundation that takes us to higher levels in life. We cannot accomplish anything or grow to our fullest potential without it. Embrace it and have faith in it. We all need it. I need it. You need it. Everyone needs it. Everybody needs love. Love always. Love daily. 365 Love.™

Have you told someone you loved them today? I have.™

Love yesterday, today and future tomorrows,™
Torion

Message in the MUSIC
Jill Scott - The Fact Is (I Need You)

Note the QUOTE!
"All you need is love." --- John Lennon & Paul McCartney

Love Always. Love Daily. 365 Love.

April

"Love is like a butterfly. It goes where it pleases and it pleases wherever it goes."
— Unknown

It Takes Adversity to Grow
April 1

Today's NOTE

Adversity is a state, condition, or instance of serious or continued difficulty. When faced with it, people become either bitter or better. Who and what a person becomes as a result of **adversity** is by choice. With faith in love, the choice would be one for the better.

It takes **adversity** to grow. You have to look at the situation closely to see the positive outcome and grow from it. That's what takes place with love. No one said that growing in love would be easy. For some it is. For others, it's a challenge. The adverse situations we are faced with sometimes make that challenge even more difficult. The key is to know that love helps you make it through those adverse situations. Love helps you overcome. Love is something good. We experience **adversity** to help us grow in love. To become better people. To humble us. To remove our egos. To make us more appreciative. To help us make better choices and decisions. To make us do the right thing. To become givers. To learn how to help others. To eliminate selfishness. To make us treat others right. To help us be fair. To help us be honest. To help us to love ourselves. To help us love. In the end, **adversity** shows a person his courage to carry on. Love always. Love daily. 365 Love.™

Have you told someone you loved them today? I have.™

Love yesterday, today and future tomorrows,™
Torion

Message in the MUSIC
Mary Mary - It Will All Be Worth It

Note the QUOTE!
"In the end, **adversity** shows a person his courage to carry on." --- John C. Maxwell

Happy Birthday, Evelyn!
April 2

Today's NOTE

Today is my girlfriend's, **Evelyn** birthday. We have been friends for over 20 years now and I love her dearly. She is like a sister to me. People who know me well, know that I speak to a lot of people and know a lot of people, but do not have many people that are REALLY, really close to me. **Evelyn** is one of only a few people I consider to be my "best" friend -- BFF.

We met when I was in college. She and I were dating Alphas and were introduced to one another through those relationships. Both of us were looking for a place to live (off campus) and became roommates. We have been best buds since then. She was one of the best roommates I have ever had. We had no major issues that we could not resolve and got along very well. We both have different personalities, but have some similarities as well. She's a talker, I'm a listener. She's outgoing, I'm more of a solo, small crowd kind of person. She's a diverse hair person, I'm the basic style hair person. She never meets a stranger, I have to warm up to people first. But she is MY friend. I feel so blessed that God has placed her in my life not just for a reason, or a season, but for a lifetime.

My girlfriend, **Evelyn** is so creative. She can think of an idea for anything and everything. You name it and she has a million ideas to make it that much better. It amazes me of how she can think of so many creative things. In addition to that, she writes poetry. She is writing a few books. She is an event planner. She has been on the Board for various charitable organizations. She is a giver. She is a hard worker. She loves scrapbooking. She loves to have fun. She loves to dance. She loves MOCHA (the coffee and her dog). She is always exploring new things -- activities, restaurants, events, etc. She is adventurous. She loves, and then some.... She is **Evelyn**, my friend.

I have watched her grow mentally and spiritually over the past several years, and she is still evolving. I know that she would do almost anything for me and I would do the same for her. We have laughed together and cried together. She has been there for me and I for her. We have supported each other in our personal endeavors. We have been an ear to listen for each other. We have held each other when we felt that our worlds were falling apart and we have lifted each other to remind us that "this too shall pass." We have given each other strength at times when we may not have even realized we were doing so. We encourage each other to be the best we can be. And we both believe that God can take care of anything and everything. We truly know each other's spirit. Regardless of what we have experienced through the years, and how we have changed, we both know that we each love.

I am thankful to **Evelyn**'s mother for brining her into this world so that we may cross paths. I am thankful to our past boyfriends for introducing us to one another. I am thankful to all the people and events that have brought us closer

Love Always. Love Daily. 365 Love.

together through good times, trials and tribulations. I am thankful for the happy moments shared and those yet to come. I am thankful for our friendship. I am thankful for our love.

So today, I want to dedicate 365 Love to my friend, **Evelyn**; in celebration of another year passed and prayers for many more to come. In celebration of her birthday. In celebration of the positive and adverse events in her life that have moved her along in her journey to become what she is destined to be. In celebration of phileo (friendship) love. Happy birthday, **Evelyn**! I love you. Love always. Love daily. 365 Love.™

Have you told someone you loved them today? I have.™

Love yesterday, today and future tomorrows,™
Torion

Message in the MUSIC
Brandy – Best Friend

Note the QUOTE!
"When it hurts to look back, and you're scared to look ahead, you can look beside you and your best friend will be there." --- Unknown

Love Always. Love Daily. 365 Love.

Keep the Faith
April 3

Today's NOTE

Today's message is going to be brief and to the point. As you go though life's struggles, don't forget that in order to make it through, you must **keep the faith**. **Keep the faith** in God. **Keep the faith** in love. God is love and love will help you get through anything.

Today was a day of heightened awareness for a few people close and dear to me going through some internal struggles. They are in a place where there is a need for them to make decisions that would change their future. That one decision will put them on a path for something better, something worse, or consistency (the same thing). The right decision is based on their faith. They have to have faith. They have to **keep the faith**. They have to know what love is. They have to do the right things and make the right moves for the right reasons. They have to believe that love conquers all and that you cannot make it through life without it.

Take a moment today and think about your faith. Think about times you have made it through because of your faith. Think about times you did not because you had no faith. You did not let go and trust that God would handle it. You did not put it in His hands. You did not believe. Sometimes we put ourselves in certain situations and want to blame others for the outcome. However, we do not take the time to think about our personal contributions and choices that brought the situation into existence. Sometimes the situation just presents itself to us. It's one of those new life challenges that we have to make it through. Regardless, when you **keep the faith**, it changes things. Love changes things. Love always. Love daily. 365 Love.™

Have you told someone you loved them today? I have.™

Love yesterday, today and future tomorrows,™
Torion

Message in the MUSIC
Marvin Sapp - Never Would Have Made It

Note the QUOTE!
"Love means to commit oneself without guarantee, to give oneself completely in the hope that our love will produce love in the loved person. Love is an act of faith, and whoever is of little faith is also of little love"
--- Erich Fromm

Love Always. Love Daily. 365 Love.

Take the First Step
April 4

Today's NOTE

There are thousands of books, articles, songs, blogs, talk shows, etc., for people to gain positive insights, lessons learned, inspiration and motivation to move them into a positive life direction. 365 Love is just one of them. Some people read or hear about positivity on a periodic basis. Others do so on a more regular basis. The key to initiating the move to a more positive direction is to act on what was read or heard. So often people talk about change, but never act on it. You have to **take the first step**. Love is a positive thought, act, feeling and emotion. In order for you to grow in it, you must act on it. You must **take the first step**.

Think about a child learning to walk. They begin by finding a way to stand. Once they learn that they can pull up on something to stand, they begin to use that same support they were able to pull up on as an object to walk around. They then let go of the object and stand with no support. They may wobble some and fall, but typically they don't give up. They will pull up on something and try again. Next, they **take the first step**. They may wobble a little and fall. They try again. Eventually, they are able to take a few more steps. Then they are walking. Before you know it, they are running. In order for the child to learn to walk, they have to act on it. They watch others to see how they walk. They take small steps to obtain the bigger goal. They do not give up. They become more and more aggressive with their progression until they eventually get it. Parents encourage them along the way. They hold the child's hand to provide some level of support until they are ready to walk on their own.

To grow, you have to **take the first step**. To love, you have to **take the first step**. To move forward, you have to **take the first step**. You have to begin somewhere. The key is to begin. You have to take one step at a time. And when and if you fall, you have to get back up and try again. You have to keep trying. You have to try some things on your own. And you may have to leverage off of the support of others. Support can come from a family member, a friend , a pastor or a book. The ultimate support comes from Love - Godly love. And with God's love, and belief in His love, you be able to keep going.

Is there a change needed in your life? Are you ready to **take the first step** to move forward with that change? Do you love and believe in love? Do you have GREAT faith? Nothing changes if you don't act on it. Nothing changes if you don't **take the first step**. Don't miss out on improving your life by not **taking the first step**. As you move forward with change, don't forget about love and the importance of love. That's what helps you keep going. Love always. Love daily. 365 Love.™

Have you told someone you loved them today? I have.™

Love Always. Love Daily. 365 Love.

Love yesterday, today and future tomorrows, ™
Torion

Message in the MUSIC
Dru Hill – **Five Steps**

Note the QUOTE!
"Faith is **taking the first step** even when you don't see the staircase" --- Martin Luther King, Jr.

Words
April 5

Today's NOTE

I went to another poetry night event this past weekend. This time, I went with some girlfriends. I had so much fun. I think I am really beginning to fall in love with this poetry thing (smile). I saw some familiar poets and some new poets. All had powerful messages to deliver with **words**. **Words** that made you want to cry. **Words** that made you happy. **Words** that made you feel some level of anger or sorrow. **Words** that made you laugh. **Words** that put you in an intimate mood. **Words** that made you think about your life and the life of others. **Words** that made you think about events taking place in the world. **Words**. God blessed those talented individuals with the creativity to deliver powerful messages through spoken **words**.

Words can hurt or heal. They can damage or build. They can motivate or discourage. They can make you feel secure or frighten you. **Words** are powerful tools like weapons and weapons can be used for good and bad. Dr. King used **words** to fight for civil rights. Comedians use **words** to make us laugh. Pastors use **words** to give praises and teach us the Word. Your **words,** in conjunction with the tone of your voice, determine how your message is received. How do you use your **words**?

- Do you use them to motivate or discourage?
- Does the tone used in the delivery of your **words** allow a person to receive your message positively? or does it have a negative impact?
- Does your choice of **words** and tone demonstrate that you are a loving person?

Think about it. There is a popular phase that says, "It's not what you say. It's how you say it." Use **words** to have a positive impact. Use **words** that show you love. Love always. Love daily. 365 Love.™

Have you told someone you loved them today? I have.™

Love yesterday, today and future tomorrows,™
Torion

Message in the MUSIC
Anthony David – **Words**

Note the QUOTE!
"**Words** mean more than what is set down on paper. It takes the human voice to infuse them with shades of deeper meaning." --- Maya Angelou

Butterfly
April 6

Today's NOTE

Have you ever taken a moment to think about the beauty of a **butterfly**? Better yet, have you thought about the process they go through to become so beautiful? A **butterfly** develops in four phases.

(1) They begin as eggs and remain in this state for 5-10 days.
(2) They then become caterpillars. As they develop, they outgrow their old skin, shedding it 5 - 6 times to reveal their new skin.
(3) Next, they form a pupa shell and remain in this state for 2 - 3 weeks. Here is where most of the development takes place. Their wings develop and grow strong so that they can eventually fly.
(4) Once this development process is complete, they go through an internal struggle to escape from the pupa shell as an adult, a beautiful **butterfly**.

If at any point in the **butterfly**'s development process something is cut short or disrupted, it never develops to its full potential. Each phase is an important part of their path to become what they are destined to be - a beautiful **butterfly**.

In life, we go through struggles to become who we are destined to be. We transform from one state to another as we learn and grow. We are the same person, but change as we experience love and life. We shed our skin. We shed those qualities that were not good or hold us back and replace them with those that move us closer to fulfilling our purpose in life. The stronger we get and the closer we get to fulfilling our purpose, we go through more struggles. These struggles assist in transforming us. When we realize that they are lessons learned and part of the process, we begin to progress even more. As we learn to love, practice love, give love and know love, we grow closer to becoming that beautiful **butterfly**.

- Where are you in your stage of development?
- Can you recall life changing events that brought you closer to love? Friendship, Brotherly, Charitable, and/or romantic love?

Love always. Love daily. 365 Love.™

Have you told someone you loved them today? I have.™

Love yesterday, today and future tomorrows,™
Torion

Message in the MUSIC
Denise Williams - Black **Butterfly**

Note the QUOTE!
"Love is like a **butterfly**. It goes where it pleases and it pleases wherever it goes" --- Unknown

Guess Who Loves You More
April 7

Today's NOTE
There is always someone who can and will love you more. Guess who **loves you more**.

- Look in the mirror and you may just be surprised at who you see.
- Your parents **love you more**. Even tough love is love. Saying "no" so that you can try, experience, remain protected and grow is still love.
- Your best friend **loves you more**. A "true" best friend does. They will be there for you through thick and thin.
- Your spouse **loves you more**. A "good" man or woman filling this role knows how to show it.
- Your child **loves you more**. Even though for some, they sometimes have a funny way of showing it, but when anyone talks about mom or dad, it is on!
- Your family **loves you more**. You may fight, not speak, laugh or play. When it is time for family to stick together, they do.
- Someone sending out a special prayer for you **loves you more**. They put aside how well they do or do not know you and pray for a better situation for you.

The ultimate one that **loves you more** is God. He **loves you more** than life itself. He is your best friend, your father, your advisor and your mentor. He is <u>always</u> there for you. Don't ever forget that. Love always. Love daily. 365 Love.™

Have you told someone you loved them today? I have.™

Love yesterday, today and future tomorrows,™
Torion

Message in the MUSIC
Raheem DeVaughn - Guess Who **Loves You More**

Note the QUOTE!
"We loved with a love that was more than love." --- Edgar Allan Poe

The Greatest Love of All
April 8

Today's NOTE
God loves all of His children. He knows what you will do before you do it. He knows everything about you. He knows that you are a treasure. He is love. He is the source of love. He wants all of His children to love. Through Him, you learn about love. You learn how to love. Most importantly, you learn how to love for yourself. It's the beginning of your journey to being able to love others and receive love from others. It's **the greatest love of all**. Love always. Love daily. 365 Love.™

Have you told someone you loved them today? I have.™

Love yesterday, today and future tomorrows,™
Torion

Message in the MUSIC
Whitney Houston – **The Greatest Love of All**

Note the QUOTE!
"Learning to love yourself is **the greatest love of all**" --- Whitney Houston

Support for Our Children
April 9

Today's NOTE
My son is playing AAU basketball for the first time this year. I spent most of the day at the gym watching hundreds of children play basketball. Almost my entire immediate family was there to show their support. From ages 6 - 18, the gym was packed with children, all in uniform representing a team effort. The gym had four courts and each team played a minimum of three games. The games on each court were almost non-stop from the AM to the PM. When my family and I left late in the evening, teams were still playing.

As I sat there and watched the children play, I noticed all of the parents. Some volunteered to help out around the gym. Some kept score. Some were coaches and assistant coaches. Some were boosters and sold t-shirts for their team. Some kept the stats. Some took care of the refreshments. Others were just there to cheer on the teams. It was an all-day event in a "hot" gym on a hot day, but the parents were there. They were in the building "representing." They applauded. They encouraged. They cheered. They fussed in an effort to direct the children to make better decisions on the court. They laughed. They were there. They were there as **support for our children**. It was a beautiful sight to see. It was a day filled with love all over the place. Everyone was nice to one another. Everyone had an appreciation for the game itself and the children...**support for our children**. Now that's love. Love always. Love daily. 365 Love.™

Have you told someone you loved them today? I have.™

Love yesterday, today and future tomorrows,™
Torion

Message in the MUSIC
Michael Jackson – You Are My Life

Note the QUOTE!
"Kids spell love T-I-M-E." --- John Crudele

It Has No Limits
April 10

Today's NOTE
Love has **no limits**. It can find you when you least expect it. It is in your place of work. It is in the church. It is in your favorite place of recreation. It is in your home. It is in your favorite restaurant or grocery store. It is in your school. It is around you as you walk down the street. It is everywhere. Quite often, people only associate love with affection; a romantic kind of love. When a person they are in love with "breaks" their heart, they doubt love. They speak negatively of love. But love is more than romance. Love is greater than romance. The greatest love is spiritual. God is love and His love is the greatest gift of all. With a strong spiritual faith in love, all other aspects of love fall into place. Charitable love comes. Romantic love comes. Family love is enhanced. Brotherly love grows. You never meet a stranger. You have a renewed vision for giving and treating others right. You have a new perspective on self-love. It is easy for you to love and be loved. Love is anything to anyone, something to someone, and everything to everyone. **It has no limits**. It is infinite. It stretches over and beyond. It goes on and on and on. Love always. Love daily. 365 Love.™

Have you told someone you loved them today? I have.™

Love yesterday, today and future tomorrows,™
Torion

Message in the MUSIC
Mary J Blige - Love **No Limit**

Note the QUOTE!
"Just because you know someone doesn't mean you love them, and just because you don't know people doesn't mean you can't love them. You can fall in love with a complete stranger in a heartbeat, if God planned that route for you. So open your heart to strangers more often. You never know when God will throw that pass at you." --- Heather Grove

I'll Be There
April 11

Today's NOTE

Alison is another one of my best friends. I have known her for over 15 years. We met at work and immediately "clicked." She is always willing to lend a helping hand in and out of the office. She taught me how to lay sheet rock so that I could finish my basement. She helped me financially during times when my finances were not as together as they are now. She opened her home to me and my children during a time of turmoil in my life. She was a shoulder to cry on at times when I was hurting during my 1st marriage. She was there to encourage and lend a helping hand when work became stressful. She was there just to check in on me and see how things were going. She was there during family issues. She was there when the children accomplished milestones in their lives. She was there to support some of the other personal endeavors in my life. She was there then and she is here now. She has always been there as long as we have been friends. She is a good friend. A great friend. One of my best friends. If you could put a label on someone who truly loves her family and friends, she would have a HUGE one. A true friend is there for you through good and bad times, happiness and sorrow, physically or in spirit. That's what love is. That's what love does. That's love.

This past week has been a trying week for Alison. Her aunt passed away in the early part of the week and her brother had a stroke on the same day. For the past week, I would call her and/or text her daily to see how she was doing. As she struggled with her emotions knowing the medical situation her brother was in, I would sometimes talk to her as she drove back and forth between cities on almost a daily basis with restless days and nights. I listened to the tears in her voice and her efforts to lift her spirits and crack a joke from time to time. I prayed for her and her family daily. I wanted her to know that I was there and "**I'll be there.**" Just as she has been there for me.

My friend found out that she lost her brother on Sunday, just short of a week later. I can only image how she must feel. See, I have never lost a close family member before. I have lost distant aunts, uncles, cousins, etc., but no one I was personally close to. My heart goes out to her during this time of bereavement. I want her to know that I care. I want her to know that I am her friend and I love her. I want her to know that **I'll be there**. Whenever she needs me, **I'll be there**. A smiling face. A shoulder to cry on. A voice to help lift her spirits. An ear to listen.... **I'll be there**. That's what friends are for. That's love. Love always. Love daily. 365 Love.™

Have you told someone you loved them today? I have.™

Love yesterday, today and future tomorrows,™
Torion

Message in the MUSIC
Michael Jackson - **I'll Be There**

Note the QUOTE!
"A true friend will always be there when the whole world left you, always cheers you up when the whole world has turned you down and never asks you to act like an angel, but he becomes your angel." --- Lloyd

Color of Love
April 12

Today's NOTE
When you think of love, what **color**s come to mind? You can think about all of the **color**s of the rainbow and associate some feeling of love to them. A **color** may be calming. A **color** may be exciting. A **color** may make you feel a sense of joy. A **color** may make you feel warm inside. A **color** may make you feel at peace. A **color** may make you feel secure. A **color** may make you smile. A **color** may make you feel romantic and so on and so on.

I can assure you that I would receive several different responses if I asked this question to several different people. This is how love is. People feel love in different ways, like different **color**s. People receive love in different ways, like different **color**s. People demonstrate love in different ways, like different **color**s. Just because someone doesn't love the way you love, doesn't mean they don't love. The key is that they love. They demonstrate love characteristics, love behaviors, love traits...**love color**s. Love comes in all shapes and sizes, big and small, different nationalities and races. It's like a huge array of different **color**s. You can mix and match **color**s to make new **color**s; more **love color**s; more love. Love always. Love daily. 365 Love.™

Have you told someone you loved them today? I have.™

Love yesterday, today and future tomorrows,™
Torion

Message in the MUSIC
Boyz II Men – **The Color of Love**

Note the QUOTE!
"Love sees no **color**, age, weight, or looks, it only sees what is in your heart." --- Shana Stanley

A Long Walk
April 13

Today's NOTE
Love can make you feel so free. It clears your mind and opens your heart to wonderful things. It's like taking **a long walk**. It could be a **walk** by yourself or with a friend, family member or romantic love. **Walk**ing serves multiple purposes. You do it to get you to a specific destination. You **walk** for health purposes. You **walk** as a hobby. You **walk** to ease your mind. You **walk** to be a part of something or for a good charitable cause. You **walk** to hold hands. You **walk** for fresh air. You **walk**. All of these are good reasons. The initial intent is good. The end result is good. It's a feeling of love. Love of yourself and/or love of another.

Just thinking about it makes me feel like taking **a long walk** right now. How often do you just take the time for **a long walk**? How often do you invite someone to take a **walk** with you...

- for no specific reason?
- to talk?
- to help motivate them to get on track with their personal fitness?
- to enjoy the beauty of the outdoors together?
- to meet your neighbors?
- to ease / clear their mind?
- to cool off?

To me, an invitation to **a long walk** is a romantic thought, depending on the mood. It's a kind gesture, depending on the person. It's healing and comforting, depending on the situation. It's a reminder of love. It's an act of love. Love always. Love daily. 365 Love.™

Have you told someone you loved them today? I have.™

Love yesterday, today and future tomorrows,™
Torion

Message in the MUSIC
Jill Scott – **A Long Walk**

Note the QUOTE!
"Pursue some path, however narrow and crooked, in which you can **walk** with love and reverence." --- Henry David Thoreau

It Makes Things Happen
April 14

Today's NOTE
Love is full of surprises. **It makes things happen.** I pray for love each day and receive it in so many different ways. I am so thankful for the love of God and all of the actions He takes to share love. The simple things in life are as much of a display of love as the grand things. A breath of fresh air is love. The ability to wake up, hear, speak, smell and touch are daily blessings and gifts of love. What a joy. Love provides all of those things.

Love **makes things happen**. You can't control it. When it comes to love, it controls you. You can try to find love, but real love finds you. You ask for the gift of love. With faith, positive thinking, and prayer the gift is yours. In God's time, it is yours. It happens. It may not be at the exact time you want it to. It may not be in the exact form you want it to be in, but it happens when you need it and comes to you how you need it. That's love. **It makes things happen**. Love always. Love daily. 365 Love.™

Have you told someone you loved them today? I have.™

Love yesterday, today and future tomorrows,™
Torion

Message in the MUSIC
Pebbles – Love **Makes Things Happen**

Note the QUOTE!
"Love is a symbol of eternity. It wipes out all sense of time, destroying all memory of a beginning and all fear of an end" --- Unknown

Your Inner Circle
April 15

Today's NOTE

My mother and I had a discussion on people in your **inner circle** a few days ago. Your **inner circle** consists of people whom you spend most of your personal time with, and who you spend your time with is a reflection of who you are. These individuals either help you progress, hold you back, or push you further behind. Positive people promote positive things and positive growth. Negative people promote negative things and have a negative impact on growth. Love is positive and knows the difference between the two. As you grow in love, you will find that you have a stronger desire to be around more positive things and positive people. You learn how to better assess the people who will remain in your life for a reason, a season or a lifetime. You learn how to asses who should be in your **inner circle**.

- Who is in your **inner circle**?
- Who do you spend most of your personal time with?

Think about five people in your **inner circle** whom you spend most of your personal time with.

- Are they positive or negative individuals?
- Do they spend more time talking about positive things or negative things?
- Do they support you, guide you and have good intentions for you?
- Do they treat other people well and promote positive thinking?
- Do they demonstrate that they are loving individuals?

As you think about the responses to these questions, assess whether your **inner circle** needs to change. With love, you sometimes have to let people go. You can still love them. However, the time they spend in your life may have to change in order for you to continue to grow. As this happens, you become better able to spread love and have a positive impact on others. Remember love is contagious. It just takes longer for some to get there than others. You should not allow someone in your **inner circle** to stunt your growth in love. You can make the effort to bring them along on your journey. However, if it is not their time, you have to move forward. Then, continue to grow by keeping love within your **inner circle**. You can't control a change others, but you can control a change in yourself. Love always. Love always. Love daily. 365 Love.™

Have you told someone you loved them today? I have.™

Love yesterday, today and future tomorrows,™
Torion

Message in the MUSIC
Whitney Houston – **I Believe in You and Me**

Note the QUOTE!
"Truly good friends are hard to find, difficult to leave, and impossible to forget" --- Unknown

Reap What You Sow
April 16

Today's NOTE

For every action there is a reaction. This is a proven fact. Scientific experiments all around the world are based on this fact. Life is based on this fact. One of the most common childhood experiments is one involving the growth of plants. You plant a seed and do all of the "right" things to make it grow. The more you do the right things to care for the plant, the healthier, more beautiful it becomes. You provide sun, water and other nourishment. The other seeds planted receive varied care. They are deprived of the right things to make them grow. You do all of the "wrong" things to them on purpose. They are mistreated and in turn have defeats and/or eventually die.

There is always an opportunity to make a change. Like with the plant experiment, you can choose to do all of the right things to revive a dying plant. The right thing produces positive results. What was done was done. You dealt with the consequences resulting in sick plant. Once you made the choice to do right, the plant was revived and was able to grow again. Sometimes there is not an opportunity to change the initial outcome. However, you can take the lesson learned and change your approach for a similar situation in the future. Using the plant experiment example again, when you do the wrong things to care for the plant, the plant may die. The wrong doing produces bad results / consequences. What is done is done. In this care, you cannot revive the dead plant. However, the next time you plant a seed you can make sure that you care for it the right way for a better end result.

Another way to think about this is the fact that **you reap what you sow**. Whatever you do has consequences. Whatever actions you take in life have reactions. Those reactions can be immediate or over a given period of time. Think about your life and the choices you have made. For those things that you did wrong, there was a reaction / consequence that you paid or will have to pay, for **you reap what you sow**. On the flip side, those things that you did right also had a reaction / positive outcome that resulted from it. In this case, **you reap what you sow** as well.

Why not choose to do the right things? Why not choose to love? For all of the good and all of the love that you put out, you will receive in return. Remember, **you reap what you sow**. You can reap the benefits today, tomorrow, next month, next year, or sometime in the future. Regardless of when, you will reap it. Everything you do comes back to you in some way. What goes around comes around. Good things happen to good people. Loving things happen to loving people. Choose to love and **reap what you sew** in a positive, abundant way. Love always. Love daily. 365 Love.™

Have you told someone you loved them today? I have.™

Love Always. Love Daily. 365 Love.

Love yesterday, today and future tomorrows,™
Torion

Message in the MUSIC
Michelle Williams - Steal Away to Jesus

Note the QUOTE!
"Be not deceived; God is not mocked, for whatsoever a man soweth, that shall he also reap." - Galatians 6:7

Something About the Name Jesus
April 17

Today's NOTE

The youth choir sang in church this Sunday. To see their little faces in the choir stand was a joy. Little children from around 3 - 10 years old raised their little voices to give praise to Jesus through song. As they repeated the chorus over and over again, tears rolled from my eyes. They were happy tears, of course. I could see and feel the emotion in their faces. Those sweet, little faces. How beautiful and magnificent it was to know that they have begun their journey to grow in love at such a young age, and the "right" kind of love at that. Also, in the right place at the right time. Awesome!

One of the songs they performed was titled "I Love You Jesus." There's **something about the name Jesus**. Hearing it over and over again through music and song enters my heart and soul in a profound way. It brings me joy. It makes me smile. It makes me feel good inside. I am grateful for His mercy. I am grateful for what He has done for me; for us. There is something about that name; that sweet name, Jesus. That's love - great love. Love always. Love daily. 365 Love.™

Have you told someone you loved them today? I have.™

Love yesterday, today and future tomorrows,™
Torion

Message in the MUSIC
Kirk Franklin – **Something About the Name Jesus**

Note the QUOTE!
"For God so loved the world that he gave his one and only Son, that whoever believes in him shall not perish but have eternal life." --- John 3:16

Love Always. Love Daily. 365 Love.

It Does Not Judge
April 18

Today's NOTE
Saturday night was poetry night again. The featured artist was a white male by the name of Justin Riley. He had an interesting piece. The poem opened with a musical intro mix from various rap artists using profanity and bitter words in judgment of others. This initially tensed up the predominantly African-American audience. However, once he began to recite his poem, its purpose became clear. He spoke of how he used to pre-**judge** others based on their sexual preferences. He spoke of how people are sometimes afraid of the unknown for not so smart of a reason. He spoke of how hatred fills people's hearts for the wrong reasons. He explained how ignorant he "used" to be and how much of a better person he "is" today. He expressed the importance of getting to know people for who they are and not judging them because of their personal preferences. People are people. They are human beings with feelings. They breathe, eat, drink, and have families. They go through life like everyone else. We are not to **judge** a person based on race, sex, nationality or sexual preference. Regardless, they are people. We are all God's children. We are all on a journey to find love, to grow in love, to share love, and to give love. There is only one **judge** - God. Love does not give us the right to **judge**. Love helps and supports. Love shares truths. Love treats people right. Love is kind. Love always. Love daily. 365 Love.™

Have you told someone you loved them today? I have.™

Love yesterday, today and future tomorrows,™
Torion

The poem made me think about this particular song and the associated music video. It touches on the same subject matter.

Message in the MUSIC
Marsha Ambrosius – **Far Away**

Note the QUOTE!
"If you **judge** people, you have no time to love them." - Mother Theresa

---

Love Always. Love Daily. 365 Love.

Pass it Along
April 19

Today's NOTE

Today is as good of a day as any other day to love. It is a good day to **pass it along**. To spread the word. To share love with others. Reach out to someone today and tell them you love them. Tell a friend. Tell a family member. Tell a co-worker. Send an e-mail or a text message. Post it on Facebook or Twitter. Pick up the phone and call someone. Make a personal visit. Once you do, tell them to **pass it along**. Spread it over and over again. Touch someone's heart and soul today. Show off your big smile (virtually or in person) and share that three word, magnificent phrase --I Love You! Watch what comes to you in return. Ready, set, go! Love always. Love daily. 365 Love.™

Have you told someone you loved them today? I have.™

Love yesterday, today and future tomorrows,™
Torion

Message in the MUSIC
Alicia Keys – **That's How Strong My Love Is**

Note the QUOTE!
"Spread love everywhere you go. Let no one ever come to you without leaving happier." --- Mother Teresa

---

Love Always. Love Daily. 365 Love.

Cherish It
April 20

Today's NOTE

I've heard a number of people recently (men and women) talk about how they let a good person they were in a relationship with get away. This was communicated to me through their song, through their poetry, via talk shows or personal conversations. When you carefully listen to the core of their message, post actual realization is that they did not know how to love or neglected to demonstrate love. See, some people get so used to something good, that they take it for granted. They assume the person is always going to be there. They do not put the same energy into the relationship to maintain it, as they did to establish it. They forget that love evolves. It is a consistent emotion and act. When you truly love something, you **cherish** it. When you truly love someone, you should **cherish** them as well. Then again, some people try so hard to keep a person, that they become controlling and selfish and forget that all it takes is love. Love is neither of those two behaviors. So, they wind up losing the person anyway. They forget to **cherish** who they love most. Some prioritize other things above the person they love, assuming that they know they are loved, and forget that where you spend your time and energy is a reflection of what matters to you most. Love realizes this. Love involves quality time. Love involves words of affirmation. Love involves physical touch. Love involves gifts. Love involves acts of service. Love **cherish**es. The key is to always love. God is love and He comes first. When you align your spirit, thoughts and prayers with love, you become more loving. Love becomes a part of who you are and eventually spreads effortlessly. It does not require a second thought, because it will be a part of who you are and will happen naturally. The character itself and the behaviors are a consistent part of who you are.

- Have you lost someone you truly loved because you did not know how to or neglected to love them?
- Has someone lost you as a result of that same question?
- How has that experience changed you for the next relationship?
- Does this change involve your personal growth in love?

Think love. Act love. Show love. Love always. Love daily. 365 Love.™

Have you told someone you loved them today? I have.™

Love yesterday, today and future tomorrows,™
Torion

Message in the MUSIC
Brian McKnight - **Cherish**

Note the QUOTE!
"Love is the irresistible desire to be irresistibly desired." ---- Mark Twain

Never Go Away
April 21

Today's NOTE
Today was a very busy work day for me. Meetings, e-mails, phone calls..... Thinking, reviewing, writing..... Up the hall, down the hall, upstairs, down stairs..... By the time I got home, I just wanted to kick back and relax. Of course, I resorted to my favorite relaxation technique, listening to music. I know that I can always rely on some good music. I found the perfect song to soothe me - **Never Go Away** by Boyz II Men. It is such a peaceful and tranquil love song, performed so gracefully. It is soothing and relaxing just like I need it to be. It makes you fall in love with love. It makes you want to hold on to love. It makes you wish that love would **never go away**. And it is definitely possible. I am so in love today and every day. I am so in love with love and all that it has to offer. I am so in love with all that it has brought and has yet to bring. I know that it will **never go away**. Love always. Love daily. 365 Love.™

Have you told someone you loved them today? I have.™

Love yesterday, today and future tomorrows,™
Torion

Message in the MUSIC
Boyz II Men - **Never Go Away**

Note the QUOTE!
"Time is too slow for those who wait, too swift for those who fear, too long for those who grieve, too short for those who rejoice, but for those who love, time is eternity." --- Henry Van Dyke

Keep it Going
April 22

Today's NOTE
Love continues to grow. Each day I experience a renewed dose of love and my desire to **keep it going** keeps growing. Today (in 2011), I am excited to introduce the beginning of the new 365 Love products line. Please take a moment to visit my web site at www.365lovedaily.com. View the *Products* page to see what's currently available and what's coming in the near future. I have so much more in store for you. So, be sure to visit again soon. Help spread love and **keep it going** by purchasing one or more of my products and/or sharing the 365 Love site and messages with others. I am always looking forward to what is in store for me, you and others as we continue to grow in love. Love always. Love daily. 365 Love.™

Have you told someone you loved them today? I have.™

Love yesterday, today and future tomorrows,™
Torion

Message in the MUSIC
The Floacist – **Keep it Going**

Note the QUOTE!
"Faith makes all things possible. Love makes them easy" --- Unknown

---

Love Always. Love Daily. 365 Love.

Support is Persuasive
April 23

Today's NOTE

For the past few months, I have been attending poetry events on a consistent basis. You could say that I have become a regular. My love for it motivated me to invite family and friends. They, in turn, invited others. One could say that they have become regulars too (smile). We've even been given a name by the host -- "The Family." I've found it to be soothing to the soul. I love the positive energy that comes from the poets and the type of crowd it draws. Regulars get to know one another and everyone is super friendly. That's love; an environment of positive, friendly love that spreads as new faces enter the place. It's another testimony to prove that love is contagious.

My daughter came with me two weeks ago on a slow night. We let the host know that she could sing. He in turn asked her to come up and do a song. She was not prepared to do so, because this was poetry night, so she sang a capella with no music. The crowd loved her and requested another song. She returned with me again this Saturday and was asked to sing again. She performed the first song and, once again, was asked by the crowd to do another. Now that's love; good, positive, supportive love. By request of the owner, she was asked to sing an original song that I wrote as the second song. She performed this song the last time she was there and they really liked it. Because it was done a capella, I sung the chorus for her (while sitting in my seat) to give her an opportunity to sing ad lib. Everyone loved her voice and the song again! This time, there was a new twist to it. After this particular crowd heard the song, they decided that they wanted to hear "mama" sing. I refused. You see, I have not sung in front of an audience in over 8 years. I still LOVE music, but I don't open up to really sing very much anymore. The host gave me the Shrek Kitten goo, goo eyes. My girlfriend's friend kept on me about it. Then, the crowd started at me. They kept on me. They got on me so hard, that I finally did it. I gave them a sample of "And I'm Telling You I'm Not Going" by Jennifer Holiday. I received a standing ovation. A few of the men fought over me as I was singing (in a cute, humorous way). It was flattering. It was supportive. It was friendly love. Good people in a good place doing good things, supporting one another. You see, **support is persuasive**. Support is love. Love persuaded me to share a hidden gift that was buried inside of me for so many years. My girlfriend was surprised. My daughter was surprised. My cousin was surprised. Everyone who knew me was surprised. Those that didn't know me expressed their appreciation for the surprise. What a wonderful evening with family and friends. New friends and old friends. What a display of brotherly, friendly, positive, supportive love. Can you see how easy it is to spread? Has there ever been a time when you were able to encourage someone who was resistant to try something new or participate just by demonstrating that you supported them? Maybe it was done to you? Love is awesome, right? Love always. Love daily. 365 Love.™

Have you told someone you loved them today? I have.™

Love Always. Love Daily. 365 Love.

Love yesterday, today and future tomorrows,™
Torion

Message in the MUSIC
Jennifer Holiday – **And I'm Telling You I'm Not Going**

Note the QUOTE!
"All, everything that I understand, I understand only because I love." --- Leo Tolstoy

---

Love Him Like I Do
April 24

Today's NOTE
This weekend was a celebration of Jesus. I was blessed with the opportunity to attend a dinner play at the church on the evening of Good Friday. I then topped the weekend off with a magnificent church service on Easter Sunday. I am so grateful for God's love for us. He loved us so much, that He gave His only begotten son, Jesus. Wow! He did that for me. He did that for you. He did that for us. I have to glorify Him and all that He has done and yet to do. That is an incredible kind of love.

Today was a beautiful day. This is a day that the Lord has made. Let us rejoice and be glad in it. A nice afternoon in the park topped the day off. God sure does know how to love. He gave us a beautiful day like today. He provided us with the natural beauty of the grass, flowers and trees. He surrounded us with people we love to share in all of this beauty. He loves us so much. He loves us all of the time. That's why I **love Him like I do.** Love always. Love daily. 365 Love.™

Have you told someone you loved them today? I have.™

Love yesterday, today and future tomorrows,™
Torion

Message in the MUSIC
Deitrick Haddon – I **Love Him Like I Do**

Note the QUOTE!
"For God so loved the world, that he gave his only begotten Son, that whosoever believeth in him should not perish, but have everlasting life." --- John 3:16

Still
April 25

Today's NOTE
I am **still** in love. Why not? There is so much to be in love with. There is so much to love. There are so many people to love. There are so many people out there that share love. Each day I am surrounded by more and more people that give love and receive it in return. I am a living testimony that when you surround yourself by positive people and positive things, when you think positive, and when your actions are positive, you continue to grow in a positive direction and more positive things begin to happen for you. Love happens for you. It is a wonderful feeling that becomes more of the norm than the abnormal. I am **still** in love. Why not? Love always. Love daily. 365 Love.™

Have you told someone you loved them today? I have.™

Love yesterday, today and future tomorrows,™
Torion

Message in the MUSIC
Brian McKnight – **Still**

Note the QUOTE!
"Do you love me because I am beautiful, or am I beautiful because you love me?"
--- Cinderella

Love Always. Love Daily. 365 Love.

A Simple Note
April 26

Today's NOTE
The man that I love whispered the words to a beautiful love song in my ear. And while he cannot really sing (smile), it was the thought that made it so special. The spontaneous gesture. The choice of song. The choice of words. The kind gesture. The act itself. The overall timing. The simplest thing. Love in a simple form. Think about it. **A simple note** of love. Love always. Love daily. 365 Love.™

Have you told someone you loved them today? I have.™

Love yesterday, today and future tomorrows,™
Torion

Message in the MUSIC
Jennifer Hudson - If This Isn't Love

Note the QUOTE!
"No man is worth your tears, and when you find the man who is, he'll never make you cry." --- Unknown

---

Love Always. Love Daily. 365 Love.

Senior Citizens
April 27

Today's NOTE

I stopped by the grocery store the other morning and overheard a game of Bingo taking place. As I approached the self-checkout lane, I noticed a group of **senior citizens** at the tables in the deli section. It was a joy to see them together, having such a great time in each other's company. I saw the smiles on their faces. I saw them laugh. I saw the excitement in their eyes as they called out "Bingo!" The winner of each game had an opportunity to choose two grocery items from the baskets in the front of the room.

I spoke with the customer service agent and found out that this was done on a regular basis. Several area stores used to host it, but this particular store was now the only one that allowed this activity to take place. She mentioned that the **senior citizens** loved coming together to play Bingo. I could definitely tell. I commended the store owner and/or manager for doing such a good thing. I have faith that they will be blessed 10 times over for being so charitable. That's love. Charitable, unconditional love. Did you feel it? I did. Love always. Love daily. 365 Love.™

Have you told someone you loved them today? I have.™

Love yesterday, today and future tomorrows,™
Torion

Message in the MUSIC
Mary Mary - I Got It

Note the QUOTE!
"Love one another and you will be happy. It's as simple and as difficult as that." --
- Michael Leunig

Love Always. Love Daily. 365 Love.

Be Ever Wonderful
April 28

Today's NOTE
Be ever wonderful. Be full of good things. Be full of love. Take each day for what it is. See the beauty in it. Look inside your heart and soul and love "you." Love yourself. Love who you are. Know that no one is perfect. You are imperfectly perfect (smile). Have good character. Demonstrate love in all that you are and all that you do. Beauty is in the eye of the beholder. It's in your eyes and mine. It's what's on the inside that matters most. **Be ever wonderful.** Know who you are. Know what you want to be. Reach for it. Set goals. Reach for those things that make you a better person. Once a goal is reached, set a new one. Don't give up! Let your setbacks be setups for something better. Strive to be better than better. Know that you are meant for greatness. Believe in it. Have faith in it. Be good to yourself and others. Study love. Know love. Be love. **Be ever wonderful.** Love always. Love daily. 365 Love.™

Have you told someone you loved them today? I have.™

Love yesterday, today and future tomorrows,™
Torion

Message in the MUSIC
Earth, Wind & Fire – **Be Ever Wonderful**

Note the QUOTE!
"Tell me who admires and loves you, and I will tell you who you are." --- Charles Austin Sainte Beuve

---

Love Always. Love Daily. 365 Love.

Jeannie and Danny
April 29

Today's NOTE

I have a strong belief in love. And yes, I do believe in fairy tale love. I believe in happily ever after love. I believe in soulmates. I believe that there is somebody for everybody. I believe that people can have long lasting, loving relationships. I love love.

Jeannie works for me, and over the past few years I have been privileged to get to know her more personally. She never meets a stranger. She embraces others with love and cares about their well being. She is the mother of her work team and has several children (co-workers) in the work place. She loves her family and is open to sharing the joy they bring to her life as they grow older. She makes you feel like you belong. She makes you feel loved. That's what loving people do. Jeannie and I had the opportunity to talk this week and it brought joy to my heart to hear her love story. The relationship she has with her husband is truly a blessing. It is a confirmation that true love exists and can be everlasting. I felt so good about it that I had to write about it for 365 Love. So, today I'd like to share the story of **Jeannie and Danny**.

Jeannie and Danny will be married for 45 years in June of this year (2011). They have been together since Jeannie was 12 years old and married when Jeannie was 17 years old. This is the only man she has ever been with. When you see them together, you can feel the love in the room. She speaks so positively of him and their relationship. And he does the same. They are a team. They are partners. They are in it together. They are one. They spend time together. They support one another. They do not let the opinions of family and friends break the bond they have with one another. Their love of spending time together has kept them together. They genuinely like one another. They shop together and visit friends together. They are genuinely good people. They are good to each other and they are good to others. They definitely love one another.

As Danny began his retirement a few years ago, they worked as a team to adjust their lifestyle to compensate. Without being told to do so, Danny now ensures that Jeannie has absolutely nothing to do when she comes home from work. The house is clean and her meals are prepared. You name it, he makes sure that she and the home are taken care of since he is retired and she is still working. She in turn is appreciative of him and his efforts. That's love - supportive, caring, considerate, humble, appreciative love.

Jeannie and Danny are a living example of love. I could go on and on about this, but I think my summary says enough. I know that God is watching over them. I pray that their story touches your life and others. Let it encourage you not to give up on love. Let it increase your belief and faith in love. Let it help you find joy in the love of others. Let it motivate you to grow in love. Love always. Love daily. 365 Love.

Love Always. Love Daily. 365 Love.

Have you told someone you loved them today? I have.™

Love yesterday, today and future tomorrows,™
Torion

The music video for today's song visually tells the story of two children that fell in love at a young age and stayed together through grade school and adulthood. When I saw it, I immediately thought about **Jeannie and Danny**. Someone else had the same belief as I do when they wrote this song and put this video together. Someone believed in love.

Message in the MUSIC
Charlie Wilson – You Are

Note the QUOTE!
"Don't find love, let love find you. That's why it's called falling in love, because you don't force yourself to fall, you just fall." --- Unknown

Love Always. Love Daily. 365 Love.

Doctor's Visit
April 30

Today's NOTE

Think about the process you go through when you make a **doctor's visit**. In order for the doctor to determine what is wrong and provide a corrective action to make you feel better, you have to provide him/her with your symptoms. You have to tell what you are feeling. You have to tell everything going on with you. You have to be honest. You have to reveal things that you are doing well. You also have to reveal bad behaviors and habits. You have to reveal it all. Your symptoms help the doctor determine what type of tests to perform. They help determine where the doctor should look and how they should handle you in the process. Leaving out some of the details may lead to a false diagnosis which in turn may not truly correct the problem. The more information you provide, the more helpful the doctor can be. There are a number of medical TV shows that support this concept (i.e. House, Grey's Anatomy).

Today I want to encourage you to look inside yourself and do a personal assessment on how you love. The same **doctor's visit** principle should be applied as you conduct your own personal assessment. You have to think about everything you do that is right. You also have to think about everything you do that is wrong. You have to be honest and true to yourself. You have to reveal all of the symptoms.

Ask yourself these questions to start:

- Are you good to yourself and others?
- Do you treat people with respect?
- Do you let go of anger?
- Do you help others in need?
- Do you have a forgiving spirit?
- Are you a positive thinker?
- Do you appreciate the simple things in life and what others do for you?
- Are you a sharing / team oriented person?
- Do you tell those you love that you love them?
- Do you believe in love?
- Where are you strong in love?
- Where can you improve with love?

Think of other questions to ask yourself during your personal **doctor's visit** to assess how you love. Write it all down. Think about it again. Reflect on it. Put together an action plan to serve as your personal prescription to grow in love. Set goals to improve. Make a conscious effort to improve each day. Even if your assessment shows that you are doing a great job in your personal growth with love, there is always room for improvement. God is love. God is good. Love is good. Love is doing the right things, for the right reasons, for the right people, at the right time... all of the time. Love always. Love daily. 365 Love.™

Have you told someone you loved them today? I have.™

Love yesterday, today and future tomorrows,™
Torion

Message in the MUSIC
India Aire -- The Truth

Note the QUOTE!
"I believe that to truly Love, is the ultimate expression of the will to live. A heart that truly loves is forever young." --- Unknown

Love Always. Love Daily. 365 Love.

Love Always. Love Daily. 365 Love.

Love Always. Love Daily. 365 Love.

May

"He who wants to do good, knocks at the gate; He who loves, finds the door open."

— Rabindranath Tagore

I Never Lost My Faith
May 1

Today's NOTE

I often take time out to reflect on yesterday, take action today, and plan for a better tomorrow. In reflecting on past yesterdays, I take an assessment. In other words, I make note of things done well and opportunities for improvements. This can also be considered assessing life's lessons learned. You cannot grow if you don't take action on lessons learned and keep doing the things done well or make changes based on the opportunities for improvement.

Reflecting again on past yesterdays, regardless of good decisions or bad decisions, good experiences or bad experiences, positive advice received or negative advice received, **I never lost my faith**. **I never lost my faith** in God and all that He can do. **I never lost my faith** in love.

As a teen, I used to worry about what people said about me. My father reminded me that they talked about Jesus. I immediately stopped worrying about that. I let go and let God handle it. **I never lost my faith**.

During my divorce, a few family and friends suggested I "take him to the cleaners" to get back at him. I knew that I did not want that. I just wanted to get it over with and move on. I remembered that God said, "Vengeance is mine." I moved forward not asking for anything out of the relationship. I asked God to forgive me if my decision to divorce was not His will and prayed for strength to move on in a positive direction. I let go and let God handle it. **I never lost my faith**.

Newly joining the single life after 18 years of being with the same man, a few friends made an effort to encourage me to explore lots of different men. Some made efforts to discourage me from loving again because of their past hurts. Some spoke negatively of love and relationships. I knew this was wrong. I knew that none of that was part of who I was. I knew that love existed and was possible. I believed in lessons learned. I chose to do what was right. I chose to keep an open mind and open heart about love. I am now the happiest I have ever been as an adult. I let go and let God handle it. **I never lost my faith**.

I experienced disappointment in a person who was once a good friend, due to my discovery of a different character trait / spirit inside of them that was not aligned with my personal and spiritual beliefs. I prayed about it and changed the relationship as appropriate in order to move forward in love. I was able to realize that the person was in my life for a reason and a season. I was able to reflect on the lessons learned. I let go and let God handle it. **I never lost my faith**.

During the past four years, I have continued to grow in love. I have further evolved in love of self. I have a renewed spiritual relationship with God. I have experienced a new kind of love from a man who knows how to love in return. I

Love Always. Love Daily. 365 Love.

have a new love of family and friends. I have continued to look at life's challenges as a journey to become a better me; a journey to fulfill the purpose He has for me. I have been able to let go of all that is not good for me. All because **I never lost my faith**. Love always. Love daily. 365 Love.™

Have you told someone you loved them today? I have.™

Love yesterday, today and future tomorrows,™
Torion

Message in the MUSIC
Tramaine Hawkins – I Never Lost My Praise

Note the QUOTE!
"God allows us to experience the low points of life in order to teach us lessons we could not learn in any other way. The way we learn those lessons is not to deny the feelings but to find the meanings underlying them." --- Stanley Lindquist

Share Your Joy
May 2

Today's NOTE
When you are good to others, good comes back to you. When you show love to others, love comes to back to you. If you have doubts, try it for yourself. Spread love and **share your joy**.

- Make a conscious effort to be nice all day. Do something special for someone for no apparent reason. Verbalize your appreciation for the simple things done for you by others.

- Make a conscious effort to share a smile all day. Give eye contact and smile at someone when passing them in the hallway or at the store.

- Make a conscious effort to let people know how good you feel all day. Even if you are in an OK mood, think about something that makes you feel good and speak it into existence. Add that special smile to it to top it off.

I guarantee it will all come back to you in return. Someone will share their joy with you. Someone will be nice to you. Someone will share a smile with you. Someone will tell you how good they feel. Someone may even provide you with a special compliment because they feel the positive energy coming from you. It may be during the same day or another day, but it will be come back to you. You will be amazed at how much thinking and speaking positive thoughts can change the way you feel and how you make others feel. It actually feels good inside. You experience how easy it is **to share your joy**. You experience how easy it is to love. Keep it going. Keep sharing. Keep loving. Love always. Love daily. 365 Love.™

Have you told someone you loved them today? I have.™

Love yesterday, today and future tomorrows,™
Torion

Message in the MUSIC
Miki Howard – Come Share My Love

Note the QUOTE!
"He who wants to do good, knocks at the gate. He who loves, finds the door open." ---Rabindranath Tagore

I'm Here
May 3

Today's NOTE

Life is full of challenges. And the world we live in introduces us to both the good and bad. Sometimes the weight of the world can hit us in so many different directions that we sometimes lose sight of the good. That's an easy thing to do with all of that pressure.

I want to constantly remind you that the glass is always half full. Whenever things feel like they are at their worst, stop, take a deep breath, and focus on something good. Tell yourself, "**I'm here**. I'm still here." That in itself is a blessing. That in itself is something to be thankful for. Reflect on all that you have overcome and tell yourself once again, "**I'm here**." Be glad about the life you have in you. You are stronger than you think you are. Be thankful that you are still able to enjoy so many things that life has to offer. Constantly tell yourself:

- **I'm here.**
- I did it.
- I made it through.
- I made it to another day.
- I have so much more to look forward to.
- I am one step closer to something bigger and better.

Be glad. Be proud. Lift your head up. Keep your head up. Love yourself. Love life. Love to love. Love always. Love daily. 365 Love.™

Have you told someone you loved them today? I have.™

Love yesterday, today and future tomorrows,™
Torion

Message in the MUSIC
Fantasia – **I'm Here**

Note the QUOTE!
"Life is 10% of what happens to you and 90% of how you react to it." ---- John Maxwell

Quiet Time
May 4

Today's NOTE
Everyone should take time out for some **quiet time** every once in a while. **Quiet time** allows you the opportunity to enjoy a moment of silence. A moment of peace. A moment of relaxation and reflection. A moment to meditate. A moment that allows you to treat yourself to a simple pleasure. Time that is taken for the love of you. No TV. No phone. No computer. No music. No children. No disturbances. Just **quiet time**. Your time. Your break. Your peace. For you and only you. I had a few hours of **quiet time** today. Did you? Love always. Love daily. 365 Love.™

Have you told someone you loved them today? I have.™

Love yesterday, today and future tomorrows,™
Torion

Message in the MUSIC
Kirk Franklin – My Life, My Love, My All

Note the QUOTE!
"We need **quiet time** to examine our lives openly and honestly... spending quiet time alone gives your mind an opportunity to renew itself and create order."
--- Susan L. Taylor

Love Always. Love Daily. 365 Love.

You Pulled Me Through
May 5

Today's NOTE

We go through life experiencing many things. We experience happy times and sad times, joy and pain, ups and downs, the good and the bad. Your being here today is a confirmation that regardless of what you have been through, you made it through. Part of growing in love is to realize and acknowledge that others helped you get to where you are today. It may be a few people or many, but someone had an impact on your life and helped you move in a positive direction. When things were down, that person helped lift you up intentionally or unconsciously. That's love. God puts people in our lives to make a difference. He uses others to help us grow and fulfill our purpose in life. You can't always move forward alone. You may have to lean on someone from time to time whether it be for a few minutes, a few days, or longer. It may be a small interaction or a lengthy conversation. Someone will make a difference in your life.

I dedicate this 365 Love to those who have positively impacted my life when things may not have been at their best and as I was still progressing in my journey to love. They helped **pull me through**. They helped me progress in life to make it to where I am today. So here's to:

- God --- for your unconditional love. You have always given me the strength to move forward. You placed angels in my life to guide me in Your chosen direction ....**you pulled me through**.
- Jill Harden (my mom) --- for reading my journal, going through my things when I was a child (without my permission) and providing me with opportunities that I would not have shared with you if you had not, and for the motherly love you demonstrated to me when I was hurting inside ....**you pulled me through**.
- Lovett Harden, Sr. (my dad) --- for those one sentence statements you made to me that changed my whole thought process on how I was feeling at that particular time, serving as the motivation behind "Note the Quote"....**you pulled me through**.
- Diamond Wright and Lanous Wright, II (my children) --- for bringing me joy just because you exist. Your accomplishments, kind words, small gestures, and phone calls are always at the right time without you even realizing it ...**you pulled me through**.
- Andrea Harden, Portia Bledsoe, Lovett Harden, Jr. and Jason Wise (my sisters and brothers) --- for supporting me even after I allowed who I was with to prevent me from being close to my family and caring for me when I did not realize I needed it.....**you pulled me through**.
- Evelyn King and Alison Jones --- for being there for me for so many years and through so many ups and downs (too many to spell out here)......**you pulled me through**.

Love Always. Love Daily. 365 Love.

- Gwenette Moore --- for being so positive through my entire work career, never hearing a negative thought come from you and encouraging me at times when you did not realize the impact it had to my heart and spirit .....**you pulled me through.**
- Warren Scandrick --- for all of the private talks and support. You were a true mentor, friend, boss, father and brother who always knew the right things to say ... **you pulled me through.**
- Michael Copeland --- for being there for me when I felt my heart was at its lowest, for being a true friend, calling me every morning to motivate me, and getting me out of the house from time to time.....**you pulled me through.**
- Jerryl Palmer--- for helping me to grow spiritually, buying me my first study bible and studying with me, being a good friend when I needed one, being there as I began to grow in love, listening to me when I was down and being "tough" for me when I could not be tough for myself (smile)...**you pulled me through.**
- David Kent, Jr. --- for being my friend first and showing me how a man can love a woman unconditionally, for understanding when I had to let go, for supporting me through everything regardless of how close or distant our relationship was, for supporting my spiritual growth and guiding me to my new found church home, for your positive spirit when family issues were heightened and for your ongoing love .....**you pulled me through.**
- Those who have come into my life for a reason and/or a season --- for the actions you had in my life that caused a positive reaction. You helped me move forward even if I had to move backwards for a short period of time to get there .....**you pulled me through.**

Who has impacted your life and helped pull you through? They are a blessing to you. Recognize and acknowledge the unconditional love that they shared with you. That's love. Love always. Love daily. 365 Love.™

Have you told someone you loved them today? I have.™

Love yesterday, today and future tomorrows,™
Torion

Message in the MUSIC
Jennifer Hudson – **You Pulled Me Through**

Note the QUOTE!
"Maybe God put a few bad people in your life, so when the right one came along you'd be thankful." --- Andrea Kiefer

A Golden Life
May 6

Today's NOTE

A golden life is one that is marked by peace and prosperity. **A golden life** is one that is free of mental stress or anxiety. **A golden life** is one that is of mutual harmony. **A golden life** is one that thrives and flourishes. **A golden life** is one of good fortune. **A golden life** is one that is splendid, glorious and joyous. **A golden life** is one that is happy. **A golden life** is one that is delightful and pleasing. **A golden life** is one full of love.

Is your life golden? The answer is a personal choice. It's a conscious decision made by you. It's your mind set on where you are and where you want to be. It a decision to see the glass as half full. It's seeing life as lessons learned. Choose love and choose **a golden life**. Love always. Love daily. 365 Love.™

Have you told someone you loved them today? I have.™

Love yesterday, today and future tomorrows,™
Torion

Message in the MUSIC
Jill Scott – **Golden**

Note the QUOTE!
"You must love yourself before you love another. By accepting yourself and fully being what you are, your simple presence can make others happy." --- Unknown

---

Love Always. Love Daily. 365 Love.

Breast Cancer Walk
May 7

Today's NOTE

I participated in the Susan G. Komen Race for the Cure 5K **Breast Cancer Walk** today. This is my second year participating and I was just as excited this year as I was last year. I was honored to be in the presence of so many people coming together for a positive cause. Thousands of people coming together as individuals, friends, family members and businesses. People coming together due to the loss of someone to breast cancer, a person currently dealing with breast cancer, or a breast cancer survivor. People coming together because they care. People coming together because of agape love. There were mothers, fathers, children, aunts, uncles, cousins, grandmothers, grandfathers, sisters, and brothers in attendance. This included those with disabilities and parents with children in strollers. You name it, they were there. They were there to support a cause. I am in awe of the celebrations that took place throughout this event--- before and after the race. The monies raised. The volunteers who supported the event. The positive messages shared. The motivation of the speakers. Love was EVERYWHERE. What a good place to be. What a good cause to support. What a great way to energize my soul and spirit as I continue my journey for personal growth in love.

To all who participated in the **breast cancer walk** and those who wanted to, but could not for some reason.... I thank you. The recipients of the contributions thank you. The survivors, the sick, the healing and those who have passed away thank you. God thanks you. We thank you for giving of yourself and your time unselfishly to help someone other than yourself. That's love; an incredible, magnificent kind of love. Love always. Love daily. 365 Love.™

Have you told someone you loved them today? I have.™

Love yesterday, today and future tomorrows,™
Torion

Message in the MUSIC
Mary J. Blige – Give Me You

Note the QUOTE!
"What we have done for ourselves alone dies with us; what we have done for others and the world remains and is immortal." --- Albert Pike

---

Love Always. Love Daily. 365 Love.

A Mother's Love
May 8

Today's NOTE

Today is a celebration of mothers across the world. As a mother myself, I have a great appreciation for who mothers are, all mothers do and endure, and how mothers love. **A mother's love** is one that is unique in itself. At birth, there is a certain bond that is established between a mother and her child. A child recognizes her voice, her smell, and her touch. Mothers make their children feel safe. They know that **a mother's love** is one that is secure. Children run to their mother when they hurt themselves and need a band aid for their little "boo boo." **A mother's love** is caring and affectionate. It has a sense of calmness to it. It is dependable and nurturing. Mother's hurt when their children hurt. They feel joy when they see their children accomplish milestones in life from birth to adulthood. They are there to give that special hug and kiss at just the right time.

A mother's love can be compared to no other. Regardless of what their children do or don't do, they still love them. And sometimes that love has to be demonstrated by tough love. Mother's worry because of their love. They want the best for their children because of their love. They make decisions because of their love. They neglect giving to themselves so that they can provide for their children first because of love. They free up their time because of our love. They wake in the middle of the night to check on their children because of their love. They try their best to be the best mother they can be because of their love. All that they do is because of their love.

To all the mother's everywhere, today I celebrate you. To my mother, sisters, aunts, cousins, grandmothers and friends who are mothers, I celebrate you. I celebrate you for all that you are and all that you do. I celebrate you because of your love. Your special, storge, affectionate love. Love always. Love daily. 365 Love.™

Have you told someone you loved them today? I have.™

Love yesterday, today and future tomorrows,™
Torion

Message in the MUSIC
Kem - **A Mother's Love**

Note the QUOTE!

"Mothers are the people who love us for no good reason. And those of us who are mothers know it's the most exquisite love of all" --- Maggie Gallagher

---

Love Always. Love Daily. 365 Love.

If Tomorrow Never Comes
May 9

Today's NOTE

So often we put off for tomorrow what can actually be done today. We go through each day doing the same thing over and over again, planning to do something new or better later. We don't think about our actions today feeling that we can wait to deal with the reactions tomorrow. What **if tomorrow never comes**?

- Is your life in a good place today?
- Do you demonstrate love on a consistent basis?
- Do you let others know you love them and how much you love them?
- Do your daily actions represent someone who loves?
- Do your actions make people feel good about you and how you treat them?
- Have you given of your time and /or other resources to help someone other than yourself?
- Have you held on to something longer than you had to?
- Have you let go of things you know are not good for you in order to move forward in love and happiness?
- Did you let go and let God handle your worries?
- Will you have regrets?

Think about it. It's so easy to keep doing the same thing. It's so easy to neglect yourself and others. It's also easy to have regrets. It's just as easy to start loving. Love has no cost. It's a mind set and a way of doing things. You don't know what you don't know. But when you know, love is doing the right things and making the right choices. Love is a positive response to all of the questions posed above. Love is growing spiritually. Don't live a life of regrets because tomorrow no longer exists for you or someone you love. Tomorrow is not promised to anyone. Make a conscious effort to love today and every day. Do it now. Right now. Love always. Love daily. 365 Love.™

Have you told someone you loved them today? I have.™

Love yesterday, today and future tomorrows,™
Torion

Message in the MUSIC
Lyfe Jennings -- **If Tomorrow Never Comes**

Note the QUOTE!
"We must become the change we want to see." --- Ghandi

Tell Her When She Looks Beautiful
May 10

Today's NOTE

Most people don't realize that it's the simple things that matter most. It's the little things that don't cost a thing that make a difference. It's love in its simplest of forms. Most people don't think about it this way. Some people feel that love is exhaustive and takes a lot of energy to act on. However, those are the ones who do not fully know the true meaning of love and are still in the early stages of learning how to love. Love is natural. When you love, it comes easy. When you know how to love yourself and you know how to love others, love is effortless. Everyone should strive to find out more about what love is and build on it. Grow in it. Continue to practice it. It will make a positive difference in your life and the life of those you love.

I often hear about the simple things that a man (or woman) stops doing to demonstrate love to their significant other. It amazes me that it's the same story and the same things every time ----No compliments. No communication. No quality time. No respect. No display of affection. No help around the house. No support. No, no, no, no, no...... Ladies and gentlemen, these simple things matter. They are important to a lasting relationship. They are important in love. While time may change some things, the simple, basic things are still needed to make a person feel special. Don't take for granted that just because you are in the same place every day, he or she knows that you love them. No. It does not work that way. It should not work that way.

I have been on both ends and can relate to how these same simple things have an impact on a relationship. I have been with a man who dished out those same "no's" over an extended period of time and it was not a good feeling. While I have always loved myself, I still sometimes felt that need to be loved by my significant other. However, the "no's" did not make me feel that way. On the other hand, I have been with men and am with a wonderful man now that provides all of those same things as "yeses" on a consistent basis. No questions asked. Effortlessly. Naturally. I _always_ feel loved. And when two people love, and love is reciprocated on both ends, the love in the relationship magnifies itself.

One of the simplest things you can do to make a woman feel loved is to **tell her when she looks beautiful**. Say it with compassion and meaning. Look in her eyes. Smile at her. Wow! What a magnificent feeling that is. A man can be told that he is handsome and good looking as well. While he may not react the same way as a woman, I know that it is good for the ego (smile). I encourage you to think about simple ways to demonstrate your love on a consistent basis.

Love Always. Love Daily. 365 Love.

- Do something she/he wants to do
- Help out around the house with something that you used to do (but stopped doing), or would not normally do
- Cook dinner for him / her
- Do something special for him/her when you know it's been a hard day at work
- Do something special just because
- Give a kiss when she/he walks in the door from work
- Give a kiss just because
- Sit on the couch and hold each other
- Sit down together and just talk about life and how your day went
- Say "thank you" just because of who they are
- Say "I appreciate you" for all that she/he does for you and/or your family
- Write her/him a note with some kinds words in it
- Send a text message just to let her/him know that you are thinking about them.

Most importantly....love. Tell him/her that you love them. Never forget about it. Never forget to say it. Never neglect to show it. Never neglect to act on it. Keep it in your thoughts. Keep it a part of your daily actions. Keep it growing. Love always. Love daily. 365 Love.™

Have you told someone you loved them today? I have.™

Love yesterday, today and future tomorrows,™
Torion

Message in the MUSIC
Vivian Green – **Beautiful**

Note the QUOTE!
"You don't love a woman because she's beautiful, she's beautiful because you love her." --- Unknown

One Hundred Ways
May 11

Today's NOTE
One hundred represents the number of tiles in a standard Scrabble set. It's equal to the number ten multiplied by itself. It represents the number of United States Senators. It represents the number of years in a century. It represents the number of pennies that make up a dollar. It is the basis of percentages. It represents the number of yards on a football field. It is the operator phone number in the United Kingdom. With one hundred representing so many things, can you think of **one hundred ways** to love? **One hundred ways** to love yourself? **One hundred ways** to love others? **One hundred ways** to become a better you so that you can be better to and for someone else? Take some time to really think about it. If it comes easy to you, you are in a good place on your journey to personal growth in love. If it takes you some time, that's OK. You are still in a good place. It just lets you know that you are in the early stages of a great work in progress. We all have to start somewhere. Now, write it all down and act on it. Love always. Love daily. 365 Love.™

Have you told someone you loved them today? I have.™

Love yesterday, today and future tomorrows,™
Torion

Message in the MUSIC
James Ingram – **One Hundred Ways**

Note the QUOTE!
"To find someone who will love you for no reason, and to shower that person with reasons, that is the ultimate happiness." --- Robert Brault

---

Home
May 12

Today's NOTE

A house with people just existing in it is just that, a house. A house filled with love and people who love is a **home**. A **home** is always filled with love. It's in every room, around every corner, and in the front and the back yard. It's in the attic and the basement. In a **home**, love is everywhere. You can feel it, breathe it, and smell it. You can't hide it even if you tried. It's a place where family can always go. It's a place where there is laughter and happy tears. It's a place of comfort when there is sadness that causes painful tears. It's a place where there are people who genuinely care about and love one another. It's a place where life's struggles may come in, but the family love helps kick those struggles out. It is a place of peace, hope, happiness and joy. It is mama's Sunday dinner. It is family get togethers. It is talking smack to one another while playing a game of Spades. It is children laughing and playing in the back yard. It's a place where pictures of the family cover the entire wall in the hallway. It's the place you run to when the street lights come on at night because you know you will get in trouble if you're not there on time. **Home** is the place where you put tick marks on the corner of the wall to measure your growth each year. It's the place where you decorate your wall with your favorite superstar. It's the place where you stay up all night as a child trying to hear Santa on the roof top. It's the place where brothers and sisters fight each other for wearing each other's clothes, but fight for one another if the neighborhood bully tries to mess with family. It's a place of discipline. **Home** is the place where tough love sometimes means having to let a child leave the house to experience life and learn to be more appreciative and humble before returning. It's a place of forgiveness and open arms. It's love...love...love....love...love... love. Love always. Love daily. 365 Love.™

Have you told someone you loved them today? I have.™

Love yesterday, today and future tomorrows,™
Torion

Message in the MUSIC
Stephanie Mills – **Home**

Note the QUOTE!
"Love begins at **home**, and it is not how much we do...but how much we put in that action." --- Mother Teresa

---

Love Always. Love Daily. 365 Love.

Today's Present
May 13

Today's NOTE

How do you feel when you are given a present? ...a present you did not expect? It's not a holiday, a birthday, a wedding or any other special occasion. It's just another day. It is a present given just because. Maybe you feel like a big kid. Or maybe you feel anxious and excited. You can't wait to open it. You can't wait to see what's inside. You are automatically happy and filled with joy just knowing that you received this present, this gift. You feel special. You are thankful. You feel loved.

Well, you can feel like that every day. Each day is a new day. Each day is today. Today is the present. And **today's present** always brings something new and different. **Today's present** is a special gift given to us because we are loved. The gift of a new day and **today's present** is never guaranteed. So, to wake up and receive this gift each and every day is a blessing. Why not be excited? Why not be happy and full of joy? Why not be anxious for what **today's present** has to offer? Why not be thankful? **Today's present** is new, different and unique. It is especially designed for you. Everything given to you in **today's present** is yours. Be happy and filled with joy. Feel anxious and excited. Feel special. Be thankful. Live to love and appreciate **today's present**. Love always. Love daily. 365 Love.™

Have you told someone you loved them today? I have.™

Love yesterday, today and future tomorrows,™
Torion

Message in the MUSIC

Luther Vandross – Here and Now

Note the QUOTE!

"Yesterday is history. Tomorrow is a mystery. And today? Today is a gift. That's why they call it the present." --- Unknown

The Performing Arts
May 14

Today's NOTE

Have you ever thought about the love found in **the performing arts**? God gives us life and love. And with that, we each are given unique gifts to share love throughout our journey to fulfill His purpose for us. Some are blessed with the ability to share their gifts through **the performing arts**. Today, I had the pleasure of seeing The Atlanta Ballet perform a new work entitled, "Ignition - New Choreographic Voices." It was magnificent. All I could think about was love in many different ways. I thought about love through the music, the songs, the dances, the poetry, the visual effects and more.

A musician can create and play pieces that make the mind envision different emotions. Those of happiness and joy. Those of peace and serenity. Those of pain and suffering. It's all in the gift of music. A musician can use an instrument to hold a note that can make you hold your breath or cause your heart to beat faster. They can put the right notes together to play at the right rhythm to create the right mood. They can create love through **the performing art** of musicianship.

A visual artist can create a scene to make the background and foreground come to life. They can change lighting to bring about a certain effect. They can allow you to see more or less. They can create a thought of a large scene with just a few items on stage. They can make you feel that the floor is moving when it is not. They can create love through **the performing art** of visual artistry.

A dancer can move their body in a way that demonstrates power and strength. They can express the words of a song without words. They can dance to silence and you can actually hear something being said. They can move in a way that makes you feel an emotion. They can create a mood as magical as a magician himself. They can create love through **the performing art** of dance.

A singer can sing words and sounds musically to share a thought, a story or a moment in time. Their voice can bring chill bumps to your skin. They can make you laugh and cry. They can hold a note to make you stand on your feet anxiously awaiting the next one. They can raise the hair on your arms. They can create love through **the performing art** of singing.

A poet can put all of the right words together to express expressions. They can touch you without using their hands. They can share thoughts from the heart. They can find the right words to say what others cannot. They can educate and motivate. They can create love through **the performing art** of poetry.

The visual artist sets the mood of the scene for the musician, who provides music for the dancer, who dances to the voice of the singer, who changes notes along with the musician, who also plays for the poet, who adds that special blend to

Love Always. Love Daily. 365 Love.

make it all about love. It's the creation of love through **the performing art of performing arts**. Love always. Love daily. 365 Love.™

Have you told someone you loved them today? I have.™

Love yesterday, today and future tomorrows,™
Torion

Message in the MUSIC
India Aire – Beautiful Surprise

Note the QUOTE!
"Love isn't an emotion or an instinct, it's an art." --- Mae West

Remember Your Fingers
May 15

Today's NOTE

Today's church program included a reference to the Five Finger Prayer. It brought out interesting points about fingers that I never really thought about before. I was able to leverage off of the same concept to share thoughts about love.

There are five fingers on your hand. Each has a specific purpose that can serve as a reminder for you to love.

1. The THUMB is nearest to you. Use this as a reminder to demonstrate love to those close to you. They should be easy to remember. They are in your life on a regular basis and / or have had a strong impact on your life.

2. The POINTING finger is next to the thumb. This finger is typically used to point, direct or teach. Think about ways you can teach others to love. Tell someone something that is loving. Place positive people in your inner circle so that you can learn from them and continue to grow in love.

3. The TALLEST finger is in the middle. This finger should be a reminder of leadership. Love is contagious, so by demonstrating it on a consistent basis, you are actually leading by example.

4. The RING finger is the fourth finger. It is considered the weakest finger. As you continue your journey to grow in love, think about those areas you know you need to improve on. Be honest with yourself. Make a conscious effort to improve on them. Think about others that are weak and/or are in need and pray for their personal growth in love.

5. The PINKY finger is the smallest finger. This finger should be used to remind us that the smallest, simplest things matter. They are key in demonstrating love.

Remember that love does not take much to act on. It can be as simple as a phone call or an act of service. Be consistent and **remember your fingers**.

- When you wash your hands, **remember your fingers**.
- When you wave "hello" or "goodbye", **remember your fingers**.
- When you put your jewelry on, **remember our fingers**.
- When you point at someone or at something, **remember your fingers**.
- When fold your hands to pray, **remember your fingers**.

Remember your fingers when you need to be reminded of different ways to love. Love always. Love daily. 365 Love.™

Love Always. Love Daily. 365 Love.

Have you told someone you loved them today? I have.™

Love yesterday, today and future tomorrows,™
Torion

Message in the MUSIC
Jill Scott – Do You Remember Me

Note the QUOTE!
"Do more than belong: participate. Do more than care: help. Do more than believe: practice. Do more than be fair: be kind. Do more than forgive: forget. Do more than dream: work." --- William Arthur Ward

---

Love Always. Love Daily. 365 Love.

Moment in Time
May 16

Today's NOTE
Use each **moment in time** wisely. Make each **moment in time** count. Be the best that you can be. Do the right things and treat people right. Be positive and uplifting. When you spend that **moment in time** doing things aligned with love and sharing love with others, it can be a moment remembered for a lifetime. It is rewarding and fulfilling to self and others. There is so much to be gained. For once that **moment in time** is lost, you cannot get it back. Love always. Love daily. 365 Love.™

Have you told someone you loved them today? I have.™

Love yesterday, today and future tomorrows,™
Torion

Message in the MUSIC
Cherish – **Moment in Time**

Note the QUOTE!
"Time is free, but it's priceless. You can't own it, but you can use it. You can't keep it, but you can spend it. Once you've lost it, you can never get it back." --- Harvey MacKay

---

Unbreakable
May 17

Today's NOTE
True love is **unbreakable**. It's a love that is so strong, nothing or no one can tear it down. It's strength comes from spiritual love, self-love and the love of others. It's strength provides the ability to block out or remove oneself from negative energies, so that that positive energies remain and are maintained. It's strength grows from lessons learned. It is unselfish, loving and caring. It's strength is strong in faith and does not allow worldly influences to break it down or tear up the good in it. It's strength plants seeds that grow into beautiful, strong roots and leaves, and spread healthy pollen. That's what love is. That's what love does. That's what makes love **unbreakable**. Love always. Love daily. 365 Love.™

Have you told someone you loved them today? I have.™

Love yesterday, today and future tomorrows,™
Torion

Message in the MUSIC
Alicia Keys – **Unbreakable**

Note the QUOTE!
"Love is indestructible. Its holy flame forever burneth; from Heaven it came, to Heaven it returneth." --- Robert Southey

Be Happy With Yourself
May 18

Today's NOTE

I reflected upon a book I read titled, *The Four Agreements*, by Don Miguel Ruiz. The first agreement notes that you should "be impeccable with your word." The author talks about this being the correct use of your energy in the direction of truth and love of yourself. He also notes how this is one of the toughest of the four agreements and how difficult this is for some people. Impeccable means without sin. We are born in a world of influence with TV, parents, peer pressures and opinions that dictate, mold, encourage, and/or require us to be "like" something or someone else. We in essence lie about who we really are trying to be what others feels we should be like. When you love yourself, you are able to be who you are. When you love yourself, you are able to be free and love others. When you love yourself, you can **be happy with yourself**. When you love, you are impeccable with your word. You use your words for good, to say good things and to bring about positive energy. You are honest with yourself and others.

This part of the book made me think about a song I wrote in February 2004 entitled, *What If I*. I wrote it for my daughter's singing group, Az1. They would practice it all of the time, but never actually had a chance to record it or perform it live during the 4 years they were together.

What If I

What if I.... Stayed in the bed all day
Just wasted all my life away
Didn't even take the time to play
No dreams, no hope, no inspiration, no remorse, no motivation
Didn't care, didn't share, just going straight no where

Then I wouldn't be myself (Be myself)
I would be somebody else (Somebody else)
I may not have this house I call my home
And all the precious things I own (I own)
The love that fills my air, my special place, my favorite chair
What if I, what if I, What if I –

Then I wouldn't be myself (Be myself)
I would be somebody else (Somebody else)
The friends I speak to every day
May not be with me here today (Today)
The things that made me grow up strong
May not have ever come along
What if I, what if I..... Oh no, I'm very satisfied

Love Always. Love Daily. 365 Love.

What if I...Were young again
I'd see all of my child hood friends
Change the way my story ends
Tell that guy I used to really like how I felt when he was in my sight
Fall in love and be his bride
Move out to the countryside

What if I... Tried to be just like you
And do all the things you like to do
Change my hair, buy new clothes like the ones you wear
Say all the things that you do and move the way you like to move
I'd be a brand new version of me and do all kinds of crazy things

Then I wouldn't be myself (Be myself)
I would be somebody else (Somebody else)
No unique personality that defines me as being me
I wouldn't do the things I do (Things I do)
'Cause I would really be like you
What if I, what if I.... Oh no, I I'm very satisfied

What I am today was destiny.
And that's the way it was meant to be.
The pain I've felt, the love I gave, were always meant to be that way
And I am happy being me with that special kind of quality
Growing stronger every day, loving me as I am this way –

Then I wouldn't be myself (Be myself)
I would be somebody else (Somebody else)
I may not have this house I call my home
And all the precious things I own (I own)
The love that fills my air, my special place, my favorite chair

What if I, what if I.... Oh no, I'm very satisfied
© 2004

Be happy with yourself. You are special. You are unique. Be impeccable with your word. Be honest with yourself and love who you are and who you are meant to be. Work on your personal progress and self improvement opportunities. Continue to grow in love. Love always. Love daily. 365 Love. ™

Have you told someone you loved them today? I have. ™

Love yesterday, today and future tomorrows, ™
Torion

Love Always. Love Daily. 365 Love.

Message in the MUSIC
Ashanti -- Shine

Note the QUOTE!
"Remember happiness doesn't depend on who you are or what you have; it depends solely upon what you think." --- Dale Carnegie

Don't Take it Personal
May 19

Today's NOTE
When negative energy comes your way, **don't take it personal**. Taking things personally is a energy drain. Think about it. Why bother? When someone claims that you are or are not a certain way, you love yourself to the point where you **don't take it personal**. When someone acts in a negative manner, you love yourself to the point where you **don't take it personal.** When you are given constructive feedback, **don't take it personal**. You love yourself enough to realize areas that you need to work on to grow in love. When you love, you are happy with who you are and what you do. True love of yourself prevents negative actions and opinions from changing your mood or behavior. True love of yourself prevents you from reacting or getting upset. Love does not influence you to have negative thoughts about yourself. Opinions do not make you question yourself when you are doing good things and/or what is right. You are aware that it's just that, an "opinion." You know who you are. You know that you love. You know that you love yourself enough to remain positive and **don't take it personal**. You do not let it drain your positive energy. When you **don't take it personal**:

- you are happier
- you are able to live
- you enjoy life
- you are at peace
- you love

Learn to love. Be more like love. Love yourself. Love always. Love daily. 365 Love.™

Have you told someone you loved them today? I have.™

Love yesterday, today and future tomorrows,™
Torion

Message in the MUSIC
Monica – **Don't Take It Personal**

Note the QUOTE!
"To love oneself is the beginning of a life-long romance." --- Oscar Wilde

It Makes You Smile
May 20

Today's NOTE
Love is a beautiful thing. Just the thought of **it makes you smile.** You wake and fall asleep thinking about that special someone and **it makes you smile.** You hear a song on the radio that reminds you of someone and **it makes you smile.** You pass by a special place that brings back wonderful memories and **it makes you smile.** You look in the mirror and **it makes you smile.** Someone special to you achieves a major, life accomplishment like graduating from school, a special honor, a new career, a promotion, etc. and **it makes you smile.** You look over at the person next to you and **it makes you smile.** You look at a photo and **it makes you smile.** You see someone smiling at you, and **it makes you smile** too. You hear a special someone laugh and **it makes you smile.** Love, **it makes you smile.** Love always. Love daily. 365 Love. ™

Have you told someone you loved them today? I have. ™

Love yesterday, today and future tomorrows, ™
Torion

Message in the MUSIC
Floetry – Sometimes **You Make Me Smile**

Note the QUOTE!
"Every time you smile at someone, it is an action of love, a gift to that person, a beautiful thing." --- Mother Teresa

The Beauty of a Flower
May 21

Today's NOTE
How often do you take the time to realize **the beauty of a flower**? How often do you think about the color, the pleasant smell, the shape, the delicacy, the process in which it grows? The purpose of the flower is reproduction through pollination. Pollination allows for the movement of pollen from one flower to another by wind or by animals. Their specific design encourages that transfer. Some flowers are even able to self pollinate.

The beauty of a flower brings symbolic meanings with it. Red roses are symbols of love, beauty and passion. Daisies are symbols of innocence. Irises/lilies are symbols of resurrection and life. Not to mention the many uses of flowers to include christenings, weddings, tokens of love, household decoration, celebrations, worship, etc. All of these things are pleasant and good. All of these things are peaceful and calming. All of these things are love.

When you love, it spreads from one person to another like **the beauty of a flower**. That's the nature of love being contagious. Love spreads in a variety of methods to include what you do and what you don't do. Love spreads through your actions and your words. Love is best shared when you love yourself first. Love has many symbolic meanings and uses. Love is the four loves and the five love languages. Love is like the **beauty of a flower**. Love always. Love daily. 365 Love.™

Have you told someone you loved them today? I have.™

Love yesterday, today and future tomorrows,™
Torion

Message in the MUSIC
India Aire - **Beautiful Flower**

Note the QUOTE!
"Love is the only flower that grows and blossoms without the aid of the seasons."
--- Kahlil Gibran

Lately
May 22

Today's NOTE
Lately I've had the feeling of love. **Lately** I've shared love with others. **Lately** I've helped someone believe in something they felt they could not accomplish. **Lately** I've motivated someone to move forward with their dreams. **Lately** I've given a hug and a kiss to someone I love. **Lately** I've taken time to say "I Love You." **Lately** I've taken time out to do something good for me. **Lately**, I've thanked God for His many blessings. **Lately** I've smiled at the thought of someone else. What have you done to show love **lately**? What have you done for Love **lately**? Love always. Love daily. 365 Love.™

Have you told someone you loved them today? I have.™

Love yesterday, today and future tomorrows,™
Torion

Message in the MUSIC
Tyrese – **Lately**

Note the QUOTE!
"Love is the master key that opens the gates of happiness." --- Oliver Wendell Holmes

Medicine
May 23

Today's NOTE

Medicine is used to relieve or eliminate pain. It's used to cure a virus or infection. It's used to control or calm a symptom that may otherwise be extreme in nature. It's used to heal. Some **medicine** must be taken with restrictions. The restrictions can include a certain time of the day, with or without something else, a specific number of times, a minimum quantity, or only when a certain criteria is in place. Regardless, the overall goal of **medicine** is to improve your personal health situation.

Love is like **medicine**. It's a deep faith that changes your entire outlook on life. It's a feeling that serves as a preventive measure. Love can cure an ailing heart. It can ease or eliminate pain. It brings about inner peace that soothes and calms. It takes time for some to grow in it and that growth is a process. Love is healthy. When you feel good inside and are not stressed, love contributes to good health. Even when your health may not be good, love slows up the process and allows you to remain in positive spirits. Love allows nature to take its course according to His will. When you love, you are positive. You have faith. You let go and let God handle things. You don't allow negative thoughts to cloud your mind. Constant negative thoughts are known to lead to health issues. Constant positive thoughts are known to improve health issues. Love is good **medicine** for the mind, body and soul.

- Think about how you feel when you let the worldly struggles fill your thoughts.
- Now think about how you feel when you are happy or made someone else happy. That's love.
- Think about how you feel when you constantly reflect on how someone treated you badly, your mistakes, or bad finances.
- Now think about how you feel when you take life's past experiences as lessons learned and make a conscious effort to move forward. That's love.

Learn to love and grow in love so that you can use that love to heal. Love to bring daily happiness to your life and the life of others. Love for a long lasting, fulfilling life. Let love be your **medicine**. Love always. Love daily. 365 Love.™

Have you told someone you loved them today? I have. ™

Love yesterday, today and future tomorrows,™
Torion

Message in the MUSIC
Musiq Soulchild – **Medicine**

Note the QUOTE!
"Love life, engage in it, give it all you've got. Love it with a passion, because life truly does give back, many times over, what you put into it." --- Maya Angelou

I Finally Know
May 24

Today's NOTE

I finally know what love is. You see, it's been around since the beginning of time. It's been with me all of my life, all of the time, every time, every day, and in every way. I sometimes overlooked it, misunderstood it, underestimated it, fought it, neglected it, held back on it or misjudged it. **I finally know** that love is inside of me. I can feel the positive energy flowing within me as I wake each day. I feel His love embrace me with open arms. I look in the mirror and smile knowing that I have an inner beauty that gives off, projects and attracts love. **I finally know** how love allows me to better position myself around positive things and positive people. I have a stronger relationship with family and friends. I am able to spread positive energy to others through the transference of love. **I finally know** that love gives more love, brings more love, spreads more love, and adds more love. I can see love, feel love, hear love and touch love, that is truly love. **I finally know** that love is good and is in all that is good. Thank you, God. **I finally know.** Love always. Love daily. 365 Love. ™

Have you told someone you loved them today? I have. ™

Love yesterday, today and future tomorrows, ™
Torion

Message in the MUSIC
Boyz II Men – **I Finally Know**

Note the QUOTE!
"Love, true love, is that which can give the most without asking or demanding anything in return." --- Mazie Hammond

Looking Out
May 25

Today's NOTE

I attended my niece's graduation today. It was a joyous occasion. Family and friends gathered to celebrate what is considered to be one of life's greatest milestones. It was a celebration of the transition from child hood (or teen hood) to that of a young adult. As I looked around, I could see smiling faces coming from proud parents and friends. I heard loud cheers to further confirm that. The cameras snapped in an effort to capture those "Kodak" moments. Video cameras recorded as another means to capture the moment. It was a celebration to note that each child had completed a core set of curricula of fundamentals to move forward in life.

God is so good. It was amazing to know that 100% of the class graduated at a time when the school drop-out rate was high and the high school graduation test failure rate prevented and discouraged students from graduating. God was **looking out** for the Benjamin Elijah Mays High School class of 2011. Graduates obtained over 10 million dollars in scholarship monies. The salutatorian was the first Hispanic to obtain this honor at the school. Additionally, she was the first person in her family to ever graduate from high school. The valedictorian had a 101+ grade point average (greater than 4.0) and received honors for character, community service, and overall contributions to his peers and the school as a whole. A high percentage of the seniors scored 1500 or higher on the SAT. God blessed the seniors with parents, family, friends, and teachers who helped them along the way. These people motivated, uplifted, inspired, lent a helping hand, listened, provided constructive feedback, and embraced them. God blessed them with people who were **looking out** for them. He gave them the strength to make it through peer pressure, puberty, and other childhood and teenage issues by giving them the mental capacity to achieve. That's love. That's a **looking out** kind of love.

Today, I send out a prayer to every graduate. This includes those from yesterday, today and future tomorrows. I know that there was/is someone special and powerful **looking out** for them. I pray that their lives be filled with love, peace and happiness. I pray that they continue to move forward on a path that continually promotes personal growth. I pray that along that journey, they realize the importance of growing in love - His love, self-love, brotherly love, charitable love. I pray that they continue to be surrounded by those who are **looking out** for them and realize that through love, they can **look out** for others as well. Love always. Love daily. 365 Love.™

Have you told someone you loved them today? I have.™

Love yesterday, today and future tomorrows,™
Torion

Message in the MUSIC
Kirk Franklin – **Looking Out for Me**

Note the QUOTE!
"Children will not remember you for the material things you provided, but for the feeling that you cherished them." --- Richard Evans

Love by Jaeson Ma
May 26

Today's NOTE
I was searching through songs on YouTube today and ran across an artist I had never heard of before, **Jaeson Ma**. The title of the video itself attracted me to it, "Love." So, that's an automatic click on the link for me. The artist expresses his thoughts on what love is in the form of spoken word, simply put. I can spell it all out here, but I think the video speaks for itself. He gets it. I hope **Jaeson Ma**'s message of love spreads through this message because of His message, my message and the message of others. It's nice to hear how others love. It's nice to know that others love. It's nice to spread love and share what others have created in the process. Remember, love is contagious. And like the Energizer bunny, it keeps going, and going, and going, and going, and going...... Enjoy! Love always. Love daily. 365 Love.™

Have you told someone you loved them today? I have.™

Love yesterday, today and future tomorrows,™
Torion

Message in the MUSIC
Jaeson Ma - Love

Note the QUOTE!
"A man is not where he lives, but where he loves." --- Latin Proverb

I Love Music
May 27

Today's NOTE

I cannot go a full month without mentioning the fact that **I love music**. A good R&B classic, Jazz or gospel song will get my day up and going, and keep it going, any time. In the car, I mostly listen to good music on 104.1 FM or 107.5 FM. I get to hear R&B, Gospel and Jazz sounds from artists such as:

- Aretha Franklin, The Commodores, Lenny Williams, Luther Vandross, Brian McKnight
- Whitney Houston, EnVogue, Kem, Eric Benet, Jill Scott, New Edition, Musiq Soulchild
- The Clark Sisters, Tramaine Hawkins, BeBe and CeCe Winans
- Kirk Franklin, Mary Mary, Marvin Sapp, J. Moss
- Kenny G, Al Jarreau, George Benson, Will Downing, Wynton Marsalis
- …and there are too many of my other favorites to name here…..

At home, I listen to a little bit of everything. I listen to a little rap to get my bounce on, a little country to get a change of pace, some pop to put more diversity into the pot, and even a little rock and classical at times. R&B, Gospel and Jazz are my favorites. I just love music, any kind, and all kinds. And every day, I wake and fall asleep to music.

I love music because it preaches to the soul. **I love music** because it has a way of saying things that others cannot always find the words to say. **I love music** because it is healing. It has a way of preaching to the soul. **I love music** because it just makes you feel good all over, inside and out. **I love music** because it makes you remember the good, the bad, the happy, the sad, the lesson learned, and the accomplishment of moving forward. **I love music** because it counsels and helps you grow. **I love music** because it calms with words and sounds that bring peace to your heart and your home. **I love music** because it makes you fall in love, stay in love, desire love, and become more like love. **I love music** because I love. Love always. Love daily. 365 Love.™

Have you told someone you loved them today? I have.™

Love yesterday, today and future tomorrows,™
Torion

Message in the MUSIC
O'Jays – **I Love Music**

Note the QUOTE!
"Music speaks what cannot be expressed, soothes the mind and gives it rest, heals the heart and makes it whole, flows from heaven to the soul." --- Unknown

In More Ways Than One
May 28

Today's NOTE
Love can be described **in more ways than one**. There are many words that can be used to describe what it is, what it means and what it does. There are many words to define its core in order to be as descriptive as possible. It can be described in your own words or in the words or others. Its meaning can be described in a favorite song, movie, TV show, book, dance, life experience, picture, etc. I could go on and on about it; about love.

- Love is like Maxwell house," Good to the last drop."
- It makes you feel like Campbell's soup, "Mmm, mmm, good."
- It has you thinking like Toyota, "Oh, what a feeling!"
- It's better than Porshe, "There is no substitute."
- When love allows you to let go and let God, it's like the promise made by Allstate, "You're in good hands."
- When others share it, it provides support like Home Depot, "You can do it. We can help"
- When you discover all that love brings, it reminds you of Best Buy, "Thousands of Possibilities. Get yours."
- And with all the possibilities love brings, it's like AT&T, "Your world. Delivered."
- The stronger you grow in faith, you become prepared like Ford, "Built for the road ahead."
- Then it's like Martha Stewart, "Sharing the good things every day."

Love always. Love daily. 365 Love.™

Have you told someone you loved them today? I have.™

Love yesterday, today and future tomorrows,™
Torion

Message in the MUSIC
Jennifer Hudson – Feelin' Good

Note the QUOTE!
"If you would be loved, love and be loveable." --- Benjamin Franklin

Sick and Tired of Being Sick and Tired
May 29

Today's NOTE

God is love and love is Godly. Love is giving. It is not selfish. Love is sharing and caring. Love is all things good. All words good. It does not hurt. Love listens and understands. It is patient and kind. For those who are going through something or are holding on to something that is not these things, love is the way. And this love may not be with or from the person you are going through something with. This love is His love. God's love. This love is self-love. Love of self. When you believe in love, have faith and love yourself like God loves you, it becomes that much easier to let go. To grow. To know that love will move you forward in a positive direction.

Love allows you to act when you finally get **sick and tired of being sick and tired**.

- When you're **sick and tired of being sick and tired**, you can quit that bad habit that is causing you to lose everything.....your home, your family, your friends, your job, and/or your life.
- When you're **sick and tired of being sick and tired**, you can let go of the man/woman that curses you with his/her words in an effort to lower your self-esteem and make you feel that you are nothing when God says that you are His child and you are something.
- When you're **sick and tired of being sick and tired**, you can leave that job that makes you unhappy because you are mistreated, disrespected, underpaid and taken advantage of. You have faith and know that there is something out there better for you.
- When you're **sick and tired of being sick and tired**, you can let go of the child that has grown to be disrespectful, disobedient, verbally and/or physically abusive to you as a parent that raised them and provided for them.
- When you're **sick and tired of being sick and tired**, you can let go of the "so called" friend that talks about you, takes from you, uses you, and mistreats you. You know that your true friend is God and He will provide "real" friends that will be there for you.
- When you're **sick and tired of being sick and tired**, you can let go of the person who continues to be unfaithful to you with other women/men, acknowledges your awareness, and does not care. You know that you are better than that and should never have to be "seconds". You deserve to be the one and only one.
- When you're **sick and tired of being sick and tired**, you can let go of that relationship you have with a married person knowing that nothing good happens from nothing good. There is someone out there for you. When you get God, you get right.
- When you're **sick and tired of being sick and tired**, you can see and act on those personal things that are holding you back and preventing you from

growing in love...procrastination, laziness, anger, selfishness, insecurity, jealousy, envy ....

- When you're **sick and tired of being sick and tired**, you can let go of the person who cannot provide love in return and is not unwilling to try in an effort to make things better. You will be able to pray that they will someday learn and progress, but move on so that you can personally progress.
- When you're **sick and tired of being sick and tired**, you can let go of the person who physically abuses you, makes you believe that it's always your fault, and blames you for all of "his/her" issues. You know that love does not hurt and these actions are not done out of love.
- When you're **sick and tired of being sick and tired**, you can forgive yourself for anything you may have done in the past where the guilt is still holding on to you. You will be able to take it as a learning experience, put actions into place to prevent it from happening again, and move forward. You know that if God forgives us for our sins. We can forgive ourselves.
- When you're **sick and tired of being sick and tired**, you can and will move on.
- When you're **sick and tired of being sick and tired**, you will let go and let God.

What are you holding on to that you know you need to let go of? At what point will you be able to say that you're **sick and tired of being sick and tired?** Let go and let God handle it. Let go and let love handle it. Love always. Love daily. 365 Love.™

Have you told someone you loved them today? I have.™

Love yesterday, today and future tomorrows,™
Torion

Message in the MUSIC
Kelly Price – **Tired**

Note the QUOTE!
"It breaks your heart to see the one you love is happy with someone else, but it's more painful to know that the one you love is unhappy with you." --- Unknown

Call Somebody
May 30

Today's NOTE
Call somebody to tell them you love them. Pick up the phone, dial those 10 - 11 digits, open your mouth and express yourself. Share how wonderful your day was. Tell someone something special. Let someone know that you were thinking of them. Open your heart and your ear and listen to what they have to say. Show that you care. **Call somebody** just because today is today. Let someone know that you took time out of your very busy day to think about them. Send them a humongous, oversized hug and smile through the phone that can be felt in the tone of your voice. **Call somebody** because your call just may be the one to help make someone's day. Your call may lift the spirits of someone at that specific moment in time, just when it is needed most. Your call might be the one to make a difference. **Call somebody** because you love. What are you waiting for? Go ahead. **Call somebody**. Love always. Love daily. 365 Love.™

Have you told someone you loved them today? I have.™

Love yesterday, today and future tomorrows,™
Torion

Message in the MUSIC
Janet Jackson – **Call** on Me

Note the QUOTE!
"I love you, not because of what you have, but because of what I feel. I care for you, not because you need, but because I want to. I'm always here for you, not because I want you to be with me, but because I want to be with you." --- Harry

Never Alone
May 31

Today's NOTE
You are **never** alone. There are times when you may feel that there is no one out there for you. No one to talk to. There is no one you can turn to or trust. No one to express yourself to. You feel that you have no one to call. You feel that no one would understand or listen. Or maybe you are embarrassed or ashamed. You don't want to talk to a stranger because they don't know you. You feel that everyone is against you vs. for you. When these feelings and other negative feelings cross your mind, stop and take a few deep breaths. Then remember your faith. Remember love. His love. And remember that you are **never alone**. Remember that there is always someone there. Open your heart, mind and soul, and feel His presence. Know that God is always there. Know that love is always there. So often we want to look to others for healing. However, you have to remember that when things get too unbearable, the first person you should look to is God. And with his everlasting love, you are **never alone**. When we pray to Him, he delivers. He may have to help us work on ourselves in the process. He is our friend. Our best friend. And through His friendship, other friends will come. We grow on the inside and out. We learn to trust and have hope. We learn to love. Love always. Love daily. 365 Love. ™

Have you told someone you loved them today? I have. ™

Love yesterday, today and future tomorrows, ™
Torion

Message in the MUSIC
Brian McKnight – **Not Alone**

Note the QUOTE!
"It is astonishing how little one feels alone when one loves." --- John Bulwer

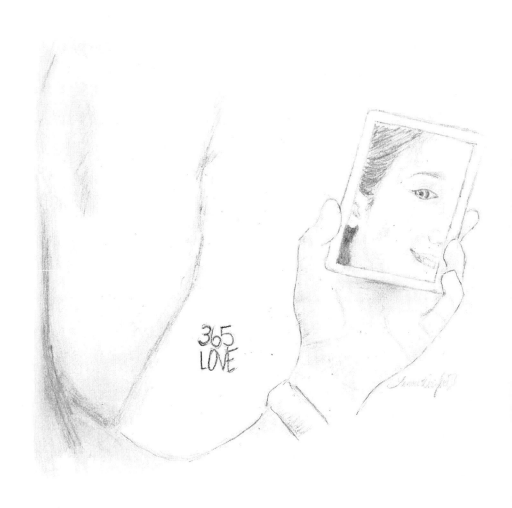

Love Always. Love Daily. 365 Love.

June

"Happiness is looking in the mirror and liking what we see."
— Mahatma Gandhi

About You
June 1

Today's NOTE

Love is all around you and **about you**. The intent is for you to love. Your life's plan includes a journey mapped for your personal growth in love. You can fight it. You can resist it, but you can't hide from it. It's in your destiny. Your choice to read and continue reading 365 Love is an indication of that. As you grow in it, you will begin to notice more things around you, **about you**.

- Has there ever been a time when you were going through something and heard someone tell a story that seemed as if they were talking **about you**? They may have come to you for advice, or shared a story about a family member or friend.
- Have you ever read a book, e-mail, magazine article, newspaper clipping, greeting card, etc. and the wording seemed as if it was **about you**? The intent was to reveal, confirm or heal.
- Have you been at church and the pastor delivered a sermon about a specific topic you felt was all **about you**? A confirmation, a revelation, a change request, or a need to take action was brought to your attention.
- Have you listened to a song on the radio and felt that the words were all **about you**? It was a personal experience you were going through or the answer to something troubling your heart.

All of these examples are ways for love to find you and enter your heart. They are ways to deliver messages to you. They wake you up, bring change in you, reveal something to you and help you grow in love. They are just for you. They are **about you**. Listen. Make a mental note and take action. Love always. Love daily. 365 Love.™

Have you told someone you loved them today? I have.™

Love yesterday, today and future tomorrows,™
Torion

Message in the MUSIC
Raheem DeVaughn – **You**

Note the QUOTE!
"Love doesn't sit there like a stone, it has to be made, like bread; remade all of the time, made new." --- Ursula K. LeGuin

If Only You Knew
June 2

Today's NOTE
Love is incredible. And it's amazing what can be done when you are filled with it. In surrounding myself with love and positive thoughts of love, I find that I come across some of the most wonderful stories. These stories are uplifting and bring joy and happiness to my heart. These stories are confirmations that people love. These stories show love, feel love, and know love.

Oprah Winfrey granted Valentine's day wishes on one of her shows. For this particular show, a woman submitted a video clip describing how much her husband loved Patti LaBelle, which happens to be one of my favorite recording artists. She asked Oprah to make her wish come true by providing an opportunity for her husband to sing with Patti Labelle. Her wish was granted. To keep the surprise a secret, the husband was informed that he was invited to the Oprah show to sing for his wife. He chose "**If Only You Knew**" as the song to perform as an expression of his love for her. Shortly after he began to sing, Patti Labelle came out from behind singing with him. What a surprise! This brought automatic tears of joy from me (and his wife). What a wonderful way to express love. The video clip submission provided the means for the gift of a duet with a husband's favorite artist out of the wife's love for him. The husband chose to sing a beautiful love song to his wife out of his love for her. Patti LaBelle gave of her time and talents out of her love for bringing joy to others. Oprah used her love for giving to grant this special wish. **If only you knew...** That's what love can do. Love always. Love daily. 365 Love.™

Have you told someone you loved them today? I have.™

Love yesterday, today and future tomorrows,™
Torion

Message in the MUSIC
Patti Labelle – **If Only You Knew**
(see Oprah Show - Valentine's Day Surprise on YouTube)

Note the QUOTE!
"We loved with a love that was more than love." --- Edgar Allen Poe

The Singer, Musician and Song Writer
June 3

Today's NOTE

I was blessed with the opportunity to attend the Brian McKnight, *Just Me* concert today. If my family and friends are reading this, they all know that he is my favorite recording artist. I call him my "boyfriend." Brian just doesn't know this (smile). All jokes aside. When you get down to the real reason that I am so fond of Brian McKnight, it's really because of his gift of giving love to others as a **singer, musician and song writer**.

Today's show was just that. It was very intimate. And for the first time, out of all of the Brian McKnight concerts I have ever been to (and that's a lot), he decided to give totally of himself. As the concert title notes, it was *Just Me*. There were no background singers, no built in tracks and no band. It was just Brian, his voice, the piano, the keyboard, the guitar, his songs and his words ---- **the singer, musician and songwriter**. He presented his artistic gifts to us. He shared his appreciation for the love of music, the spiritual upbringing that serves as his foundation, the artists who inspired him, and the gift of life through his children.

First, the voice of the **singer**. He has a range that is out of this world. The things he does with his vocals bring joy to the heart and soul of the listener. He has passion for what he does and you can tell that he loves it. He adds a little sense of humor to it every once in a while also. When he speaks to the audience, you can tell how humble he is. He knows where his gifts come from and does not take that for granted.

Second, the music of the **musician**. He plays music on the instruments in the same manner he uses his voice, with love. There is passion and feeling in the notes played with every instrument. A true gift. A true blessing. The music written by Brian adds a special touch to the songs he writes and sings. The melodies are perfect in setting the mood to make one feel love.

Lastly, the **song writer**. I cannot think of one song written by Brian that I do not like. And every one of his love and life songs touch my heart in some way. As of June 2011, he has 15 albums (10 original, 2 Christmas, and 3 Best of). I have listened to every single word, from every song, from every album. Each and every one is filled with love - romantic love, family love, spiritual love, brotherly love, lessons in love, setbacks and steps forward.

I love love and I love music. I tend to become fond of artists who frequently sing and write about love in a way that further promotes all aspects of it. Brian McKnight is that dominant artist for me. There are times when I may be going through something, times when I am feeling super good, or times when I just want to hear some good loving music. These are times when I pull up all of Brian's albums on the computer or my iPod, click the shuffle button, turn up the volume, and hit play. I am inspired once again that love exists and it is out there.

Love Always. Love Daily. 365 Love.

I am uplifted and encouraged. I am constantly filled with love, song after song, after song, after song. Thank you, Brian, for sharing love with me and so many others. Thank you for giving of yourself as **the singer, musician and songwriter**. Love always. Love daily. 365 Love.™

Have you told someone you loved them today? I have. ™

Love yesterday, today and future tomorrows,™
Torion

Brian McKnight closed the show by bringing his sons on stage to perform a song with him. Enjoy!

Message in the MUSIC
Brian McKnight – **Rest of My Life**
(LIVE concert performance with Sons)

Note the QUOTE!
"Words make you think a thought. Music makes you feel a feeling. A song makes you feel a thought." --- E. Y. Harburg

The Power of Love
June 4

Today's NOTE
Love is powerful. First and foremost because God is love. Secondly, because it is what God desires for us to do for ourselves and for others. And with that, we can accomplish almost anything. Psychologist Today notes that **the power of love** is one of the best antidepressants. I know from God's promise and personal experiences that this is true. One of the most common sources of depression is feeling unloved. This includes not loving oneself and not feeling loved by others. I am here to tell you, that **the power of love** is everywhere. We are beautiful creatures, because we are children of God. We are surrounded by beautiful things, because God made them. We are surrounded by love, because that's what God provides to us. We must reach inside our heart and soul and realize **the power of love**. His power. His love. And all that it possesses. We must realize that we are always loved. We must have strong faith in His word and His love for us. When we have faith in His love, more love comes our way. We learn to love ourselves and others. We use **the power of love** to spread love. Love always. Love daily. 365 Love.™

Have you told someone you loved them today? I have.™

Love yesterday, today and future tomorrows,™
Torion

Message in the MUSIC
Luther Vandross – **Power of Love**

Note the QUOTE!
"The way of peace is the way of love. Love is the greatest power on earth. It conquers all things." --- Peace Pilgrim

Practice
June 5

Today's NOTE

As a child, **practice** was required to learn how to read. The more you **practice**d, the more reading you were able to do. Your reading comprehension evolved and you eventually moved on to read more advanced books. Most professional athletes began playing sports in their youth. They started out by playing for the little leagues. As they continued to **practice** with various leagues at various age levels they got better. Their skills evolved. Dancers have to **practice** to ensure that they perform the moves as choreographed using certain techniques. The more they **practice**, the better they become and the more coordinated they are. Each new choreographed piece becomes that much easier. They progress in skill level and begin to perform more complex moves. It takes **practice** to become a great musician. It takes **practice** to become a great doctor. It takes **practice** to learn how to drive a car safely and with a certain level of expertise. It takes **practice** to construct a house or office building that is safe and stable. Without **practice**, there is no growth, there is no change. Things remain the same, fail or fall apart. Greatness can never be accomplished with no action and no **practice**.

Practice is required to develop, maintain and perfect any skill, job, or talent a person possesses. The more you **practice**, the more natural it becomes. **Practice** in itself is a journey. There are wins and losses and ups and downs, as with any learning effort. The point is to take the lessons learned, **practice** again, and keep going. **Practice** is also required to develop, maintain and continue to grow in love. The more you **practice** love, the better you are with love. It comes naturally. It becomes effortless. Treat love as you would any other skill that you are trying to develop and watch how it evolves in you and others. As you continue your life's journey, don't forget the importance of **practice**. **Practice** love always. **Practice** love daily. **Practice** 365 love. Love always. Love daily. 365 Love.™

Have you told someone you loved them today? I have. ™

Love yesterday, today and future tomorrows, ™
Torion

Message in the MUSIC
Aaliyah -- Try Again

Note the QUOTE!
"Practice means to perform, over and over again in the face of all obstacles, some act of vision, of faith, of desire. Practice is a means of inviting the perfection desired." --- Martha Graham

The Only One for Me
June 6

Today's NOTE

I've found it. Something magnificent. Something more than choice words one could use to describe it. It gives and receives. It helps and heals. It brings comfort. It soothes. It uplifts and inspires. It has no demand that is not worth fulfilling. It embraces the mind, body and soul. It glorifies. It praises. It is deserving of anything, everything and all things good. It is good. It has purpose and meaning. It creates greatness. It takes your heart and fills your heart. It shares and cares. It protects. It wakes me and takes care of me. It watches over me. It provides for me. It keeps me warm inside and out. It makes me smile. It brings joy and happiness. It is the goodness in both night and day. It is up and down. It is all around. It costs nothing, but is worth everything. It is plentiful and abundant. It is simple and complex. I hear it, see it, smell it, touch it and feel it. It means the world to me. It is everything to me. It is **the only one for me**. It is love. Love always. Love daily. 365 Love.™

Have you told someone you loved them today? I have.™

Love yesterday, today and future tomorrows,™
Torion

Message in the MUSIC
Brian McKnight – **The Only One for Me**

Note the QUOTE!
"We picture love as heart-shaped because we do not know the shape of the soul."
--- Robert Brault

Love All Over Me
June 7

Today's NOTE

Love is beautiful. When you embrace it, practice it and make it a part of who you are, you receive it in return. You see things and people differently. You are always surrounded by love and more love. At this moment in my life, I can honestly say that I have **love all over me**. I give it, I share it and I receive it daily. I know about it, seek to learn more about it and continue to grow in it. I am a living testimony that when you put your life in the order of love, you receive more love in return. It magnifies and multiplies itself. My life is full of love. At home, in the work place and throughout the day, I have **love all over me**. God continues to bless me with His love and surround me with the love of worldly blessings, family and friends. He has also blessed me with my future husband.

My future husband (fiancé).... I smile at the thought of him. With him, I know how much a man can love a woman and how much a woman can love a man. When he is with me, I feel **love all over me**. When he is away from me, I feel **love all over me**. We are best friends. We have a true we vs. me relationship. We pray together and attend church together. He has my best interest at heart and I have his. We communicate well with one another. We are respectful of each other's feelings. We know how to talk to one another so that we can hear and understand what is being said. We discuss the present and the future together. We are able to give and receive feedback to one another and are both willing to improve and/or change as needed. We listen and understand with no heightened emotions, no yelling, and no animosity. We never depart, end a conversation, or end the evening angry with one another. We say, "I love you" frequently and daily. We share small kisses with one another. We hug and hold one another often. We take care of one another at times when we are not feeling well. We send text messages to express that we are thinking about one another. We uplift, inspire and motivate each other. We demonstrate PDA (Public Displays of Affection) whenever we are together. We support one another in all that we do. We are protective of one another, but not controlling over one another. We do lots of things together, but give each other personal time as well. We are secure in who we are and our relationship with one another. I support all of his hobbies and he supports mine. He will go with me to a doll show and I will go with him to a car show. We cook together. We have fun together. We take walks around the neighborhood or the park together. We bring out the best in each other. We have fun together. Others can feel the love we have for one another (including strangers). We are consistent with who we are, how we treat each other, and how we love. And it gets better and better with each new day. As you can see, he has love all over him and I have **love all over me**. We love always. We love daily. We love 365. Love always. Love daily. 365 Love.™

Have you told someone you loved them today? I have.™

Love yesterday, today and future tomorrows,™
Torion

Message in the MUSIC
Monica - **Love All Over Me**

Note the QUOTE!
"A loving relationship is one in which the loved one is free to be himself -- to laugh with me, but never at me; to cry with me, but never because of me; to love life, to love himself, to love being loved. Such a relationship is based upon freedom and can never grow in a jealous heart." --- Leo F. Buscaglia

Well Done
June 8

Today's NOTE
As you grow in love, you should always do your best. You know when you put your best foot forward and when you do not. You know when you are prepared and when you are not. You know when you practice and when you do not. You know when you do what is right to do and when you do not. You know when you treat someone well and when you do not. You know when you push yourself and when you do not. You know when you put your all into it and when you do not. The point is, you know. And no matter what the outcome, when you know you did your best, you know it. When you do your best, you are happy with the end results. You are happy with yourself. You are less judgmental of yourself. You avoid self-abuse and regret. You can be honest with yourself and say, "**Well done**." Doing your best is different for different things and at different stages in your life. It's different depending on your physical and mental abilities at that point in time. It's different based on the things you know and don't know, but it is your best and you know it. Love yourself enough to always do your best. Always do your best when you love. And when God looks down on you, he too will be happy. He will smile and say, "**Well Done**." Love always. Love daily. 365 Love.™

Have you told someone you loved them today? I have.™

Love yesterday, today and future tomorrows,™
Torion

Message in the MUSIC
Deitrick Hadden - **Well Done**

Note the QUOTE!
"Remember, there are no mistakes, only lessons. Love yourself, trust your choices, and everything is possible." --- Cherie Carter-Scott

He's Done Enough
June 9

Today's NOTE
People rarely, openly acknowledge the simple things in life. Those things that come to us naturally. Simple things like the sun, the trees, the birds and the bees, the rain, and the air... nature itself. A beautiful day. A blessed day. God's every day gifts to us. Gifts of love. His love. He gives so much to us. He gives so much of Himself to us. He provides so much for us. Recognize it and appreciate it. Realize that each day you wake, you receive a new present. A gift. And if He doesn't do another thing for you, know that with all that He has already done, **He's done enough**. Feel good about it and give thanks for it. That's love. Love always. Love daily. 365 Love.™

Have you told someone you loved them today? I have.™

Love yesterday, today and future tomorrows,™
Torion

Message in the MUSIC
Beverly Crawford - **He's Done Enough**

Note the QUOTE!
"Though our feelings come and go, God's love for us does not." --- C.S. Lewis

Love Always. Love Daily. 365 Love.

Choose Heaven
June 10

Today's NOTE
Life is about choices. You choose how you look at life. You choose how you feel about life. You choose how you view reality. It's your choice. You can choose to be happy or sad. You can choose to love or hate. You can choose to feel good or bad. You can **choose heaven** or hell. You will find that when you choose love, you choose a life filled with happiness. When you choose love, you **choose heaven**. You have a different perspective on what others may view as negative.

- Death is a celebration of life and a transition to a better place.
- A bad experience is a lesson learned.
- A struggle is a test that leads to personal growth and a testimony.
- The rain is God's way to providing nourishment to the earth.
- The glass is half full vs. half empty.

Choose love and **choose heaven**. **Choose heaven** on earth. Love always. Love daily. 365 Love.™

Have you told someone you loved them today? I have.™

Love yesterday, today and future tomorrows,™
Torion

Message in the MUSIC
Patti LaBelle - **When You've Been Blessed**

Note the QUOTE!
"There's only one path to **Heaven**. On earth, we call it love." --- Unknown

Don't Worry Be Happy
June 11

Today's NOTE
Today is another great day. It's a wonderful day. It's a new day that is different from yesterday or any other day. It is your day. It's a day to love and be loved. Everything about it is good. Everything is going to be the best it can be. Everything is going to be just fine. Everything will be taken care of. So, **don't worry, be happy.** Put a smile on your face, get excited and look forward to what the day has to offer. Love always. Love daily. 365 Love.™

Have you told someone you loved them today? I have.™

Love yesterday, today and future tomorrows,™
Torion

Message in the MUSIC
Bobby McFerrin - **Don't Worry Be Happy**

Note the QUOTE!
"Happiness is not found at the end of the road, it is experienced along the way. So take not for granted each moment of your life and you will find a reason to be happy each day." --- Unknown

When Your Heart is Hurting
June 12

Today's NOTE

Life is full of ups and down. We go through these ups and downs to make us better people. They guide us in fulfilling our purpose in life. They help us become more like love. Sometimes we get it the first time and are able to move forward. Other times, we may have to go through something again and again before we get it, learn from it and grow from it. Love helps us to deal with all that we go through. Love is always there. God is always there, even **when your heart is hurting**. Sometimes you have to hurt before you heal.

When Your Heart is Hurting

When your heart is hurting
Say a prayer
And know that God is always there
To comfort you and keep you warm
To give you strength throughout the storm

When your heart is hurting
Close your eyes
Take a deep breath, hold it, then let out your sigh
Raise your head high and feel your faith
Know that God is with you in your space

When your heart is hurting
Let go and let God
It may take time, but you have to start
Right here, right now, with no delay
Not tomorrow, but on this specific day

When your heart is hurting
And the pain is hard to bear
Know that love is everywhere
It may not be with who or what you want, indeed
But God will surround you
With who and what you need

When your heart is hurting
Find a place
To ask for God's mercy and grace
To help you move forward and love yourself
To better prepare you to give love and receive love from someone else

Love Always. Love Daily. 365 Love.

When your heart it hurting
Don't deny
Love is the answer and this is why
God is always good and this you know
So just let go and watch your heart heal and grow, and grow and grow
© 2011

Love always. Love daily. 365 Love.™

Have you told someone you loved them today? I have.™

Love yesterday, today and future tomorrows,™
Torion

Message in the MUSIC
Cat Cole - Hurt Before You Heal

Note the QUOTE!
"Love comes to those who still hope even though they've been disappointed, to those who still believe even though they've been betrayed, to those who still love even though they've been hurt before." --- Unknown

---

Love and Basketball
June 13

Today's NOTE
Almost every weekend, family and friends get together for a friendly game of basketball at a neighborhood community park. The ladies cheer, keep score and provide refreshments. The men play the game and get a good work out in the process. People from all over the surrounding neighborhoods come to join in the game as well. It always starts with one person just messing around on the hoops. Then it becomes a game of one on one, three on three, a full 5 on 5 team and a full team with people waiting. Strangers come together every week to play basketball. Whether you are called by name, shape, skill set, or look, a unique relationship is established through a friendly game of basketball. Everyone around laughs, jokes and fellowships. It's like never meeting a stranger. Eventually, everyone knows everyone in some way. Teams form and you see support from within the teams and for the other team. Old play against the young. Old play with the young. Older players encourage and support the younger players. Younger players kid with the abilities of the older players. Big players impress and sometime intimidate the smaller players. Smaller players amaze the larger players. People come who have not played in years, but get the fire and energy back in them to play. It doesn't matter. You see people enjoying people, fellowshipping with people, being good to people, being kind to people, sharing with people, given to people, learning from people and having fun with people. It is an incredible sight to see. And it is consistent week after week after week. That's love. Consistent and contagious love. **Love and basketball.** Love always. Love daily. 365 Love.™

Have you told someone you loved them today? I have.™

Love yesterday, today and future tomorrows,™
Torion

Message in the MUSIC
Lil Bow Wow - **Basketball**

Note the QUOTE!
"Basketball doesn't build character. It reveals it." --- Unknown

Pray Big
June 14

Today's NOTE
Someone needs a prayer today. Someone is going through something today. Someone needs a special prayer to make a difference today. Someone needs spiritual love today. Someone needs someone to think about them today. Someone is weak and needs strength today. Someone needs you to pray because they don't have the strength or the words to pray for themselves today. Someone is hurting inside and cannot see how to move forward today. Someone is lost and cannot find their way today. Someone needs a helping hand and a friend today. Someone needs to be reminded that they are loved today. Someone needs a sign that everything is going to be alright today and every day. Someone needs you and your prayers based on your unique and personal relationship with God. That someone may be a perfect stranger, a family member, a friend, or it may even be you. Get on your knees, close your eyes and pray. **Pray big**. **Pray big** out of love. **Pray big** because of love. **Pray big** for love. Love always. Love daily. 365 Love.™

Have you told someone you loved them today? I have.™

Love yesterday, today and future tomorrows,™
Torion

Message in the MUSIC
Deitrick Haddon - Won't Stop Praying

Note the QUOTE!
"Pray, and let God worry." --- Martin Luther

Somewhere Over the Rainbow
June 15

Today's NOTE
Rainbows can be observed whenever there are water drops in the air and sunlight shining from behind. Another way of looking at it is rain, supported by sun, results in something beautiful, magical, colorful and full of life. **Somewhere over the rainbow** there is beauty. There is support. There is good. There is love. A tear drop from the eye of a hurting soul, supported by God's love, care and healing, results in something good. When we hurt, know that His love is there to support us, like with the rainbow, and we can and will make it through. When the tears fall, know that they are just temporary and sometimes necessary for something good to follow. It results in something magical and great. It produces something eye opening the brings happiness and joy to your life and the life of others. When the sun supports the rain, when God's love support you, the outcome is as beautiful as a rainbow. He is watching over you, me, and us always. Love always. Love daily. 365 Love.™

Have you told someone you loved them today? I have.™

Love yesterday, today and future tomorrows,™
Torion

Message in the MUSIC
Patti LaBelle - **Somewhere Over the Rainbow**

Note the QUOTE!
"Let no one who loves be unhappy...even love unreturned has its rainbow." --- James Matthew Barrie

Living or Existing?
June 16

Today's NOTE
Tomorrow is not promised. In the end, a dash will be placed between the year you were born and the year you pass away. Your entire life will be represented by a dash. What can be said about your dash? How do you feel about where your life is right now, at this very moment? Are you **living or existing**? Take a moment to think about these and other questions.

- Do you go through life just existing, doing day to day things? or are you truly living by doing things you love?
- Do you spend time worrying about what you don't have? or are you thankful and appreciative for all that you do have?
- Do you spend time blaming others for who you are and where you are? or do you forgive and move on by choosing your own happiness?
- Do you linger on past hurts? or do you move forward and start something new and different realizing the lessons learned from past experiences?
- Do you stay in a dead end job that you don't like? or do you step out on faith and find something that you love to do even if it means starting over or changing careers?
- Do you mistreat people? or treat people with respect, regardless of where they come from, what they look like and what they have or don't have?
- Do you surround yourself with negative people who make you feel bad, gossip and/or do bad things? or do you surround yourself with positive people who uplift, help you to grow and encourage you?

Life is too short, even when it is long lived. Enjoy life by **living** it. Enjoy life by loving it. Love yourself enough to live your life. Do good things for you and do good things for others. Be good to yourself and be good to others. Love always. Love daily. 365 Love.™

Have you told someone you loved them today? I have.™

Love yesterday, today and future tomorrows,™
Torion

Message in the MUSIC
India Aire - Beautiful

Note the QUOTE!
"Laugh as much as you breathe and love as long as you live." --- Unknown

---

Love Always. Love Daily. 365 Love.

Time
June 17

Today's NOTE

Time waits for no one. So often we wait on it assuming that we will have more of it later. So often we waste it thinking that we will be able to make up for it. So often we take it for granted just existing with no plan for it. **Time** is precious and valuable. It is provided to us on a limited basis. It is not infinite or limitless. It has a start and an end. Once **time** is gone you cannot get it back. The **time** you have is always here and now.

What about your **time**? What have you done with it? What are you doing with it? What do you have planned for it? How much quality do you put into it? Make your **time** count. Make it matter. Do something meaningful and significant with it. Love, live and care for yourself and others with your **time**. Enjoy life with your **time**. Share life with your **time**. Be the best that you can be with your **time**. Know when it is important to be patient with **time**. Know when to ensure that there is quality invested in your **time**. Remember to say, "I love you" with your **time**. Never forget about the value of **time**. Love always. Love daily. 365 Love.™

Have you told someone you loved them today? I have.™

Love yesterday, today and future tomorrows,™
Torion

Message in the MUSIC
Musiq Soulchild - **Time**

Note the QUOTE!
"**Time** is more valuable than money. You can get more money, but you cannot get more **time**." --- Jim Rohn

---

Love Always. Love Daily. 365 Love.

Work in Progress
June 18

Today's NOTE

For some, it's easy to love. It comes to them naturally. All that they do is based on love. There are no thoughts about it. They choose to do the right things, they treat people well, they take care of themselves and they take care of others. They are unselfish and giving. You know when you are around them, that they are good people. You feel it in their spirit. For others, it's a **work in progress**. But that's OK. When you don't know what you don't know, you just don't know it. When you know and don't act on it, that's an area that needs to be improved upon. But when you know and make an effort to practice what you know, that's a good thing. When you know about love and strive to further develop in love, that's a **work in progress**. It takes more time for some than others. It all depends on how much work needs to be done to get to a place where love is. The **work in progress** is different for everyone because everyone has their own personal experiences from the past and the present. Everyone has different people that impacted their lives and are currently a part of their lives. Some have more to go through and get through than others, but the **work in progress** itself is a plus. It's a step in the positive direction. It's a plan to move forward with personal growth in love. Growing in love is also realizing that others are a **work in progress** as well. We have to be patient and understanding of where we all are on our journey to love. We cannot expect others to think, act and react in the same manner as we do based on where they are in love. As you reach certain levels, you will be better able to determine this for some people.

Where are you with your **work in progress**? Are you at the beginning stages of growing in love? Are you still at a place where you are learning to truly love yourself? Have you evolved to a point where you can begin learning how to love others? Are you almost there? If so, keep it going. If not, don't stop now, keep going. Keep going until you reach the ultimate goal of love. Love always. Love daily. 365 Love.™

Have you told someone you loved them today? I have.™

Love yesterday, today and future tomorrows,™
Torion

Message in the MUSIC
Mary J. Blige – **Work In Progress**

Note the QUOTE!
"Love has its own time, its own season, and its own reasons from coming and going. You cannot bribe it or coerce it or reason it into staying. You can only embrace it when it arrives and give it away when it comes to you." --- Kent Nerburn

A Father's Love
June 19

Today's NOTE

We are children of God. He is our Father. He cares for us like no other. He is there for us when things are going well for us and when we are hurting inside. He provides for us. He protects us from things that are not good for us. He gives us what we need, when we need it. However, he does not always give us what we want, because He knows what is and is not good for us. He gives to us even when we don't deserve it. He disciplines us when we do wrong in an effort to lead us in a positive direction. He sometimes has to let us go our own way and make mistakes in order to learn to trust in Him. Regardless of how much wrong we do, He still loves us. When we go in the wrong direction, His love for us provides guidance to push us in the right direction. He is forgiving. He is love.

That's what a father is. That's what a father does. **A father's love** is one that has the best interest of his children at heart. He aims to provide the best for his family. He is unselfish and caring. He knows love and spreads its teaching throughout his family. Decisions made and actions taken are always intended for the greater good of his family and his children. He teaches His (God's) word to us. Know that just because a man has children does not mean he is a father. A father demonstrates love. Some men love from the start. Some men take time to love. Some men eventually get it together and love later in life. Some men never fully love and that is unfortunate. Regardless of where your birth father is in love, know that you always have a Father who is there for you. He is your heavenly Father and He loves you unconditionally. He will always love you. He is the one who knows best how to demonstrate **a father's love**. Love always. Love daily. 365 Love.™

Have you told someone you loved them today? I have.™

Love yesterday, today and future tomorrows,™
Torion

Message in the MUSIC
Whitney Houston – I Will Always Love You

Note the QUOTE!
"God loves each of us as if there were only one of us." --- St. Augustine

Don't Give Up
June 20

Today's NOTE
Life will pull you in a number of different directions - up, down, left, right, around, sideways, backwards, forward, diagonal. Regardless of where you end up at any given point in time, **don't give up.** Don't ever give up. **Don't give up** on life. **Don't give up** on hope. **Don't give up** on love. God would never give up on you. So **don't give up** on yourself. Throw away, trash and discard of any negative energy preventing you from thinking any differently. Be the best that you can be and keep on keeping on. Something great is in store for you. Everything happens for a purpose and a reason. Everything has a meaning and the best is yet to come. Love is the answer to everything and can overcome anything. Fulfill your purpose in life. Fulfill your purpose in love. Love always. Love daily. 365 Love.™

Have you told someone you loved them today? I have.™

Love yesterday, today and future tomorrows,™
Torion

Message in the MUSIC
Deitrick Hadden – God Didn't Give Up on Me

Note the QUOTE!
"Anyone can give up. It's the easiest thing in the world to do. But to hold it together when everyone else would understand if you fell apart, that's true strength." --- Unknown

It's About You
June 21

Today's NOTE
You read the book, heard the sermon, saw it on TV, heard the song, and then some. You immediately thought to yourself, "Boy, I wish ____ could hear this." or "____ really needs to read this." You thought about what you heard or read, and how it would impact someone else in an effort to change them for the better. Or maybe even to change them to who you want them to be for you. You wanted to change others. Not once did you think about how any of those messages applied to you. We often think of how to change others. However, some of us never take the time to think about how change is needed in ourselves. The first place to look is in the mirror at you. Love begins with you, self-love. When you love yourself, you can assess various messages and look within to determine change that is needed. We are able to be honest with ourselves about the change needed. And once we change ourselves for the better, for ourselves, and in alignment with love, we are able to share love with others. We are able to appropriately balance those inspirational messages and walk the walk and talk the talk. So the next time you are in church, at a seminar, in discussions with a friend, listening to the radio, or reading a good book or 365 love note, look at yourself. Somewhere in there, **it's about you**. It's about a change needed in you. It's about how you can and should love you. Love always. Love daily. 365 Love.™

Have you told someone you loved them today? I have. ™

Love yesterday, today and future tomorrows, ™
Torion

Message in the MUSIC
Tonex – Work on Me

Note the QUOTE!
"If you aren't good at loving yourself, you will have a difficult time loving anyone, since you'll resent the time and energy you give another person that you aren't even giving yourself." --- Barbara De Angelis

---

Love Always. Love Daily. 365 Love.

Give Yourself to Others
June 22

Today's NOTE

Love gives. With giving, there is charitable love. This includes giving of yourself and your time for the benefit of others. Some people share themselves on a regular basis. Others do it periodically, but they share. My sister has a gift of motherly love where she always looks after others. This includes my mom, my grandmother, other siblings, nieces, nephews, friends, co-workers and acquaintances. You name it, she is always willing to help others. It's a natural love gift that she has. It's how she loves. I would say that acts of service is one of her primary love languages. Other givers include the pastor of the church who gives of his/her time doing sermons for his church and others, counseling, mentoring, coaching, sponsoring, etc. It is in his calling, and his will to help others. Others invest time working for charitable organizations, nursing homes, shelters, etc. always giving of themselves to care for, help and love others. I challenge you to give yourself to love, for love and out of love. **Give yourself to others**. Show that you care. Lend a helping hand for the benefit of someone other than yourself. It starts with just a little bit of your time. Regardless of how small or large, your time means a lot to someone in need. Love always. Love daily. 365 Love.™

Have you told someone you loved them today? I have.™

Love yesterday, today and future tomorrows,™
Torion

Message in the MUSIC
William McDowell – I Give Myself Away

Note the QUOTE!
"Love wasn't put in your heart to stay. Love isn't love until you give it away." --- Michael W. Smith

Plan for a Change
June 23

Today's NOTE
As you continue to grow, so do the things you do, how you do them and your thoughts about them. As you go through school, you change based on what you learn and who you associate with. As you grow in age, you change the habits you have and the activities you participate in. As you learn new skills, you change how you apply all the collective skills you have. Life changes you and love changes you. You are not meant to remain as you are at any given time in your life. You never stop learning, you never stop growing, and you never stop changing. You are on a constant journey for personal growth which results in change. With love, change is always in a positive direction. So, as you grow in love, **plan for a change**. **Plan for a change** in what you do for yourself and others. **Plan for a change** in how you love yourself and others. Notice how much better you feel inside. Notice how much happier you are. Notice how much of a positive impact you have on the lives of others. Notice how much you appreciate the little things that love and life have to offer. Notice how good things become. Notice how you worry less. Notice how much brighter your days become. Notice a change - change for the better. Continue to grow in love. Learn about it, talk about it and be about it. Love always. Love daily. 365 Love.™

Have you told someone you loved them today? I have.™

Love yesterday, today and future tomorrows,™
Torion

Message in the MUSIC
Yolanda Adams – Still I Rise

Note the QUOTE!
"God loves us the way we are, but too much to leave us that way." --- Leighton Ford

Happy Tears
June 24

Today's NOTE

We are all born to fulfill a purpose in life. Each purpose is as different and unique as we are as individuals. Our purpose may be as big as that of the President of the United states, a NFL/NBA player, a Nobel Peace Prize Winner, or a multi-platinum recording artist. Our purpose may be of a smaller magnitude in making a difference in the life of one specific person, a group of people, or several people in ways that may not be as publically recognized. Regardless of how big or small that purpose is, we all have one or more. We just have to find it, realize what it is and act on it.

My grandmother is a giver. She is used to giving of herself to family members in need. Some of those same family members who are on the receiving end of the giving, may or may not always show appreciation for her kindness. She will be 95 years old on June 29, 2011 and is perfectly healthy for the most part. She is not on any type of medication for any personal ailment and has never been her entire life. I have never heard her say a curse word and have never seen her cry about anything. Her skin is practically blemish free. In addition to my grandmother being a giver, she is also stubborn. She likes to give, but does not like to receive. She does not like others to do for her and will moan and groan at the thought of someone helping her do something. I guess she has been independent for so long, she wants to remain that way. She does not like to go many places and is basically at a point in her life where she is comfortable with just being at home.

My sister visits my grandmother on almost a daily basis. She takes her food and helps to keep the house clean for her. She "jumps bad" at those who try to take advantage of my grandmother and is the ring leader in getting family members together when my grandmother has special needs. In essence, my sister makes sure everything is comfortable for her.

Over the past few days, my sister uncovered a number of things that made her realize that my grandmother was in need. She has been hiding the fact that she cannot fully care for herself, and her skin and other things needed to be addressed. My sister gathered family members to come to the rescue. She, my mom, my cousin and my niece took care of things. They collectively worked together to clean her bedroom and wash her body and her hair. While my sister and niece were taking care of some other things, my mom moisturized my grandmother's skin with lotion. At that point in time, my grandmother began to cry. It was the first time anyone ever saw her cry, including my mother. She cried hard and long. She thanked everyone for tending to her and told them that God would bless them. The tears she could never cry came out that day - **Happy Tears.** They were tears that let her know she is truly loved. She does not always have to do it alone. She does not always have to be the giver. Regardless of what life's struggles have presented to my grandmother, on that day, she felt loved;

Love Always. Love Daily. 365 Love.

unconditional, family love. The kind of love that you cannot buy. The kind of love that comes from the heart. The kind of love that comes from within.

My sister often times has discussions with me about why others are not as caring or concerned as she is when it comes to certain situations. I continually remind her that everyone is different. We love differently. And because someone does not love like you do, does not mean that they do not love. We just all have different ways of showing it. Additionally, we are all in different places in our life on our journey to grow in love. We all have strengths and weaknesses when it comes to where we are with love. This week, I realized my sister's purpose. Her life situations and motherly intuition put her in a place to be able to provide special care for my grandmother. To be that guardian angel. To put things in order to ensure that she is OK. To lead and encourage the family to help out when needed. She is fulfilling her purpose. This weekend was just that. She was a special gift born to care for a special person - God's child, my grandmother.

This week was proof that God will provide. He will provide us with what we need, when we need it, how we need it and with how much we need. He will send us angels, hidden messages and then some. He will use us to help others. To my sister, Portia, thank you for your loving heart. You positioned yourself to love our grandmother in a way that allowed her to release and have a moment of peace in her heart. You provided a foundation for her to shed **happy tears**. You showed her how much she is loved. You showed family how much you love. While we all are on personal journeys to grow in love, in more ways than one, you have the ultimate agape love for our grandmother. I love you dearly. Love always. Love daily. 365 Love.™

Have you told someone you loved them today? I have.™

Love yesterday, today and future tomorrows,™
Torion

Message in the MUSIC
Kirk Franklin – He Will Supply

Note the QUOTE!
"You will find, as you look back upon your life, that the moments that stand out are the moments when you have done things for others." --- Henry Drummond

Love Always. Love Daily. 365 Love.

Holding On
June 25

Today's NOTE
There is strength in your faith. The stronger your faith, the stronger you are. As you go through all that life has to bring, the strength of your faith keeps you **holding on**. Love keeps you **holding on**. It gives you the ability to see the brighter, positive side. It gives you the ability to see the glass as half full vs. half empty. It is up vs. down. It is good vs. bad. Love keeps you **holding on** knowing that greatness and great things are possible. Love keeps you **holding on** to your faith. Love keeps you **holding on** to a brighter today and future tomorrows. Love keeps you **holding on** to the belief that you can do it. You can do just about anything you set your mind to do. Love keeps you **holding on**, when you are ready to give up on something that is truly meant for you to achieve or make it through. Love keeps you **holding on** when you are ready to quit on something you were destined to complete. Love gives you the strength to do whatever is possible for you to fulfill your purpose in life by **holding on**. Recognize life as a developmental tool in your personal growth in strength, love and faith. A personal growth that continues to provide you with the ability, when needed, to keep **holding on**. Love always. Love daily. 365 Love.™

Have you told someone you loved them today? I have. ™

Love yesterday, today and future tomorrows, ™
Torion

Message in the MUSIC
J. Moss - **Holding On**

Note the QUOTE!
"When you have come to the edge of all light that you know and are about to drop off into the darkness of the unknown, faith is knowing one of two things will happen: There will be something solid to stand on or you will be taught to fly." --- Patrick Overton

---

Love Always. Love Daily. 365 Love.

Your Will vs. His Will
June 26

Today's NOTE
Often times you want what you want, when you want it, how you want it, and with whom you want it with. God gives us what we need, when we need it, how we need it, and with whom we need it with. That's the difference between **your will vs. His will**. We have control over how we feel and the choices we make. However, God has the ultimate control. He determines the final outcome of all that we do. When your choices are aligned with your will and are not aligned with His will, He will always redirect you toward the correct path by any means necessary. He knows what is best for you better than you do. God's love is one with a greater plan for you than you may have for yourself. That's **your will vs. His will**. He has all the answers to everything you go through. And everything you go through has a purpose and a meaning. It's all designed to guide you in the direction to love - to love more, to love better. Love always. Love daily. 365 Love.™

Have you told someone you loved them today? I have.™

Love yesterday, today and future tomorrows,™
Torion

Message in the MUSIC
Trin-i-tee 5:7 – I Will Lift

Note the QUOTE!
"God has editing rights over our prayers. He will edit them, correct them, bring them in line with His will and then hand them back to us to be resubmitted." --- Stephen Crotts

Permission to Be Happy
June 27

Today's NOTE
You have God's **permission to be happy**. You have His permission to love and be loved. If you are not willing to be happy on your own, to love on your own, I assume that maybe you are waiting to receive permission to do so. Permission has officially been granted today and every day for the rest of your life. Now that you have **permission to be happy**, feel free to act on it and use it to love. Absorb it in all that you do. Wake up to it. End your day with it. Make each day great because of it. Enjoy every moment of it. Let go of all that has been holding you back. The past is now behind you so that you can move forward. This permission gives you the extra strength and support you need to do so. There are no excuses. The chains have been removed and you are free to love. You are no longer held captive because you have His **permission to be happy**. Love always. Love daily. 365 Love.™

Have you told someone you loved them today? I have.™

Love yesterday, today and future tomorrows,™
Torion

Message in the MUSIC
Yolanda Adams – Be Blessed

Note the QUOTE!
"Love is a symbol of eternity. It wipes out all sense of time, destroying all memory of a beginning and all fear of an end." --- Unknown

Your Reflection
June 28

Today's NOTE
When you look in the mirror, **your reflection** appears. You see a duplicate image of what you look like physically. You see yourself on the outside. You see your skin color, your facial perfections and imperfections. You see the exterior you. Take a moment to look harder at **your reflection** to see the real you in you. Think about what **your reflection** would look like if the mirror revealed who and what you are on the inside; the core of who you are; your soul and spirit. What would **your reflection** of your character look like? What would **your reflection** of how you feel about yourself and others look like? What would **your reflection** of how you love look like? Think honestly and truthfully about these questions. Only you know the answers. Others may make assumptions. You can hide who and what you are from others, but you cannot hide it from yourself. You cannot hide it from God. Does **your reflection** show inner beauty? Does **your reflection** show that you love? Does **your reflection show** that you have good character? Does **your reflection** show that you are a work in progress? Others can tell you what they see, but until you see the real you, nothing can be done to become a better you. Whatever **your reflection** shows, put a plan in place to improve upon it. Put a plan in place to grow in love. Love is the key to a magnificent inner reflection that magnifies the beauty of the outer reflection. Love always. Love daily. 365 Love.™

Have you told someone you loved them today? I have.™

Love yesterday, today and future tomorrows,™
Torion

Message in the MUSIC
Christina Aguilera – **Reflection**

Note the QUOTE!
"Happiness is looking in the mirror and liking what we see." --- Mahatma Gandhi

---

Love Always. Love Daily. 365 Love.

POW!
June 29

Today's NOTE

One of my best friends has her own unique way of letting those near and dear to her know that they are loved. She puts her hands together to form the shape of a heart, places it over her heart and then tosses it to you while exploding her fingers and saying, "**POW!**" You may also get a text message, a voice mail message, a verbal message, a post it note, etc. with a "**POW!**" on it at any time. She uses it with her grandchildren on a regular bases and they love it. To see and hear little children share that unique message of love in return is simply adorable. She is sharing her unique message of love with them and they in turn are learning to love. That is exactly how it should be.

"**POW!**" is Alison's way of saying, "I love you with all my heart." She never really broke it down beyond that. However, I would say it is a loving way of giving someone a **P**iece **O**f **W**onderful (**POW**). After all, love is a wonderful gift to give. And when you give love, it continues to spread to others. It's contagious. It keeps going and going and going. So, today I am going to spread it more. Alison shared this with me, and I am now sharing it with you. The next time you want to let someone know how much you love them, remember your heart, remember my best friend, Alison, and give them a big **POW!** Love always. Love daily. 365 Love.™

Have you told someone you loved them today? I have.™

Love yesterday, today and future tomorrows,™
Torion

Message in the MUSIC
Mary J. Blige – Share My World

Note the QUOTE!
"You can learn a lot from people who view the world differently than you do."---Anthony J. D'Angelo

---

Love Always. Love Daily. 365 Love.

Just Fine
June 30

Today's NOTE
You are going to be **just fine**. You have decided to keep your head up and be a positive thinker. Your negative experiences have transitioned into positive lessons learned. Your glass is always half full vs. half empty. You have decided to be truthful and thoughtful with words you share with yourself and others. You know that your words make a difference in how you and others think. You use them to share loving thoughts. You have learned that people are who they are. You know that you cannot always change others, but you can change what needs to be changed in yourself. You can share love and have faith that love is contagious. You have decided that you will communicate effectively. You talk things out and ask specific questions to get the answers to what you need to know. You have decided to be the best that you can be because when you are at your best, you are satisfied with who you are and what you have accomplished based on what you know and don't know. Your dedication, commitment and drive in being your best demonstrates how much you love yourself and how what you do and don't do may have an impact on others. You have decided to love. You share and spread the gift of love to others. You are friendly with others. You are charitable and give of your time to help others. This includes those who may not be able to help themselves. You are romantic and share a special kind of love with your spouse, significant other or special friend. You are family oriented and demonstrate love in the things you do with your family. You have decided that you love yourself enough to let go and let God handle any of life's challenges presented to you. Your faith and belief in God's love for you is strong. And with all of that love inside of you, you are going to be **just fine**. Love always. Love daily. 365 Love.™

Have you told someone you loved them today? I have. ™

Love yesterday, today and future tomorrows, ™
Torion

Message in the MUSIC
Mary J. Blige – **Just Fine**

Note the QUOTE!
"Being happy doesn't mean that everything is perfect. It means that you've decided to look beyond the imperfections." --- Unknown

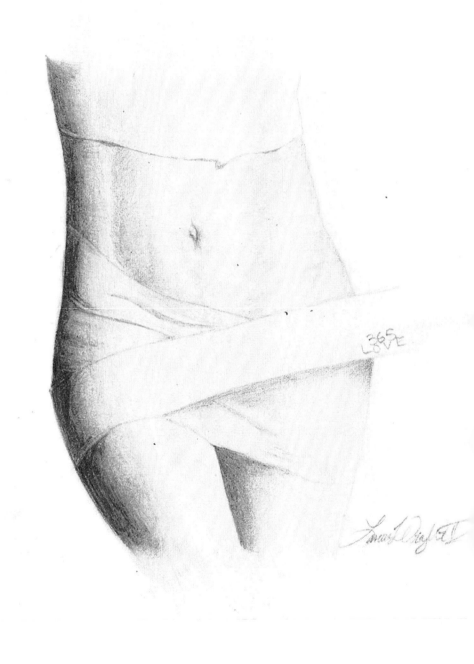

Love Always. Love Daily. 365 Love.

July

"Hate leaves ugly scars, love leaves beautiful ones."

— Mignon McLaughlin

Single with Triplets
July 1

Today's NOTE

God is so good. He sends His angels down on a consistent basis to touch our lives in some way. They provide confirmation of His love and how much He loves us. They also remind us of how He helps us make it through, regardless of the circumstances.

I had the privilege of meeting a young lady today as part of a college campus tour I took my son and niece on. We shared a seat on the shuttle as part of the tour. And while I only had an opportunity to converse with her briefly, I was automatically uplifted by her presence. She was the single mother of three talented, handsome, well mannered, African-American boys (young men). All were seniors getting ready to graduate from high school. She was **single with triplets**. I was in awe. This one woman managed to get three boys through high school with good academic grades at a time when the media and peer pressure are strong, negative influences on our youth. She did it.

I am the mother of two. Both of my children were blessed with the opportunity to be raised by both of their parents in the same household for most of their childhood. And they still have both of their parents as part of their lives today. I recall how much work it was to have one child with two parents in the household. As a new mother, I immediately began to have a greater level of appreciation for other mothers and an even greater level of appreciation for single mothers. So, to think of this mother, **single with triplets**... Wow! What an incredible woman. During our brief interaction, I found out that her husband walked out on her when she was 3 months pregnant leaving her to raise her sons alone. While they all appear to be physically fit, they personally chose not to play sports. Two play string instruments in the orchestra and one is into mass media / production. All have been good students in school and are exploring opportunities to attend college to further their education. They have written essays that were published in local news publications and were the winners of various essay awards.

When we exchanged names, I was amazed to find that her name was NuLuv. Her name included my favorite word. The word I share with others on a daily basis. The word I wear imprinted on my clothing, my favorite jewelry pieces, and my bedroom wall. The word that is greater than great. God's word....Love. The time spent with NuLove reminded me of how much God loves His children. I don't know what her life was like while these boys were growing up, but He made a way for her to care for them so that they grew up to be healthy, strong and educated.

So, when you think raising your one child is tough, think again. When you think about some of the things that you are personally going through, think again. When you allow something small to drain your energy because you can't let go, think again. Think about NuLuv, **single with triplets**. She did it. God made a way. He made a way for her and He will make a way for you. I don't know how

Love Always. Love Daily. 365 Love.

hard or easy it was for her, but she did it. I don't know if there were times that she felt like giving up, but she didn't. I don't know how much help she had from others, but God provided her with the help she needed. Now look at what she has accomplished. I am so proud of her. She is definitely a strong, inspirational woman just by her mere presence and motherly accomplishments alone.

If this 365 Love note happens to one day cross NuLuv's path, I thank her for sharing a small piece of herself with me. I thank her for sharing the love she has for her children. I thank her for reminding me that God will make a way for anything and everything. I thank her for providing yet another confirmation of God's love. Love always. Love daily. 365 Love. ™

Have you told someone you loved them today? I have. ™

Love yesterday, today and future tomorrows, ™
Torion

Message in the MUSIC
Heather Headly – I Know the Lord Will Make a Way

Note the QUOTE!
"When you are a mother, you are never really alone in your thoughts. A mother always has to think twice, once for herself and once for her child." --- Sophia Loren

Scars
July 2

Today's NOTE

A **scar** is a result of the body's process to patch up the skin and other body tissues after an injury. An injury does not become a **scar** until the wound has completely healed. This can take many months or in worst cases, it can take years. No **scar** can be completely removed. However, in some cases its appearance can be improved.

People often refer to **scars** as mental or physical. And most often we think of a **scar** as negative or something not appealing to the eye. It stands out or draws attention to itself. But who says a **scar** has to be represented in this manner. Love makes **scars** beautiful. Love turns a **scar** into something a person can appreciate, have respect for, learn from and/or admire.

A friend of mine dealt with a personal illness from childhood through most of her early adulthood. In her 30's she underwent a surgery that left a permanent **scar** across her stomach. Once healed, she began to wear her cut off shirts and flaunt her stuff. While others may have noticed the **scar** and questioned why she would show it, to her, it was beautiful. It was a reminder of all that she had gone through and survived. It was something beautiful, because for so many years of her life, she was covered. She was hidden. To her, she turned what others may have felt was negative, into a positive, glass is half full experience. She was able to reveal herself and acknowledge that something good happened to her. It was a blessing.

As a participant in the annual breast cancer walk, you get the opportunity to see and meet lots of breast cancer survivors. Some of the survivors had to have one breast removed and made a decision not to have it artificially replaced. This left a beautiful **scar** for them. They are proud to walk around with their body as is. It is a reminder of their struggle and their survival. It is inspiration to other breast cancer patients, making a statement that it is OK and that there is hope. It is their appreciation for another chance to live and the parts of their body that are remaining, as is. It is a display of love. It is a blessing.

Others may have mental **scars** from a life threatening experience, mental abuse, verbal abuse, physical abuse, or some other situation. This includes life-long insecurities formed from learning to love one-self or being teased by someone else (who was even less insecure of themselves and didn't realize it). These **scars** are carried around for extended periods of time to include years. However, once a person learns about the meaning of love and learns to love themselves, they use these **scars** as lessons learned. Through love, they become one of God's messengers, being used to make a difference to someone else. They provide testimonies about their **scars** to others. They inspire those with similar **scars** so that they can make it through whatever they are dealing with. They inspire others to love.

Love Always. Love Daily. 365 Love.

In each of these situations, a personal choice is made to look at the **scar** in a positive manner. That's what love does. Love helps us to see the good in everything that happens to us. That's the power love possesses. When it grows inside of you, happiness is always yours, even with **scars**. Make love a part of who you are and how you choose to be. Love always. Love daily. 365 Love.™

Have you told someone you loved them today? I have.™

Love yesterday, today and future tomorrows,™
Torion

Message in the MUSIC
Whitney Houston – Miracle

Note the QUOTE!
"Hate leaves ugly **scars**, love leaves beautiful ones." --- Mignon McLaughlin

Vacation
July 3

Today's NOTE
I took a 10 day **vacation**. During this time, I spent quality time with family and friends, handled some planning activities for a personal event I was working on, touched based with some old friends via phone, lent a helping hand to a few close friends, listened to music, enjoyed a few local artists in concert, watched movies, danced, roller skated, attended birthday celebrations with family, and continued to share love through 365 Love notes. I enjoyed every day and everything about each day. My **vacation** time did not include work for work. I used it to do things out of love, love of myself and others.

I often hear people say they don't have time for a **vacation** or break from work. I used to be that same person, but I eventually realized God wants us to take time for ourselves too. He wants us to take care of everything He gives to us, including ourselves. While we need to work to make a living, we also need rest, relaxation and fun. We need to use some of our time to enjoy the simple things in life. We need to use some of our time to share love with others beyond the workplace. We need to use some of our time to love ourselves beyond the workplace. We need to use some of our time to rejuvenate and find joy in taking a **vacation**. Love always. Love daily. 365 Love.™

Have you told someone you loved them today? I have. ™

Love yesterday, today and future tomorrows, ™
Torion

Message in the MUSIC
Janet Jackson – Enjoy

Note the QUOTE!
"Happiness consists of living each day as if it were the first day of your honeymoon and the last day of your **vacation**." --- Unknown

Knowledge, Learning, Training, Education and Development

July 4

Today's NOTE

I have over 15 years of experience in the **training** and management fields and have a deep passion for both of them. I love helping others accomplish things they did not know or feel they were able to do. I love helping others learn something new or build on an existing skill. It's the "aha" moments coming from the learner/staff that bring me the most joy. I also enjoy developing staff to improve upon their current performance levels, and/or move into higher level positions or other careers. Knowing that I have contributed to helping someone become successful in a current or future job brings me additional joy. Understanding some key terms is helpful in my process of helping others.

- **Knowledge** is familiarity with something acquired through experience or *education*.
- **Learning** is acquiring new or modifying existing *knowledge*.
- **Training** allows a person to acquire specific *knowledge*. It is typically short term and for a current job.
- **Education** is the process by which people learn and gain *knowledge*. It is considered medium term and for a future job.
- **Development** is the continuous process of acquiring *knowledge* where 80% of it comes from experience. This is more long term and ongoing.

I have the same passion for promoting love as I do for **training** and management. Once you gain **knowledge** of love, you are familiar with it. Begin using it and practicing it. Continue your **learning** process by reading more about it and surround yourself with others who love. **Learn** something new that helps you grow in love and expand upon your existing **knowledge** of love. Teach (or **train**) others to love so that they can begin practicing what they **learned** from you. Even the simplest forms of love make a difference. Continue to gain more **knowledge** by further **educating** yourself. The more you know, the wiser you become. The more you **learn**, the easier it is to do. It becomes more natural. You can never learn too much. You should always **educate** your mind. And keep it going. Ongoing **learning** is a part of the overall **development** process. You are your own vessel of **knowledge**. Open your heart to share love and share your **developmental** experiences with others. Apply what you **learn** about love on a consistent basis and see how much of a difference it makes in your life and the life of others you choose to share with. Remember, love is contagious. Love always. Love daily. 365 Love. ™

Have you told someone you loved them today? I have. ™

Love yesterday, today and future tomorrows, ™
Torion

Message in the MUSIC
Stephanie Mills – I've **Learned** to Respect the Power of Love

Note the QUOTE!
"**Learn** to get in touch with silence within yourself, and know that everything in life has purpose. There are no mistakes, no coincidences, all events are blessings given to us to **learn** from." --- Elizabeth Kubler-Ross

Laugh a Good Laugh
July 5

Today's NOTE

Today I took a moment to **laugh a good laugh**. I laughed because the beginning of my work day ended almost the same way it began. I laughed because I knew that I was being sent a hidden message or messages. I sat and thought of several messages, both serious and humorous, and I laughed. I laughed and it felt good.

The hallway from the employee entrance to the elevators that take me to my office at work is literally like walking the Green Mile. It is long. This morning, I made it from the parking garage all the way to my desk and noticed that I left my laptop in the trunk of my car. Of course I can't do any work without that. So, with my keys in hand, back down "the mile" I went to my car and then back to my desk again. My work day was a long one and when I was finally ready to leave, back down "the mile" I went to the parking garage. I was ready to go home. Once I made it to my car, I realized I left my keys in my laptop bag at my desk. And I can't go home without my keys, right? So, once again, as my work day began, so it ended, back down "the mile" I went to my desk and back to the parking lot. Once I finally made it to my car, again, I **laughed a good laugh**. I told myself that I was just being stalled because even though I was ready to go home, it really wasn't time for me to go. There was a hidden message there. So, I was fine with it. Since I've gained a few pounds, maybe it was a sign for me to begin my work out plan (smile). Or maybe I was to be reminded that I have a memory and could recall where my laptop and keys actually were. Or maybe I was being protected and kept safe so that I would not encounter another situation if I had left at an earlier time. Or maybe it was intended for me to just have some peace time by walking down the calming halls of "the mile" again, and again, and again. Regardless, **I laughed a good laugh**. I laughed at myself. And it actually felt good. Sometimes you have to just do that, laugh. Open up your smile and laugh. It's your own private, personal session of fun. Laughter is good for the soul. Laughter is even better when you love. Love always. Love daily. 365 Love.™

Have you told someone you loved them today? I have.™

Love yesterday, today and future tomorrows,™
Torion

Message in the MUSIC
Mary Mary – God Has Smiled on Me

Note the QUOTE!
"I believe that imagination is stronger than knowledge, myth is more potent than history, dreams are more powerful than facts, hope always triumphs over experience, laughter is the cure for grief, and love is stronger than death." --- Robert Fulghum

Drawing of You
July 6

Today's NOTE

They say that a picture or drawing speaks a thousand words. It can also tell a story. It's amazing what the eye can see and what the mind can image just from looking deeply at a work of art. You can see happiness or sorrow. You can see good or bad. The initial idea comes from the artist. He typically draws what he feels in his soul about the object presented in front of him. And the beauty in his artistry comes out on paper. If someone was to create a **drawing of you**,

- What story would it tell?
- How do you think the artist would see you?
- How would you see yourself?
- How do you think others would see you?
- What type of energy would appear in the **drawing of you**?
- Would it come out in your smile?
- What about your eyes?
- And your lips, what message would they send?
- That nose of yours, with its unique characteristics, what would it tell the artist about you?
- Your inner self that transcends outwardly, would it show?

A person of love looks for the best in you. They see what others cannot, but they can also see reality right in front of their eyes. The love you have on the inside can always be seen on outside. And people take notice. Let the **drawing of you** be a reflection of the love you demonstrate. Let it be plentiful and vibrant, full of life and color. Let it glow and make heads turn because it represents so much love. Let it radiate love. Love strong and make it easy for the artist to see your beauty in his **drawing of you**. Love always. Love daily. 365 Love.™

Have you told someone you loved them today? I have.™

Love yesterday, today and future tomorrows,™
Torion

Message in the MUSIC
James Fortune – **Draw Me**

Note the QUOTE!
"In art the hand can never execute anything higher than the heart can inspire." --- Ralph Waldo Emerson

Try It
July 7

Today's NOTE
Sometimes, we let the opinions of others determine what we will and will not do. We let someone else's words persuade us to think a certain way or act a certain way. You have your own mind and you are in control of you. You are fully capable of making your own decisions, your own choices. You know the difference between right and wrong. You know the difference between good and bad. Knowing these things means you know at least a little something about love. Love is what is right and love is what is good. You can use a number of other words to break it down and make it more complex, but the basic foundation is as simple as that.

We learn by hearing and seeing things repetitively. The more you see or hear the same thing, the more likely you are to act on it and remember it. So, why not place your focus on practicing to be more like love? Doing the right things. Practicing things that are good. Making the right choices. Choosing to do good things. **Try it** once. Then **try it** again and again. You don't need to consult with someone else to do something you know is the right thing to do. You can decide for yourself to love, be loved and practice love. You can decide to treat yourself and others well. Go on. **Try it**. Try love, today, tomorrow and the day after that, and the day after that. Never allow someone else to take your ability to love away from you. Hold on to your own personal desire to love. Keep it in your mind, heart and soul. Love always. Love daily. 365 Love.™

Have you told someone you loved them today? I have. ™

Love yesterday, today and future tomorrows, ™
Torion

Message in the MUSIC
Whitney Houston - **Try It** On My Own

Note the QUOTE!
"God doesn't require us to succeed. He only requires that you try." --- Mother Teresa

---

Become a Blessing
July 8

Today's NOTE

Become a blessing to someone. Share a piece of yourself with someone other than yourself. Give of your talents, your time, your testimony and/or your financial blessing. Give charitable love.

If you have a special talent, don't let it go to waste. God gives us gifts to use for good. When we don't use them, He takes them away from us. Use your God given gift to make a difference to someone else. Use it to help them learn something new. Use it to help brighten their day. Use it to inspire them to become a better person. Use it to **become a blessing**.

There is value in time. Once you lose it, you cannot get it back. And when you give it, it can make things happen. If you have time to give, use it to help someone else. Volunteer for a good cause. Spend time with someone who has no one to spend time with them. Share a moment with someone in need of a mentor or the elderly in need of a friend. Use it to **become a blessing**.

If you have been through a life changing event and made it through, share your story with someone to give them hope. Share your testimony to let them know they are not alone. Share your triumph to serve as a living confirmation that they can make it through. Use your experience to help them hold on to their faith. Use it to **become a blessing**.

If you are blessed financially, share some of what you have with someone in need of financial support. Contribute to a non-profit organization, or help a family member, friend or stranger. Donate supplies to a school in need or contribute funds to help rebuild a community. Use it to **become a blessing**.

Use your blessing to **become a blessing** to someone else. God will smile at you for doing something good. He will smile for your demonstration of His greatest gift, love – agape, charitable, love. Love always. Love daily. 365 Love.™

Have you told someone you loved them today? I have.™

Love yesterday, today and future tomorrows,™
Torion

Message in the MUSIC
Mary Mary – God in Me

Note the QUOTE!
"God blesses you to **become a blessing**." --- Unknown

Love Always. Love Daily. 365 Love.

Stop Competing with the Jones'
July 9

Today's NOTE

It's nice to win. It's nice to be the best. It's nice to have the best. But **stop competing with the Jones'** just to be better than or have more than someone else. God gives us each our own unique gifts. Everyone is not meant to be classified as "the best" by people, or have "the best" of everything. God puts His own classification on who we are and what we have. He wants us to be the best that we can be with what He has defined our purpose to be. There is always going to be someone with more money, a nicer house, a fancier car, a nicer body, nicer clothes, a better job, more creativity, more accomplishments, etc. If you keep trying to keep up with the Jones', you will lose who you are. You will lose out on learning to truly live. You will lose out on discovering the true meaning of love.

God created us all differently, each with a different purpose. Everyone is not meant to do the same thing the same way. Everyone is not meant to be alike. Be happy for those who have more than you. Be happy for those who have gifts that are different than yours. Put your envy in the toilet and flush it. Watch it go down the drain. And if you left some behind, flush that toilet again until you know it is all gone. Love does not envy. Be satisfied with you, what God has allowed you to have, and what you are yet to become. Be happy knowing that you are meant to be different and unique. Be happy knowing that you have a totally different purpose than anyone else. **Stop competing with the Jones'**. If you must compete, compete to be your own personal best. Compete to be the best that you can be for you. Everything else will fall into place from there. It is then that you will be satisfied with who you are and all that you have that is meant for you. And the lives you touch through love will be your greatest reward. Love always. Love daily. 365 Love.™

Have you told someone you loved them today? I have. ™

Love yesterday, today and future tomorrows, ™
Torion

Message in the MUSIC
Usher – Just Be You

Note the QUOTE!
"Always be a first-rate version of yourself, instead of a second-rate version of someone else." --- Unknown

Because It's the Right Thing to Do
July 10

Today's NOTE
Why love? **Because it's the right thing to do.** Because in fulfilling our purpose in life, we are meant to love. We are meant to love in a way that has an impact on life, our life and the life of others. We are meant to love and teach others to love in return. We are meant to share and spread love in a way that brings happiness, joy and peace. We are meant to live a life of purpose and meaning. We are meant for greatness, greatness found within doing our best in all that we do. God wants us to love. He loves us and wants us to love in return. Why? **Because it's the right thing to do.** Love always. Love daily. 365 Love.™

Have you told someone you loved them today? I have.™

Love yesterday, today and future tomorrows,™
Torion

Message in the MUSIC
Donnie McClurkin – Great is Your Mercy

Note the QUOTE!
"See, you don't have to think about doing the right thing. If you are for the right thing then you'll do it without thinking." --- Maya Angelou

---

Forgive Somebody
July 11

Today's NOTE
Love forgives. If you are holding on to hurt, anger or pain as a result of a past or current relationship or situation, let it go. Just let it all go. You have to find it in your heart to forgive and let go. When you hold on to pain and anger, it drains your personal energy. It holds on to you and keeps you from moving forward. It keeps you from loving to your fullest potential. You are held hostage in your own emotions. You allow someone or something else to maintain a hold on you when they have moved on and the situation is over and done with. Then again, the person you may need to forgive might be you. You may need to forgive yourself for something you have done personally and are wearing the guilt for. God loves you. He is a forgiving God. And if He can forgive, so can you. That's what love does. That's what a loving heart does. **Forgive somebody** right now, today. If it is hard for you to do, have strong faith and pray for the strength to let go. Pray hard and mean it. **Forgive somebody** so that you can move forward in fulfilling your purpose in life. **Forgive somebody** so that you can continue to grow in love. Love always. Love daily. 365 Love.™

Have you told someone you loved them today? I have.™

Love yesterday, today and future tomorrows,™
Torion

Message in the MUSIC
Kelly Price – Healing for My Soul

Note the QUOTE!
"If you want life to be greater for you, you have to **forgive somebody**." --- Rev. R. L. White, Jr.

The Sky
July 12

Today's NOTE
I sat in a seat next to the window on the airplane today. After take-off, I saw the city get smaller and smaller. Once we reached a certain altitude, my view was that of blue skies full of white clouds. All I could think about was how beautiful it was. How peaceful it was. How serene it was. How pure it appeared to be. The clearness in the blue of **the sky**. The fullness of the white in the clouds. If I could smell the air, it would be so refreshing. If it were possible to lay on the clouds, it would be so relaxing and comforting. I felt blessed for that moment of peace. I felt blessed for that moment of calmness. I felt blessed that I was able to see **the sky** up close and up high. I felt love. And I was thankful that God gave someone the ability to create the airplane so that others could witness such beauty in **the sky**. It's another one of the simple things in life that we think so little of. Another one of God's creations. Another perspective on love. Love always. Love daily. 365 Love.™

Have you told someone you loved them today? I have.™

Love yesterday, today and future tomorrows,™
Torion

Message in the MUSIC
Earth, Wind and Fire – Keep Your Head to **the Sky**

Note the QUOTE!
"Look what happens with a love like that, it lights the whole **sky**." --- Haflz

An Action Verb
July 13

Today's NOTE

An action verb is used to describe how to take action on something. It is used to express action or the performance of an action. Action is doing. Action is moving forward. Action is having something to take place. Love can be defined as a noun or **an action verb**. The **action verb** for love is *to love*. It's meaning is to have affection for, or to have a strong liking for. And there are many ways to love. Read it, absorb it, embrace it, and act on it.

- Love God
- Love spiritually
- Love others
- Love people
- Love family
- Love friends
- Love me
- Love you
- Love hard
- Love smart
- Love deep
- Love long
- Love forever
- Love with meaning
- Love great
- Love a lot
- Love more
- Love big
- Love abundantly
- Love high
- Love infinitely
- Love with heart
- Love much
- Love all over
- Love respectfully
- Love honestly
- Love truthfully
- Love with integrity
- Love peace
- Love harmony
- Love balance
- Love the unloved
- Love to be loved
- Love with an open mind
- Love broadly
- Love willingly
- Love uniquely
- Love music
- Love life
- Love to smile
- Love to laugh
- Love right
- Love fully
- Love unconditionally
- Love being
- Love listening
- Love hugging
- Love dancing
- Love walking
- Love talking
- Love singing
- Love romantically
- Love brotherly
- Love charitably
- Love the rain
- Love after pain
- Love eternally
- Love with understanding
- Love openly
- Love joy
- Love magnificently
- Love diversely
- Love helping
- Love sharing
- Love caring
- Love the past
- Love the present
- Love the future
- Love inspiring
- Love the positive
- Love the day
- Love the night
- Love what is
- Love what is to be
- Love each season
- Love for all reasons
- Love love
- Love always
- Love daily

365 Love™

Have you told someone you loved them today? I have.™

Love Always. Love Daily. 365 Love.

Love yesterday, today and future tomorrows,™
Torion

Message in the MUSIC
Michael Jackson – The Way You Love Me

Note the QUOTE!
"When you love, you wish to do for. You wish to sacrifice for. You wish to serve."-
-- Ernest Hemingway

Feel Good All Over
July 14

Today's NOTE

Feel good all over. Choose the feeling and bring it into existence. Your feelings are a choice made by you. The more you choose to **feel good all over**, the more it comes into existence. Think about it. Say it to yourself. Talk about it. Repeat it. Smile about it. Laugh about it. And begin to **feel good all over**. Remind yourself of love. The feeling of love, the thought of love, and the joy of love. Remind yourself of God's love and self-love. Smile at yourself and **feel good all over**. Love always. Love daily. 365 Love.™

Have you told someone you loved them today? I have.™

Love yesterday, today and future tomorrows,™
Torion

Message in the MUSIC
Stephanie Mills - I **Feel Good All Over**

Note the QUOTE!
"Sometimes your joy is the source of your smile, but sometimes your smile is the source of your joy." --- Thich Nhat Hanh

Bigger and Better
July 15

Today's NOTE
As humans, our life cycle includes growing and evolving. Part of that evolution process includes God's plan to make us **bigger and better**. We are born as babies requiring 100% dependency on the help of an adult to nourish us. We then become toddlers and learn how to walk and talk. We move on to become active children, running, playing, learning and becoming more independent. Then comes the teenage, adult hood, and elderly years. At each stage of our lives, we learn, grow and ultimately become **bigger and better**. Our experiences are meant to be lessons learned to help us "get it." They are meant to be lessons learned to help guide us in the direction of love, learning to love and loving more. We are meant to experience love by receiving it and giving it, practicing it and sharing it. Love in itself helps make us **bigger and better**. **Bigger and better** than we were the day before, and the day before that. Love always. Love daily. 365 Love.™

Have you told someone you loved them today? I have.™

Love yesterday, today and future tomorrows,™
Torion

Message in the MUSIC
Yolanda Adams – Show Me

Note the QUOTE!
"You don't have to go looking for love when it's where you come from." --- Werner Erhard

The Truth
July 16

Today's NOTE

I often tell my children that **the truth** is the easiest thing to remember. And there is **truth** in making the right choices and doing the right things. When you do the right things, good things happen. When you lie and do things you know are wrong, you eventually have to deal with the consequences of your actions. It is said that **the truth** will set you free. Well it often times keeps you free. Free internally and externally. When you lie, you have to remember the lie and one lie keeps building on the other. You have to keep track of who you told what and when. And the lie keeps growing and growing. That includes lies you tell to yourself. **The truth** makes it easy. You don't have to remember what actually happened. You don't have to worry about consequences associated with doing the right thing. You can be who you are or put things in place to become a better you. The truth is the truth. Sometimes we deny it. Sometimes it hurts. But it is what it is. There is love in **the truth**. That includes being truthful with yourself and others. Being truthful with what you say and how you say it. Being truthful with who you are. Being truthful in all that you do. Love always. Love daily. 365 Love.™

Have you told someone you loved them today? I have.™

Love yesterday, today and future tomorrows,™
Torion

Message in the MUSIC
Lalah Hathaway – **The** Naked **Truth**

Note the QUOTE!
"It (love) does not rejoice about injustice, but rejoices whenever **the truth** wins out." --- 1 Corinthians 13

Are You Listening?
July 17

Today's NOTE
Are you listening? Part of being a loving person is the ability to listen. Listen with your ears, your eyes and your heart. Sometimes we hear what is being said, but we are not truly **listening**. We hear others talking, but our heart is not open to fully understanding what is being said. We are so stuck on how we feel about what is being discussed that we block out another point of view. We see something happening as a result of the discussion and we ignore the long lasting impact because we can only see our side of things.

Listening requires holding on to your personal thoughts until the thoughts of another are fully expressed. **Listening** allows you the ability to absorb what is being said. **Listening** does not scream, interrupt or ignore. Love listens and with **listening** comes understanding. With **listening** comes understanding that another point of view may be different than yours, but that point of view matters. With **listening** comes truly hearing and the ability to make a change. **Listening** is not always having your way, but having "our" way. **Listening** is a part of love. Love always. Love daily. 365 Love.™

Have you told someone you loved them today? I have.™

Love yesterday, today and future tomorrows,™
Torion

Message in the MUSIC
Kirk Franklin – **Are You Listening?**

Note the QUOTE!
"The first duty of love is to listen."--- Paul Tillich

Love Always. Love Daily. 365 Love.

Preparing You for a Blessing
July 18

Today's NOTE
Life has its ups and downs. There are moments when you want to give up. There are moments when you want to quit. There are moments when you feel things are hopeless. You feel that you are in a position where you can't take care of your needs. You feel like you've lost it all. You feel that no one cares and no one understands. It is at these times when your faith should be its strongest. Your faith should remind you that you go through things for a reason and a season. Your faith should remind you that God is **preparing you for a blessing**. It is a blessing that is designed for you and only you. He is preparing you for something better than what you are and where you are. He is leading you to love Him more. He is leading you to love more. He is leading you to make a change. He is leading you to make a difference. He is leading you to stop talking about it, but being about it. He is leading you to stop doing what is within your will, to start doing what is within His will. And when you take His lead, your blessings will follow. Love never fails. Love is **preparing you for a blessing**. Love is a part of your blessing. Love always. Love daily. 365 Love.™

Have you told someone you loved them today? I have. ™

Love yesterday, today and future tomorrows,™
Torion

Message in the MUSIC
Kirk Franklin – **Blessing** in the Storm

Note the QUOTE!
"May your days be many and your troubles be few. May all God's **blessings** descend upon you. May peace be within you. May your heart be strong. May you find what you're seeking wherever you roam." --- Irish Blessings

Hey You!
July 19

Today's NOTE

Hey you! Yes, you! I'm talking to you. Keep your head up. Think positive. Surround yourself with positive people. Make good choices. Do the right things. Treat people right. Be impeccable with your words. Be truthful and honest. Have integrity. Help somebody. Lend a helping hand. Listen with understanding. Be a good steward of your finances. Be good to yourself. Live your life. Love your life. Appreciate the simple things. Always say, "Thank You." Value your time and the time of others. Share some of your time with others. Give. Be charitable. Reach for the stars. Stop talking about it and act on it. Do something. Pray big. Always do your best. Don't take things personal. Open your heart to love. Love yourself and others. Remember the beauty of the rainbow. Be respectful. Smile at somebody. Enjoy each moment of each day, every day. Look for the best in others. Find joy in all things. Think positive thoughts. See the glass as half full vs. half empty. Have strong faith.

Hey you! Yes, you! I'm talking to you. Love always. Love daily. 365 Love.™

Have you told someone you loved them today? I have.™

Love yesterday, today and future tomorrows,™
Torion

Message in the MUSIC
Babyface – Good to be in Love

Note the QUOTE!
"True love doesn't just fill your heart, it overflows into your whole body and soul."
--- Unknown

Today is a Good Day
July 20

Today's NOTE
Today is a good day. Why? Because it is. Find joy in it and appreciate your livelihood. Remember, it's your choice. Choose good in the day. Realize that it is another day you have to fulfill your purpose. Be glad about it. Do something with it. It is yours. Love always. Love daily. 365 Love.™

Have you told someone you loved them today? I have.™

Love yesterday, today and future tomorrows,™
Torion

Message in the MUSIC
Greg Street – **Good Day**

Note the QUOTE!
"True love cannot be found where it does not exist, nor can it be denied where it does." --- Unknown

---

Love Always. Love Daily. 365 Love.

Special
July 21

Today's NOTE
Everybody wants to feel **special**. They want to belong. They want to be needed. They want to be loved. Well, you are **special**. You are very **special**. God created you. His love for you makes you **special**. Your uniqueness makes you **special**. Nothing and no one is like you. Who you are and what you do are **special**. Doing your best is a demonstration of your **special** qualities. You have a **special** way of showing love, sharing love and being loved. Your life is **special**. You have a **special** path designed for your journey to grow in love. God loves you in a **special** way that is meant just for you. Look at yourself and smile knowing how **special** you are. Let no one convince you otherwise. Love always. Love daily. 365 Love.™

Have you told someone you loved them today? I have.™

Love yesterday, today and future tomorrows,™
Torion

Message in the MUSIC
Janet Jackson - **Special**

Note the QUOTE!
"Never underestimate the power, because love can do miracles which you never thought possible." --- Unknown

---

Love Always. Love Daily. 365 Love.

I Know
July 22

Today's NOTE
There is somebody somewhere who has gone or is going through something you are going through. This, **I know**. You can open up the Bible and read countless stories that are similar to current life situations. You can go to church and hear testimonies from the members. You can even look across the street or right next to you and find someone who has experienced or is experiencing what you are going through. **I know** there are times when you struggle to find resolution and peace in your heart. Just know that what you are going through is only temporary. Know that love will bring you through it. God's love is the first and ultimate healer. His love is above all things. Pray for strength, courage, forgiveness, healing, and wisdom. Pray your special prayer to address your needs that are within His will. Self-love comes next. Love yourself enough to let go and let God. Love yourself enough to put things in place within your control to help find your way through. Love yourself enough to see if you need to make a change in you in order to make your situation better. Love yourself enough to have the desire to love more, love often, and love again and again. Love yourself enough to truly know what love is and what love is not. **I know** love is the answer. **I know** love changes things. **I know** love sometimes takes you through things to make you a better person. **I know** love gives. **I know** love heals. This, **I know**. Love always. Love daily. 365 Love.™

Have you told someone you loved them today? I have.™

Love yesterday, today and future tomorrows,™
Torion

Message in the MUSIC
Destiny's Child – **I Know**

Note the QUOTE!
"Love allows you to get the best out of life instead of allowing life to get the best out of you." --- Torion Wright

---

Love Always. Love Daily. 365 Love.

The Good in Goodbye
July 23

Today's NOTE
Saying goodbye can be a hard thing to do. However, it's not always a bad thing to do. Sometimes, it's the right thing to do. There is **good in goodbye**. Not only is good within the word itself, there are times when good things happen by finally saying goodbye and really meaning it. There is good in saying goodbye to bad habits. There is good in saying goodbye to negative influences. There is good in saying goodbye to people that are not good to you or for you. There is good in saying goodbye to people and things that are holding you back and keeping you from growing. There is good in saying goodbye to those we love so that they can be free to learn more and grow independently and on their own. There is good in saying goodbye to the old you. There is good in saying goodbye so that God can take control of things. The **good in goodbye** allows you to say, "hello" to something bigger and better. It allows you to say hello to new people and new things. It allows you to say hello to a new and improved you. It allows you to say, "hello" to a greater love. It allows you to say, "hello" to a greater level of faith. It allows you to say, "hello" to a new experience. Think about what you need to say, "goodbye" to. Find the **good in goodbye**. Say goodbye and get ready for the love in hello. Love always. Love daily. 365 Love.™

Have you told someone you loved them today? I have.™

Love yesterday, today and future tomorrows,™
Torion

Message in the MUSIC
Beyonce – Best Thing I Never Had

Note the QUOTE!
"Don't cry because it's over. Smile because it happened." --- Dr. Seuss

Blame
July 24

Today's NOTE
So often we **blame** others for the outcome of our lives. We hold onto the past and tell stories about what "the other person" did to affect us. I was reading *The Confident Woman Devotional by Joyce Meyer* and thought about her views on Adam and Eve. She pointed out that everyone typically **blames** Eve for eating the forbidden fruit and giving it to Adam who in turn did the same. However, God created Adam first and told Adam not to eat the fruit. Additionally, Adam knew God's word (right from wrong), yet he made a choice to eat the fruit also. It's interesting that Eve is typically the one that the **blame** is placed upon. Yet both made a choice. Both dealt with the consequences and moved forward.

We make choices in life and we deal with circumstances in life. Some are within our control and others are not. While we can spend the rest of our lives pointing **blame** on others for who we are, where we are, and how we are, our future is ultimately up to us. At some point in our lives, we have the ability to make a choice. We also have to realize how our own actions or failure to act were contributors of our life situations as well. We can choose to exist and forever point **blame**, or we can make our past a lesson learned and choose to move forward. We can become whatever we want to become by choice. We can choose to be happy. We can choose to be more and do more. We can choose to let go and let God handle things. We can choose to be better as a person. Your interactions with those in your past are in your past. The past was yesterday. Today is a new day. And tomorrow is yet to come. What we make of today and tomorrow are personal choices. Stop blaming others for your livelihood. Push the **blame** aside today. Choose to forgive yourself and others and move on to a bigger and better tomorrow. Love always. Love daily. 365 Love.™

Have you told someone you loved them today? I have. ™

Love yesterday, today and future tomorrows, ™
Torion

Message in the MUSIC
Chrisette Michele – **Blame** It On Me

Note the QUOTE!
"Take your life in your own hands, and what happens? A terrible thing: no one to **blame**." --- Erica Jong

We Belong Together
July 25

Today's NOTE

There are times in our lives when it is good for us to be alone. There are also times in our lives when it is meant for us to be alone. It is during these times that we grow in love so that we are better prepared to give and receive love. However, we are not meant to be alone forever.

One of my staff members is beginning to open up to dating after being divorced for about 7 years. He gives women a hard time and has a wall up guarding his heart. I told him that when the right woman comes along, he will drop the wall for her. It may be a slow process, but it will happen. I also reminded him that God does not mean for us to be alone and that God created Eve so that Adam would not be alone. So, as man and woman **we belong together**. He agreed with me and in turn told me an interesting story.

The Bible tells us that Eve was created from the rib of Adam. As a result, there is an old saying that states, "A woman will always have a part of man with her. Accordingly, a man will never be complete until he finds the right woman. He will continue to search for her until he finds her. She is the missing part of him that when found, makes man whole again and they become one."

The one thing that I have always held strong to my heart is never allowing someone to make me lose the desire to love. And neither should you. I believe in love and have strong faith that there are other people who believe in love also. Never allow anyone to take away your desire to love. For when you do, you allow them to take control of you. Let go and let God. Again, God does not want us to be alone. So if you are holding back on loving again because of a current and/or past hurt, know that this is not aligned with God's plan for you. If you are growing in love, doing the right things, making the right choices, and fulfilling your purpose in life, know that God has a plan for you. He wants you to love. He wants you to be loved. He wants all of us to love and be loved. And when you love, love will come to you. It will come through a family member, a stranger, a brotherly friend and/or a romantic friend. Remember, it is what is within God's will, not your will. It's also when God feels you are ready, not when you feel you are ready. Love always. Love daily. 365 Love.™

Have you told someone you loved them today? I have.™

Love yesterday, today and future tomorrows,™
Torion

Message in the MUSIC
Mariah Carey - **We Belong Together**

Note the QUOTE!
"A part of you has grown in me. And so you see, it's you and me together forever and never apart, maybe in distance, but never in heart." --- Unknown

The Rain
July 26

Today's NOTE
I went to a baseball game yesterday and as soon as I got there it began to rain. And it rained, and rained and rained. Everyone wanted **the rain** to end so that they could see the game, but it would not and did not. It rained for most of the evening. Today, the sun was shining and the day was simply beautiful. It reminded me of what we go through to grow in love. **The rain** may fall, but the sun will eventually rise up and shine. **The rain** may not stop when we want it to, but it does eventually stop. And once **the rain** stops, the sun does shine. **The rain** has its purpose. It cleanses. It provides nourishment. It is a contributor to the growth of beautiful things. Flowers cannot grow without water from **the rain**. Rainbows are not formed without **the rain**. Your tears (or struggles) are a part of your personal growth in love. Once the tears stop, the sun shines and there is a beautiful end result. That's life. That's love. Love always. Love daily. 365 Love.™

Have you told someone you loved them today? I have.™

Love yesterday, today and future tomorrows,™
Torion

Message in the MUSIC
Michelle Williams - Purpose in Your Storm

Note the QUOTE!
"God didn't promise days without pain, laughter without sorrow, sun without **rain**, but He did promise strength for the day, comfort for the tears, and light for the way." --- Unknown

Forever
July 27

Today's NOTE

Love is **forever**. And **forever** is a very long time. It has no ending. It carries on to infinity and beyond. It extends past what is imaginable. It goes on and on and on. It is a number greater than the greatest number. It goes beyond the end of time. It moves consistently forward in a positive direction, endlessly. It is here today, tomorrow, the day after that, and many, many days beyond that. It reaches the highest of heights. It outlives everything and everyone.

Wouldn't you like to be a part of something good for that period of time? Something so good that lasts **forever**? Love is a choice. Choose love **forever**. Love always. Love daily. 365 Love.™

Have you told someone you loved them today? I have.™

Love yesterday, today and future tomorrows,™
Torion

Message in the MUSIC
The Floacist - **Forever**

Note the QUOTE!

"Love is not written on paper, for paper can be erased. Nor is it etched on stone, for stone can be broken. But it is inscribed on a heart and there it shall remain **forever**." --- Unknown

---

Stand Up for Love
July 28

Today's NOTE
Part of our history includes countless stories of people standing up for human rights. People stood up for civil rights, women's rights, employment rights, veterans rights, voting rights, etc. All of these historical events and many others were for a good cause. They were for the purpose of standing up for treating people right. A lot of opportunities we have today would not exist if someone did not **stand up**. In all cases, people joined together to **stand up** for the greater benefit of many. They stood up for others who may not have been as strong to **stand up** for themselves. They stood up for the collective. They stood up unselfishly. They stood up because of love. Charitable love. The love of others. A love greater than self.

We live in a world where media glorifies the bad vs. the good. Most of the popular TV shows and movies are based on sex and/or violence. Gossip columns are extremely popular. Entertainers become famous promoting disrespect for themselves, women, men, race, religion and then some. Parents can be arrested for disciplining their children and several don't discipline at all. Children are having sex as early as elementary school. Where is the love in all of this? What is your contribution to love? Do you talk about it? Do you support the TV programs and movies that promote good things? Do you read things that inspire and promote good? What about reading the Bible? Do you have a Bible? Do you spend your money on entertainment that uplifts, inspires, teaches good things, etc.? What you choose to surround yourself with has an influence on who you are. Do you surround yourself with things that are positive and represent the good in love? I think it's time for you to **stand up**. For everyone to **stand up**. **Stand up** for what is good. **Stand up** for what is right. **Stand up for love**. Learn more about it. Practice it. Share it. Grow in it. Love always. Love daily. 365 Love.™

Have you told someone you loved them today? I have. ™

Love yesterday, today and future tomorrows,™
Torion

Message in the MUSIC
Destiny's Child - **Stand Up for Love**

Note the QUOTE!
"You have not lived a perfect day, unless you have done something for someone who will never be able to repay you." --- Ruth Smeltzer

---

Love Always. Love Daily. 365 Love.

Adore
July 29

Today's NOTE
To **adore** is to worship or honor. It is synonymous to love and includes admiration and devotion. I **adore** life. I **adore** all that is and is not. I **adore** the potential of every man. I **adore** all that is good and all that strives to be and do good. I **adore** what I have and what I have not. I **adore** my family and friends. I **adore** those who came into my life for a reason, a season and a lifetime. I **adore** my spirituality. I **adore** growing in love. I **adore** giving and receiving love. I **adore** because I love. Love always. Love daily. 365 Love.™

Have you told someone you loved them today? I have. ™

Love yesterday, today and future tomorrows, ™
Torion

Message in the MUSIC
Prince - **Adore**

Note the QUOTE!
"You know when you have found your prince because you not only have a smile on your face but in your heart as well." --- Unknown

Family Reunion
July 30

Today's NOTE

The Williams **family reunion** takes place every other year. Most family members live in the state of Georgia and are primarily split between Atlanta and Savannah. The hosting city typically alternates. Lue Kent was the oldest living descendent of the Williams family at the 2011 reunion. She alone has 15 children -- 11 of her own and 4 step children. All of her children were alive and present at the 2011 Williams **family reunion.** All of Lue's children have children and most of their children have children. So imagine how big her immediate family alone is. Lue has three siblings. Two are still living. However, none of them have an immediate family as large as hers. There were at least 150 family members at the reunion.

There is a traditional basketball rivalry between the two cities where family members talk smack to one another via phone calls, e-mails and the **family reunion** Facebook page until the day of the actual reunion basketball game. They plan their basketball strategy. They even have a trophy that has been passed around over the years to the winning city. It's serious, but healthy family rivalry. After the game is over, the winning team cheers, the losing team puts on a big smile, they hug, they laugh and they become a true family of one. It's a wonderful sight to see.

Each member of the family has their own separate life to live. However, they look forward to getting together as family for the reunion. They put all other things on hold, take vacation time away from work, save up their money, and travel near and far to make sure they are present for the **family reunion**. They come as sisters and brothers, aunts and uncles, nieces and nephews, grandmothers and grandfathers, mothers and fathers, in-laws and cousins. They are all there. It's the one time of the year when the larger scale family devotes time dedicated to fellowshipping with one another. They share lots of hugs and kisses. They share childhood stories. They share family history. They meet the newest members of the family. They congratulate one another for life accomplishments achieved. There are lots of smiles. There is lots of laughter. Love is all over the place. That's family. That's love. Love at the **family reunion**. Love always. Love daily. 365 Love.TM

Have you told someone you loved them today? I have. TM

Love yesterday, today and future tomorrows, TM
Torion

Message in the MUSIC
The O'Jays – **Family Reunion**

Note the QUOTE!
"Other things may change us, but we start and end with family." --- Anthony Brandt

Who Knows
July 31

Today's NOTE

Who knows what we have to look forward to for the remainder of today? **Who knows** what tomorrow may bring? No one. We must live today and each day to its fullest. We must celebrate the simple joys in life and appreciate all that life has to offer. Let the love you share today, build on a greater love for tomorrow. For no one knows about tomorrow, but today is always a new day. Spend today giving and receiving love. Love always. Love daily. 365 Love.™

Have you told someone you loved them today? I have.™

Love yesterday, today and future tomorrows,™
Torion

Message in the MUSIC
Musiq Soulchild - **Who Knows**

Note the QUOTE!
"Today you have 100% of your life left." --- Tom Landry

Love Always. Love Daily. 365 Love.

Love Always. Love Daily. 365 Love.

August

"The quickest way to receive love is to give; the fastest way to lose love is to hold it too tightly; and the best way to keep love is to give it wings."
— Unknown

Right in Front of My Eyes
August 1

Today's NOTE
I was on the way home today and it began to rain. It went from a clear sky to hard rain, just like that, but the sun was still shining. All of a sudden, out of nowhere, a rainbow appeared. It was huge. The more I drove, the closer it became. At one point, I could actually see the rainbow end on the hood of my car. If I had been on the outside of my car, I feel that I could have put my hand right through it. What a beautiful sight. How magnificent it was. I was in awe. I have seen a few rainbows in my lifetime, but never this close, and never a clear sight of where it ended. It was so colorful and full of life. For those few seconds, I saw one of God's gifts..... **right in front of my eyes**. Then, in a matter of seconds, it was gone. The sun went away, the clouds were gray, and all that remained was the rain, rain, rain coming down. It didn't matter though. All I could think about was that rainbow. I personally witnessed what I felt was the end of a rainbow....**right in front of my eyes**. Wow! I was talking to my mother on the phone at the time and informed her of everything as it was happening. She heard the excitement in my voice as I experienced this sight. We joked about me being the treasure at the end of the rainbow because of what I experienced. But on a more serious note, I felt that it was a gift. At the end of a long day of work, after dealing with family issues, after sending out prayers for those in need, I saw it as a Piece Of Wonderful (POW). It was God's way of sharing one of His remarkable creations. It was His silent message. It was a smile. It was a way to say everything ahead of you is going to be OK. It was a moment of peace. It was a moment of serenity. It calmed and soothed me. It moved me. It was simple beauty; magnificent beauty. And there is love in beauty. Love always. Love daily. 365 Love.™

Have you told someone you loved them today? I have.™

Love yesterday, today and future tomorrows,™
Torion

Message in the MUSIC
George Benson – In Your Eyes

Note the QUOTE!
"Life is like a rainbow. You need both the sun and the rain to make its colors appear." --- Unknown

---

Love Always. Love Daily. 365 Love.

Think Happy Thoughts
August 2

Today's NOTE
Stop whatever you are doing and think about something you like. Think about something you like to do. Think about something good. Think about someone who makes you feel good. Think about a place that makes you feel good. Think about a special event that filled your heart with joy. Think about something that puts a smile on your face. **Think happy thoughts**. How are you feeling, just thinking about it? Doesn't it make you feel good inside?

For that moment, you made a choice about what your thoughts were. You made a choice to think about something that changed how you were feeling. It was easy to do. You just had to make a conscious choice to do it. Now use this same example and think about how you can feel this way all of the time. Think about how much control you have of your happiness. You control your own thoughts and you can choose to be happy when you **think happy thoughts**. Whenever you find yourself focused on something negative, make a conscious choice to turn that feeling around. Chose to change your mindset, and your mood, and **think happy thoughts**. That's positive thinking. That's looking at the glass as half full vs. half empty. That's growing in the direction of love. Love always. Love daily. 365 Love.™

Have you told someone you loved them today? I have. ™

Love yesterday, today and future tomorrows,™
Torion

Message in the MUSIC
R. Kelly – Happy People

Note the QUOTE!
"Once you replace negative thoughts with positive ones, you'll start having positive results." --- Willie Nelson

Identify Your Gift and Invest in It
August 3

Today's NOTE
What are you good at? What are your special talents? What are your special gifts? We all have special gifts. Some are pretty obvious to us. Others are not, because we don't see them as gifts, they are not easily revealed to us, or they have yet to be discovered. You may be able to sing. You may be good with numbers. You may be good with wood, cars, or electronics. You may be able to write well. You may be a great organizer. You may work well with children. You may be good at cooking. You may be good with yard work. You may be good with talking to people. You may be good with helping others. Whatever it is, **identify your gift and invest in it**. We all have a purpose in life. Our gifts are to be used to assist in fulfilling that purpose. Our gifts are given to us out of love. When we use them and invest in them, they magnify and become better and stronger. When we fail to use them, or misuse them, they disintegrate, lose their flame and are sometimes taken away from us. Use your gift to make a positive difference. Use your gift for something good. Use your gift to help others. Use your gift to inspire and motivate. Use your gift to show others how you love and how to love. Love always. Love daily. 365 Love.™

Have you told someone you loved them today? I have. ™

Love yesterday, today and future tomorrows,™
Torion

Message in the MUSIC
Ramiyah – Power from God

Note the QUOTE!
"When I stand before God at the end of my life, I would hope that I would not have a single bit of talent left, and could say, "I used everything you gave me." --- Erma Bombeck

Let it Go and Let it Flow
August 4

Today's NOTE
Sometimes you have to just **let it go and let it flow**. When you know that you have done everything within your ability to change or improve the situation and when you know that you have done your best, **let it go and let it flow**. Say your special prayer. Ask for forgiveness and/or strength. Everything will work itself out. The outcome will be the best that it can be for the situation at hand. Accept the outcome. Take life's experiences as lessons learned and **let it go and let it flow**. Change, grow, improve, do better, do more, and love. Love always. Love daily. 365 Love.™

Have you told someone you loved them today? I have. ™

Love yesterday, today and future tomorrows, ™
Torion

Message in the MUSIC
Toni Braxton - **Let It Flow**

Note the QUOTE!
"Some people think it's holding on that makes one strong. Sometimes it's letting go." --- Unknown

---

Love Always. Love Daily. 365 Love.

He Will Supply
August 5

Today's NOTE
Someone lost something today, yesterday, or this past week. It was something they felt they needed or it was something they really wanted. Regardless, it was lost against their desires, planned or unexpectedly, but what was lost was not lost in vain. There is something bigger and better on its way. God does not present us with anything we cannot handle. Everything happens for a reason and there is a purpose behind everything that He does and does not do. What we feel we need, when we feel we need it, is not always meant for us to have. And when it's all said and done, He will come through for us and **He will supply. He will supply** a new direction. **He will supply** brighter days. **He will supply** love and joy. **He will supply** everything you need when you need it. **He will supply** what is meant just for you. Have strong faith. Pray big. Love always. Love daily. 365 Love.™

Have you told someone you loved them today? I have.™

Love yesterday, today and future tomorrows,™
Torion

Message in the MUSIC
Kirk Franklin - **He Will Supply**

Note the QUOTE!
"Faith is deliberate confidence in the character whose ways you may not understand at this time." --- Oswald Chambers

My Joy
August 6

Today's NOTE
Love is **my joy**. It surrounds me. It's in the air I breathe. It's in the life I live. It covers me in all that I do. It protects me and gives me strength. **My joy** is the joy of joys. It makes me smile. It brings light to my day. It guides me and directs me. It helps me to see my way. **My joy** makes my heart beat to a harmonious melody. It changes things. It brings out the best in me. It lifts me. It is my romance. It is my first and last dance. It is my music and my song. **My joy** is eternal. **My joy** is everlasting and forever long. **My joy** is a joy to be shared. It is charitable. It's in my heart and it cares. Love is my love. My love is **my joy**. Love always. Love daily. 365 Love.™

Have you told someone you loved them today? I have.™

Love yesterday, today and future tomorrows,™
Torion

Message in the MUSIC
Chrisette Michele – Your **Joy**

Note the QUOTE!
"When you wish someone joy, you wish them peace, love, prosperity, happiness...all good things." --- Maya Angelou

Admission is Absolutely Free
August 7

Today's NOTE
We all like things that are free. One of the best ways to motivate a person to participate in something is to give them something free. Say the word "free" and heads start turning. Some of the best marketing strategies include providing a good or service that is free. Once tried for free, there is a higher probability that a person will want more. Especially, if they like it. Then they will want to do it or use it again, and again, and again.

Today I want to invite you to one of the greatest joys in the universe. It is the greatest of all great things. It is bigger and better than anything you have ever witnessed. It can be and do anything. It is ranked number one. It makes you laugh, cry, smile, and feel humility. It keeps you wanting more. It is all things good. It's something you don't want to miss. And you will never regret it. If you learn about it, and use it the right way, you can accomplish anything. If you invite others to participate, your rewards multiply. It provides you with a life filled with happiness. **Admission is absolutely free**. That's right. It doesn't cost a thing. You can't beat it. There is no better offer anywhere. Nothing else compares. So, "what's the catch?." There isn't one. Today and every day for the rest of your life, you are invited to love. Love always. Love daily. 365 Love.™

Have you told someone you loved them today? I have.™

Love yesterday, today and future tomorrows,™
Torion

Message in the MUSIC
Kem – Set You **Free**

Note the QUOTE!
"Love is a noble act of self-giving. The more you love, the more you lose a part of you, yet you do not become less of who you are. You end up complete." --- Unknown

Spread My Wings
August 8

Today's NOTE

I found love. With that, I am able to **spread my wings**. My mother did all that she knew how to do to prepare me for the world. She molded me, talked to me, and provided for me. Her life and the lives of so many others, were used as an example of things to do and not to do. My father provided words of wisdom for those moments when I needed to hear his voice. My teachers provided me with foundational information so that I could read, write and do arithmetic. Friendships provided additional life experiences. I learned. I listened. I did this, that and the other. I did it again. I tried something new. I tried things a different way. I grew. I continued to grow. And I am still growing. But when I found love, I knew it. I felt it. I noticed that I was able to **spread my wings**. Those beautiful, glorious, wings. Those wings that allow me to be free. They are connected to my mind, body and soul. Everything I have ever experienced, and every encounter I have ever had, has brought me here. It was a part of my journey. And now I am flying high. The more I grow in love, the higher I fly. The stronger my wings become. I feel the wind beneath them. I see the blue in the sky even when it is gray. I smell the fresh air even when pollution is there. I see the sun shining even on a cloudy day. What a feeling. What a joy. All because I found love. Love always. Love daily. 365 Love.™

Have you told someone you loved them today? I have.™

Love yesterday, today and future tomorrows,™
Torion

Message in the MUSIC
Troop – **Spread My Wings**

Note the QUOTE!
"The quickest way to receive love is to give; the fastest way to lose love is to hold it too tightly; and the best way to keep love is to give it wings." --- Unknown

Love Always. Love Daily. 365 Love.

Work That
August 9

Today's NOTE
Take a personal assessment of everything good about you and everything good that you do. Reach deep down inside and note everything you can think of. Make sure that what you come up with are qualities, character traits and/or strengths you possess that are truly good. Write it all down. Review everything you wrote. Now **work that**. **Work that** in a way that builds upon everything you do and share with others. **Work that** in a way that helps others. **Work that** in a way that allows you to be more and do more. **Work that** in a way that brings joy to your life and the life of others. **Work that** in a way that continues to promote good things and your personal growth in love. Build on your strengths. Maximize your strengths. And **work that**. Love always. Love daily. 365 Love.™

Have you told someone you loved them today? I have.™

Love yesterday, today and future tomorrows,™
Torion

Message in the MUSIC
Mary J. Blige - **Work That**

Note the QUOTE!
"The greatest magnifying glasses in the world are a man's own eyes when they look upon his own person." --- Alexander Pope

---

Love Always. Love Daily. 365 Love.

Give Someone Your Smile
August 10

Today's NOTE
A smile is something that requires little effort to do. It positively represents a frown turned upside down. It is contagious and transferable. It resonates with love. Love is charitable and it gives. So, why not **give someone your smile**? Something as simple as a smile can make a big difference in someone's day. It could even be the start of a change in someone's life. **Give someone your smile** and find personal joy in your contribution to sharing and spreading love. Love always. Love daily. 365 Love. ™

Have you told someone you loved them today? I have. ™

Love yesterday, today and future tomorrows, ™
Torion

Message in the MUSIC
Usher - Smile Again

Note the QUOTE!
"If you see a friend without a smile, give him one of yours." --- Proverb

The One
August 11

Today's NOTE
What are you looking for? And why are you even looking? Don't you know that I am right here? I've always been here. Right in front of your face all of the time, every time. I am **the one**. You've overlooked me so many times, but I have not and will not go away. I will never leave you. I will be here until you accept that I am all that you need. I am confident in who I am. I make you feel better than anyone else can. I wake up and go to sleep with you. I give you strength. I am always there for you when no one else is. I turn all of your frowns upside down. I am in the air that you breath. I give your heart a new rhythm to beat to. I bring joy and laughter to your life. I give you what you need, when you need it, how you need it. I am here to please. I give you a natural high that keeps you feeling good all of the time. I take away all of your worries and all of your pains. I complete you. I do things for you that no other will or can do. I make you feel good all over, inside and out, every day and in every way. I am the best thing that has and will ever happen to you. Choose me. Accept me. Receive me. Because I am **the one**. I am love. Love always. Love daily. 365 Love.™

Have you told someone you loved them today? I have.™

Love yesterday, today and future tomorrows,™
Torion

Message in the MUSIC
Mary J. Blige – **The One**

Note the QUOTE!
"There is no feeling more comforting and confusing than knowing you are right next to **the one** you love." --- Unknown

I Just Called to Say, "I Love You"
August 12

Today's NOTE
Ring, Ring, Ring! Hello, how are you today? I pray that all is well. I was thinking about you today and how much you mean to me and so many others. I thought about the good qualities in you. You are such a good person. Your light shines even when the sun is out. I am glad that I have had the privilege of getting to know you and having you as part of my inner circle. That's it. I didn't really want much. You were just on my mind and **I just called to say, "I love you."** Have a wonderful, blessed day! Love always. Love daily. 365 Love.™

Have you told someone you loved them today? I have.™

Love yesterday, today and future tomorrows,™
Torion

Message in the MUSIC
Stevie Wonder – **I Just Called to Say I Love You**

Note the QUOTE!
"If you were going to die soon and you had only one phone call to make, who would you call and what would you say? And why are you waiting?" --- Stephen Levine

---

Love Always. Love Daily. 365 Love.

A Letter to Love
August 13

Today's NOTE
Dear **Love**,

I am writing this **letter** to let you know how much I appreciate all that you are and all that you do. Because of you, I have purpose and meaning. You are part of who I am. You make me see things more clearly. You give me life and fill my heart with joy. You make me a stronger and better person. You help me to reach my fullest potential and bring out the best in me. When I am in doubt, you give me hope. You provide me the means to give and to live. I have strong faith because of you. I believe in you. I know that through you all things are possible. Thank you for being you, for being love, for your mercy and your grace. Because of you, I Love always. Love daily. 365 Love.™

Have you told someone you loved them today? I have. ™

Love yesterday, today and future tomorrows,™
Torion

Message in the MUSIC
112 – Still in Love

Note the QUOTE!
"To write a good **love letter**, you ought to begin without knowing what you mean to say, and to finish without knowing what you have written" --- Jean-Jacques Rousseau

---

Love Always. Love Daily. 365 Love.

This Moment
August 14

Today's NOTE

This moment is here. It's right here, right now. What are you thinking about at **this moment**? What are you doing with **this moment**? **This moment** is an opportunity to do something good and make a difference. **This moment** is an opportunity to change based on lessons learned from yesterday. **This moment** is an opportunity to establish a foundation to create a new tomorrow. **This moment** is an opportunity to forgive. **This moment** is an opportunity to share and to give. **This moment** is an opportunity to live. Smile in **this moment**. Laugh in **this moment**. Reflect in **this moment**. Grow in **this moment**. Move forward in **this moment**. Let go and let God in **this moment**. Love in **this moment**. Love always. Love daily. 365 Love.™

Have you told someone you loved them today? I have.™

Love yesterday, today and future tomorrows,™
Torion

Message in the MUSIC
Kelly Clarkston – A **Moment** Like This

Note the QUOTE!
"We are always getting ready to live, but never living." --- Ralph Waldo Emerson

This Too Shall Pass
August 15

Today's NOTE

I have a love for black art. One day I happened to run across a print titled, **This Too Shall Pass** by Henry Lee. It's a picture of an angel sitting with her eyes closed and wings spread wide open. Of all the many pictures in the store at that time, I purchased this one. It was in the right place at the right time. My heart told me I had to have it. Little did I know, shortly after its purchase, I began to go through a divorce. I believe that waking up to this constant reminder assisted with the rebuilding of my faith and gave me the courage to move forward during that time period of my life. It was one of the many positive reminders that I was going to be alright. It was in my face as I awakened each day and as I fell asleep each night. It was there when tears rolled from my eyes and when my heart was hurting. And it was at those times, something would cause me to look up, see those big, beautiful wings, and read, "**This Too Shall Pass**." I would dry my eyes. I would begin to think happy thoughts to calm my heart and I would thank God for all the good things in my life and all the good things yet to come. I began to gravitate more and more to love, loving people and loving things, loving behaviors and loving thoughts. My spirituality grew stronger and stronger and God set things in motion for me to become a better person, within His will and within His purpose for me.

This picture has remained on my bedroom wall since its purchase. I often look at it and let it serve as a reminder that God sends His angels to watch over of us and that whatever we are going through exists only temporarily. For with any situation, it **too shall pass**. It also reminds me of my personal growth in love over the years. The stronger my faith, the more positive my life and life experiences have become. My wings grow wider and stronger each day. As each new battle is put into action, strong faith keeps me strong and helps me to handle the situation. I wake to a constant reminder that whatever is presented to me, it **too shall pass**. While all days are not perfect, I know that love watches over me. Love changes things. Love has changed me over the years. Love can change you too. Whenever you are going through something that you find difficult to handle and can't seem to figure out how you will make it through, have strong faith and remember the angel with her wings spread wide. Think about the picture by Henry Lee. Think about my story. Think about love. And tell yourself, "**This Too Shall Pass**." Love always. Love daily. 365 Love.™

Have you told someone you loved them today? I have.™

Love yesterday, today and future tomorrows,™
Torion

Message in the MUSIC
Yolanda Adams – **This Too Shall Pass**

Note the QUOTE!
"Look at life through the windshield, not through the rear-view mirror." --- Byrd Baggett

Love Many Things
August 16

Today's NOTE
To grow in love, you have to practice love. To practice love, **love many things**. Love is all around you. It's everywhere, always, all of the time. It's easy to overlook, ignore and forget. However, part of loving is realizing the simplest of things to love and the fact that love does exist. We often take the simple things for granted. This includes basic things that are capable of loving and being loved. Today, I encourage you to love, love more and **love many things**. Love nature. Love animals. Love people. Love your haves and have nots. Love helping. Love giving. Love your neighbor. Love your friends and your enemies. Love what you have gone through and what you have made it through. Love the thought of loving. Love to smile. Love someone else's smile. Love to laugh, share laughter and be laughed at. Love your job and the opportunities that come along with it. Love your well being. Love your physical abilities. Love who you are, where you came from, and what you have yet to become. Love yourself. Most importantly, love God. Love always. Love daily. 365 Love.™

Have you told someone you loved them today? I have.™

Love yesterday, today and future tomorrows,™
Torion

Message in the MUSIC
Kirk Franklin – You Are

Note the QUOTE!
"The best way to know God is to **love many things**." --- Vincent Van Gogh

---

Love Always. Love Daily. 365 Love.

The Opportunity to Love Again
August 17

Today's NOTE
Whatever you have been through or are going through, never stop loving. Never stop having the desire to love. Never allow anyone to take love away from you. Love is the one thing you have that is uniquely yours. It is as strong as your faith is in it. It is also what you make of it, how you use it, and what you do with it. No matter how many times you feel that you have lost love or been hurt by someone you love, there is always **the opportunity to love again**. Regardless of how many steps you take in what appears to be the backwards direction, you can always turn things around and move forward. And with that forward movement comes **the opportunity to love again**. Every day is a new day to make new choices. Regardless of the results from yesterday's choices, today's choices can be different and make a difference. Today's choices provide **the opportunity to love again**, and again, and again. Fill your thoughts with this opportunity. Act on this opportunity. Watch love grow in you and spread to others because of this opportunity. And when **the opportunity to love again** comes, embrace it, hold on to it, and never let it go. Love always. Love daily. 365 Love.™

Have you told someone you loved them today? I have.™

Love yesterday, today and future tomorrows,™
Torion

Message in the MUSIC
Deitrick Hadden - You Are My Strength

Note the QUOTE!
"The freedom to move forward to new opportunities and to produce results comes from living in the present, not the past." --- Brian Koslow

Musiq's Music
August 18

Today's NOTE

I have a fond interest in the musical abilities of Musiq Soulchild. What I like most about **Musiq's music**, is the positivity and inspiration in his love songs. Additionally, the associated music videos are filled with creativity that equally match the concept of the songs allowing them to fully touch the soul. One of my favorite songs on his 2011 album, Musiqinthemagic, is, "Yes." The first time I heard it, I listened to it over, and over and over again. It brought tears to my eyes. These were happy tears of course. My heart filled with joy to hear of a man loving a woman for what she is on the inside and not what she is or becomes on the outside.

I was listening to a local radio show interview with Musiq Soulchild yesterday (in 2011). He was discussing the concept behind one of his upcoming music videos. The thought and the concept along with the choice of song brought tears to my eyes. Yes, **Musiq's music** did it to me again. The video concept is about a man in a relationship with a woman who has breast cancer. He wanted the video to inspire women who are dealing with breast cancer. He also wanted to uplift men who are in relationships with a woman dealing with breast cancer. Along with the announcement of the upcoming video for the song, "Yes", Musiq announced that he is the new ambassador for The Susan G. Komen for the Cure Circle of Promise, designed to further engage black women in the fight against breast cancer. The purpose is to raise awareness about breast cancer so that younger women know the importance of early detection and the importance of paying attention to their bodies. I participate in the Susan G. Komen walk for the cure on an annual basis, so my love for the song and the cause made this announcement that much more personal to me. My eyes filled with tears immediately, again! I thanked God for **Musiq's music** and his ability to use his music to spread love. Unconditional, charitable love.

While there are many different types of music for us to love, know that there is always a message in the music. Regardless of your personal music style and preferences, a good song can deliver a powerful message. A good song can be used as a medium to teach someone to love. And love can be found in **Musiq's music**. Love always. Love daily. 365 Love.™

Have you told someone you loved them today? I have.™

Love yesterday, today and future tomorrows,™
Torion

Message in the MUSIC
Musiq Soulchild - Yes

Note the QUOTE!
"**Music** speaks what cannot be expressed, soothes the mind and gives it rest, heals the heart and makes it whole, flows from heaven to the soul." --- Unknown

Your Difference
August 19

Today's NOTE

Reflect on your life as a whole and think about how much of that time you spent loving. Your time spent loving includes time spent loving yourself, loving others, and having loving thoughts.

Loving yourself means...
- being happy because of who you are and what you have, even if that means being alone, not because of someone else being a part of your life.
- being able to take responsibility for handling old baggage you may be carrying around.
- you are able to forgive.
- being honest with who you are and areas you need to improve in.
- you actually work to improve.
- you do not allow others to control you, mistreat you, or disrespect you.
- you always do your best at whatever you do.

Loving others means...
- being patient, kind and honest with others.
- when you have a bad day, you do not take it out on others.
- not wanting others to take responsibility for old baggage you carry around with you.
- giving without the expectation of receiving something in return.
- accepting others as they are and allowing others to be who they are without trying to control what they say, what they do, how they say it, or how they do it.
- listening with understanding.
- not participating in or contributing to gossip.
- you are happy for others and what they have, even if it is more than or better than what you have.
- you support, inspire, motive and appreciate others without envy or jealously.

Having loving thoughts means...
- you realize and appreciate the simple things in life.
- you find joy in each day regardless of what the day is or is not.
- you see the positive side of things.
- you take the lessons learned from life's experiences and put actions in place to make your life better moving forward.
- the glass is always half full vs. half empty.

Basic math teaches us that one number minus another number equals the **difference** between those two numbers (a-b=c). If you apply this concept to your life and love, what would **your difference** be? Narrow the time frame down to the past year of your life and think about the year as 100% of your time.

> *Your Difference* = 100% - % of Time Spent Loving
> REMINDER: % of Time Spent Loving = Loving Yourself + Loving Others + Having Loving Thoughts

Your Difference number determines how much growing you have to do to become a more loving person. The higher the number, the more work you have to do. The lower the number, the closer you are to being consistent with love. Realizing **Your Difference** is a good thing regardless of whether the number is high or low. It is a reality check that lets you know there is still work to do. It's a reminder that you are still a work in progress. It says that you are still learning and that you need to consistently practice love to improve. As **Your Difference** number gets lower, it shows that you are growing more and more in love. At 0%, you are there. However, to remain consistent with love, you have to continually practice it and learn about it. There are new life challenges around every corner to test your faith, how you love and how much you love. So, the battle is never over. However, it becomes that much easier to deal with, maintain and have a happy and fulfilled life. You control what you do, think, say and feel. You control who you love and how you love. It's your choice. You choose to be happy or sad. You choose to love yourself enough to love others and know when to let someone you love go because you love yourself more. As each day passes, think about **Your Difference** number and choose to love. Love always. Love daily. 365 Love.™

Have you told someone you loved them today? I have. ™

Love yesterday, today and future tomorrows,™
Torion

Message in the MUSIC
Michelle Williams - Change the World

Note the QUOTE!
"God, grant me the serenity to accept the things I cannot change, the courage to change the things I can, and the wisdom to know the **difference**." --- Reinhold Niebuhr

---

Love Always. Love Daily. 365 Love.

A Special Someone
August 20

Today's NOTE

I frequently encourage others to always be thankful. This includes being thankful for things that we as people often times take for granted such as our health, our sanity, and our ability to see, hear, smell, touch, walk, and talk. While we frequently encounter people who are healthy in mind and body, there are so many others who are not. There are children born with physical and mental disabilities. There are others who experience mental and physical disabilities and/or illnesses later in life. These individuals are cared for by **a special someone.** That **special someone** becomes a care giver for a short period of time, or for the duration of the needed care. Most times that **special someone** is a family member....a mother, father, spouse, grandparent, sibling or other family member. Other times there may be a need to obtain the care of **a special someone** in the medical field or some other specialization area such as a doctor, nurse, or special education teacher. There are also organizations founded by **a special someone** to support those with disabilities and illnesses through self help, assistance, and support. God uses these people to take care of those in need, because it takes **a special someone** to do that.

For the mother who gave birth to a child with a disability, for the spouse who has to take care of their husband/wife due to an extended illness of physical disability, and for the family member who has to take care of another family member in need, you were given the strength to endure. You were assigned by God as **a special someone** to provide care for another. Regardless of whether you care for others personally or oversee someone else who provides the needed assistance, you were chosen. You were hand-picked to care for someone in need. You were chosen because God knew you could handle it. And He is smiling at you. He is happy for your unconditional love. He feels good about your active role in the care of another, because it is a demonstration of how much you love. Love gives you the ability to care. Love gives you the ability to share a part of you, your time, and your energy. Love gives you the ability to hang in there. Love provides you with the support you need to obtain support from those who specialize in providing care for others. So, for all of the hospital visits, time off from work, missed opportunities to do other things, I thank you. Love thanks you . Thank you be being **a special someone** who is willing to help those who are unable to help themselves. It is your gift. It is within the purpose God has for you. It is a part of your journey in love. Love always. Love daily. 365 Love. ™

Have you told someone you loved them today? I have. ™

Love yesterday, today and future tomorrows, ™
Torion

Message in the MUSIC
Mariah Carey – Hero

Note the QUOTE!
"God places the heaviest burden on those who can carry its weight." --- Reggie White

Magnificent
August 21

Today's NOTE

God is so good. He provides us with gifts that are not only able to be used during our youth, but ones that we cherish, love, hold on to and continue to use later in life. These gifts keep giving by the hearts they touch.

I attended a church dance recital that I would describe as nothing less than **magnificent**. This was not your typical, children's /young adult dance recital. What was so **magnificent** about it was that over half of the dancers were in the 55+ age range. Soloists, small groups and large groups. Short, tall, slim, and heavy set. Male and female. Gray haired, passionate, extremely poised and all. From simple to complex choreography pieces. Body movements that told stories. Body movements that made you smile, laugh, and rejoice. How **magnificent**. Popular TV dance shows and dance companies around the world feature dancers who are in their youth. It is a very rare occasion that you will see a major dance performance with dancers past their 30's. I have not seen one in my lifetime, until this one. Again, **magnificent**! God provided the 55+ dancers with flexibility, creativity, poise and grace. They provide inspiration in continuing to be active as we grow older. They share their love of dance. They share love with others. They share a most **magnificent** gift. That's love. Love always. Love daily. 365 Love.™

Have you told someone you loved them today? I have.™

Love yesterday, today and future tomorrows,™
Torion

Message in the MUSIC
India Aire - Wonderful

Note the QUOTE!
"Great dancers aren't great because of their technique; they're great because of their passion." --- Unknown

Your Journey
August 22

Today's NOTE

We all have a personal journey to develop and grow in love. It's different for each of us. For some, it can be clear cut and distinct. For others it is long, confusing and sometimes full of obstacles. Regardless, it's **your journey**. And to reach your destination, to fully love, you often times have to go through some things to finally get it.

Pastor R. L. White, Jr., talked about taking a trip during church service. I felt the description of this trip could also be used to describe **your journey** to grow in love. A variation of his story is as follows:

You want to travel to New York and you happen to live in the far western or southern part of the United States. You could go by plane or train, but you decide to go by car. Along the way, there is rain and there are storms. Some of the storms are so bad, that you can't see and have to pull over. The sun eventually comes back out and you are able to continue. There are traffic jams that slow you down. There is construction in the road that causes you to take an alternate route. You have to stop for gas to refuel the car. You need to stop for some rest to stretch your legs or to sleep. You may even have a flat tire that needs to be repaired, but you keep going. Your set-backs are only temporary. Because you know where you are going and you want to reach your destination. And eventually, you're there.

That same approach can be used for **your journey** to develop and grow in love. If you want it, regardless of the road blocks, barriers, storms, set-backs, you will continue to move forward. The final destination in **your journey** is love. You know it exists. You know it is attainable. So you know that you can and will reach it. You don't give up on it. You don't let other people and other things keep you from reaching it. You keep going and going until you know you are there. The next time you experience turbulent times during **your journey** and you want to give up on love, know that it is temporary and the sun always shines after a major storm, there is always another path to take, and there is always the ability to move forward. Love always. Love daily. 365 Love. ™

Have you told someone you loved them today? I have. ™

Love yesterday, today and future tomorrows, ™
Torion

Message in the MUSIC
Lamar Campbell – Closer

Note the QUOTE!
"The road of life twists and turns and no two directions are ever the same. Yet our lessons come from the **journey**, not the destination." --- Don Williams, Jr.

There's Nothing Better
August 23

Today's NOTE
Love. That wonderful word. **There's nothing better.** You can take any feeling, emotion, or situation, add love to it, and realize the most perfect relief. **There's nothing better** than love. God is love and God is good. What could be better than that? Absolutely nothing. Choose the best feeling you have ever had....had to have love in it. Choose the most memorable, joyous occasion you have ever experienced....had to have love in it. Think about what the perfect day would be like......has to have love in it. Wake-up....love. Look around you.....love. Reflect on your past, present and future.....love. Love got you here. Love is keeping you here. Love will take you there. I tell you, **there's nothing better.** You name it, love will claim it. Reach for it. Learn about it. Practice it. Be about it. Love always. Love daily. 365 Love.™

Have you told someone you loved them today? I have.™

Love yesterday, today and future tomorrows,™
Torion

Message in the MUSIC
Luther Vandross and Gregory Hines – **There's Nothing Better** than Love

Note the QUOTE!
"The most important thing in life is to learn how to give out love, and let it come in." --- Morrie Schwartz

The Ants
August 24

Today's NOTE

We see **the ants** as tiny little pests. They sometimes run through our homes in packs, they form ant hills in the middle of our beautiful lawns, or they make us itch when they cross our feet in the grass. While we can find a number of reasons not to be particularly fond of **the ants**, we can actually learn from them by looking at their livelihood and how it relates to love and how love grows.

The ants are social, highly organized insects. They function as a unified group, working together to support their colony. Their successes can be attributed to their social organization and their ability to change habitats, use their resources and defend themselves. Once food is found, the ant that finds the food marks a pheromone trail on the way back to the colony. The pheromone trail is followed by other ants which reinforce the trail when they head back to the colony with food. If the path is blocked, a new trail is found to the same food or other food and the process is repeated.

Love works in some ways like the lifestyle **the ants**. When you love, you are able to work with others and your love draws you closer to others who love unconditionally and charitably. The more you love, the more you begin to love naturally and continually. Your love glow shines and becomes contagious. Your demonstration of love spreads to others. And as others learn about love, they reinforce it by sharing it with others. When one finds love, they spread love in a way that leaves a trail for others to follow. And the cycle continues. Love keeps spreading and spreading. It goes on and on. And when life presents you with challenges or road blocks, love keeps you going. You may have to travel a different path to continue your love journey, but you know that love still exists. The next time you see an ant, forget about the fact that it's an insect or a pest. Think about its life and think about love. Think about where it is going, what it is doing, how it is teaching and how it is learning. Follow its footsteps in how you love and spread love to others. Love always. Love daily. 365 Love.™

Have you told someone you loved them today? I have.™

Love yesterday, today and future tomorrows,™
Torion

Message in the MUSIC
Kirk Franklin – So Good

Note the QUOTE!
"The only love I know, is the love we shared, the love you showed me; a love I never knew until you came into my life...that I know is real." --- Unknown

The Little Things
August 25

Today's NOTE

Most people go through life expecting big things to happen in order to make a change. When often times, it's the **little things** that make the biggest difference. Stop and think about it for a moment.

- Saying, "I Love You"
- Receiving a call from a friend just to say, "hello."
- Sending a text message that says, "I was thinking about you"
- Giving someone a hug just because
- Saying "Thank you" or "I appreciate you"
- Giving someone a hand-picked flower
- Writing a poem or small note that came from the heart
- Drawing a picture for someone
- Opening the door for someone
- Helping someone do something they could not do
- Stopping by to visit a family member or friend
- Giving breakfast in bed
- Inviting someone to take a walk in the park
- Picking a special song that reminds you of someone and dedicating it to them
- Singing a song to someone special even when you can't sing
- ......Any act of kindness, just because.....

I could go on and on. These and so many other **little things** are symbols of love. They are acts of kindness. They don't take much to do, but have a big return on investment. They change things. They change people. They matter and they make a difference, even if the difference is for that moment in time. They are little love seeds being planted. With nourishment and consistency, they grow into big, beautiful things. They grow in love. They pollinate like flowers and continue to spread and grow. They are as natural as nature. Those **little things** that seem so little, but mean so much keep spreading around to others. It doesn't always take something big to have a big impact. Learn to love and appreciate the **little things** and watch big things happen. Love always. Love daily. 365 Love.™

Have you told someone you loved them today? I have.™

Love yesterday, today and future tomorrows,™
Torion

Message in the MUSIC
India Aire - **The Little Things**

Note the QUOTE!
"Enjoy the **little things**, for one day you may look back and realize they were the big things." --- Robert Brault

Hear Yourself
August 26

Today's NOTE
Some people spend so much time talking that they don't really take the time to hear. Not just hearing others, but hearing themselves. They don't take the time to listen -- both ways. Love listens. Love hears. Do you hear what you are saying? Do you **hear yourself**? When was the last time you took the time to **hear yourself**? To actually listen? I know a few people that will curse others out, call them out of their name, "tell them like it is", say ugly things, and/or speak lies and think nothing of it, but when the table is turned and they are on the receiving end, they are hurt and want to claim that the other person is mean. Some people just spend time talking period. The other person does not get a chance to speak or is frequently interrupted and eventually gives up. And the person talking is not talking about anything. And then there are the gossipers. They just keep talking and talking, spreading rumors, untruths, and other folks business over and over, again and again. While neither person is right, no one took the time to hear themselves. If some people could hear a recording of what they sound like talking (or yelling) it would make their stomachs turn and hopefully make a difference. And for those who it would not make a difference to, we have to continue praying for them. A wise person listens more than they speak. Love listens more than it speaks. But when love does speak, it speaks with patience, kindness and understanding. It is encouraging, honest and respectful. It is not hurtful. It does not scar or tear at a person's esteem. Take the time to **hear yourself** every once in a while. Receive it as a confirmation that you are demonstrating love or put actions in place to further your personal growth in love. Because love hears. Love always. Love daily. 365 Love.™

Have you told someone you loved them today? I have.™

Love yesterday, today and future tomorrows,™
Torion

Message in the MUSIC
Michelle Williams – Heard a Word

Note the QUOTE!
"To listen well, is as powerful a means of influence as to talk well, and is as essential to all true conversation." --- Chinese Proverb

Self Acceptance
August 27

Today's NOTE

You were born with your specific hair, face, neck, chest, arms, hands, legs and feet. You have your own voice, mind, talents, thoughts, physical appearance, and style. These things are yours. They are a part of you. Why allow society and/or someone else make you feel differently about who you are and how you look? Part of learning to love is loving yourself. And with that comes **self acceptance**. Some people spend so much time trying to be someone else that they lose sight of who they really are. They want to change who they are because of the media, because they want to be like the most popular person in the school, because of the next door neighbor or co-worker, or because they want to be liked. They want to change who they are and what they look like because their girl/boyfriend, friend, family member, or some other person told them to change in order to be who they want them to be. They may also change because they don't want to be rejected. These are the wrong reasons for wanting to change. They are not aligned with love and **self acceptance**.

When using these reasons for change, people forget they are God's creation. They forget that God personally molded them Himself. They forget that the way they are is the way God indented them to be. And when they make changes that are not within His will, he sets a new path to recreate the mold He has intended for them. Not their own personal mold, or someone else's mold, but His mold. Love opens your heart and allows you to see change that is truly needed to make you a better person for the good of you, not just because another person wants you to change to satisfy them, or because they were mean and insecure themselves. Not because you are unsatisfied with yourself because of outside sources.

Love allows you to see the greatness in your own personal appearance and qualities. Love allows you to accept rejection from others, but does not cause you to reject yourself as a result. Love allows you to accept yourself as you are and for who you are. Love brings about **self acceptance**. Love always. Love daily. 365 Love.™

Have you told someone you loved them today? I have. ™

Love yesterday, today and future tomorrows,™
Torion

Message in the MUSIC
TLC – Unpretty

Note the QUOTE!
"Be who you are and say what you feel, because those who mind don't matter and those who matter don't mind." --- Dr. Suess

Your Story
August 28

Today's NOTE

Everyone has a story to tell. I have my story and you have **your story**. If you were to tell **your story** today, what would it be? How would it start and how would it end? What life decisions brought you to where you are today? Is **your story** filled with heartache and pain? Is **your story** filled with joy and laughter? Is **your story** filled with love? If you've experienced life, it's a high probability that **your story** includes some of all of the above. When you think about **your story**, did you make good choices? Did you do good things? Can you honestly say that you are a better person now than you were then? Have you progressed in a direction that is pleasing to God? Have you enjoyed life? Do you appreciate the little things in life? Do you love?

While the past cannot be changed, the future is yet to be determined. As you reflect on **your story**, it should give you some insight on where you are and where you need to be. It should motive you to plan for a new and improved tomorrow. You know you. You know what you do and don't do. You know if you are a doer or a slacker. You know if you are good to people or nasty to people. You know if you are a giver or a taker. You know if you speak truths or lies. You know if you are a hero or a villain. God knows these things too. You are the main character in **your story**. What lesson can people learn from you? What impression will they have of you? What difference will you make? You still have time to complete **your story**. For if you are reading this today, **your story** is not over yet. Make **your story** have a happy ending. Let it teach someone. Let it motivate, inspire and uplift. Make it a positive testimony that can change lives for the better. It's never too late to change. It's never too late to create a different ending to **your story**. And it's never too late to love. Love always. Love daily. 365 Love.™

Have you told someone you loved them today? I have. ™

Love yesterday, today and future tomorrows,™
Torion

Message in the MUSIC
Ruben Studdard – **Our Story**

Note the QUOTE!
"You must have control of the authorship of your own destiny. The pen that writes **your** life **story** must be held in your own hand." --- Irene C. Kassoria

---

Love Always. Love Daily. 365 Love.

1+1=2
August 29

Today's NOTE

I have what I call a "1+1=2" analogy when it comes to things that make up a successful relationship. Basic math teaches us that the sum of any two numbers is greater than the individual numbers themselves. So, **1+1** ≠0 and **1+1** ≠1. Correct math says that **1+1=2**. When two people enter a relationship, they should add to one another. Their union should be greater than the individual. The sum of two numbers provides a correct result when both numbers are added at their full value, not 1/2 the value, not 1/3 the value, or not 1/4 the value, but the full value of each number.

- If you can pay all of your bills and I can pay all of my bills, we should have more (**1+1=2**) because in some cases, two bills will be eliminated because of the need for only one. If one person does not pay their bills, they drain from what the other person has which makes them have less than if they were by themselves.

- If you can pay your rent/mortgage and I can pay my rent/mortgage, we can only have more because there will only be one vs. two rents/mortgages to pay (**1+1=2**). If one person is not able to pay, there is no gain for the other. One person begins taking care of the other who is not contributing to the growth of the relationship in this area.

- If you know how to communicate, and I know how to communicate, we are able to communicate effectively to make things happen or make changes for the betterment of the relationship (**1+1=2**). Communication is a critical part of a successful relationship. If one person is not an effective communicator, it becomes one sided and there is a break down in its effectiveness. If communication is really bad, it can eventually drain from the relationship to the point where communication stops completely.

- If you love and I love, there is an abundance of love. If I have faith and you have faith, our joint faith brings a higher level of support and blessings (**1+1=2**). If one person does not love, conflict resonates due to jealously, envy, anger, negativity, low self-esteem and other non-loving character traits.

You cannot love effectively if you don't love yourself first. You cannot make good choices about who you chose to let in your life and who you release from your life, if you don't love yourself first. When you love yourself, you are able to work on you without having a negative impact on the life of others. When you love yourself, you are able to love others. When you love, you receive love in return. And when you receive that love in return, **1+1=2**. Love always. Love daily. 365 Love.™

Have you told someone you loved them today? I have.™

Love yesterday, today and future tomorrows,™
Torion

Message in the MUSIC
Beyonce – **1+1**

Note the QUOTE!
"You attract people by the qualities you display. You keep them by the qualities you possess." --- Unknown

Never Felt This Way
August 30

Today's NOTE

I have a phenomenal feeling. It's inside and out. It's all over me. It's in everything I do. And I've **never felt this way before**. It's a feeling of love. It's amazing how I feel now that I've found it. I can't imagine what life would be like without it. It's difficult to understand why people don't want to know it. All I can think about is how when I smile, I show it. I always want to share it. When I wake, I just have to have it. I can't wait to learn more about it. It took time for me to realize it. I love the opportunity to give it. I wouldn't want to ever lose it. And every day it gets better and better. I want to hold on to it forever. And as I continue to grow, I have it more and more. And until now, I've **never felt this way** before. That's love. Love always. Love daily. 365 Love.™

Have you told someone you loved them today? I have.™

Love yesterday, today and future tomorrows,™
Torion

Message in the MUSIC
Brian McKnight - **Never Felt This Way**

Note the QUOTE!
"We choose those we like; with those we love, we have no say in the matter." --- Mignon McLaughlin

Someone Needs You
August 31

Today's NOTE

You may be well known because of places you go often, activities you participate in, tasks you perform on the job, or special gifts you possess. You may be less known because of the things you do in the privacy of your home, neighborhood or with family. Regardless of the magnitude of your "popularity", somewhere **someone needs you**. You are an important part of someone's life. You see, we are all God's children. He uses us in small ways and big ways. And one is just as important as the other. One way He uses us is to help someone else in need.

The customer you support on your job feels good that you were able to resolve an issue that allowed them to meet a critical deadline. The coworker you were able to lend a helping hand to appreciated the support you provided. The family member you helped move or called to talk to needed that help just when you provided it. The elderly person you helped walk across the street needed your assistance. Someone was sad inside and the smile you shared as they crossed your path brightened their day. The person you let cut in front of you in your car made it to work on time and was able to keep their job because of your kindness. The song you shared at a recent performance made someone feel good inside. The child you read to learned something new. The stranger you shared a testimony with gained a new level of faith.

These are just a few examples of how **someone needs you**, but there are countless others that take place on a day to day basis. Some you consciously realize and others you don't. Every interaction you have with another person has the potential for you to help someone in need. These interactions are small doses of love. They are God's way of sharing the love He has for His children through the use of others. He uses me, you and everyone else on a daily basis. Never, ever feel that you are not needed. Somewhere **someone needs you**. You can and do make a difference in someone's life. You always have and you always will. Love always. Love daily. 365 Love.™

Have you told someone you loved them today? I have.™

Love yesterday, today and future tomorrows,™
Torion

Message in the MUSIC
Anne Murray – You Needed Me

Note the QUOTE!
"In helping others, we shall help ourselves, for whatever good we give out completes the circle and comes back to us." --- Flora Edwards

Love Always. Love Daily. 365 Love.

Love Always. Love Daily. 365 Love.

September

"Love yourself, for if you don't, how can you expect anybody else to love you?"
— Unknown

Catch Yourself

September 1

Today's NOTE

You're on your way. Each day brings you closer and closer to more love. You are learning to open your eyes, your mind, your ears and your heart to love. You are working on yourself and learning to love yourself and others better in the process. You are learning what love is and is not. Now comes the real test. The world is yours to conquer or be conquered by. Where you end up is based on strong faith and love. I have faith that you will end up on the positive side of things when you love. You have self-love, charitable love, brotherly love, romantic love and family love. And with that, you are now prepared to **catch yourself**.

- When the world leans hard on your shoulder and you begin to have doubts, **catch yourself**. Remember, it's only temporary. Always take it as a lesson learned.
- When people let you down and disappoint you, **catch yourself**. You know that you can only control your actions and not the actions of others.
- When you lose something or someone you love, **catch yourself**. You know that everything and everyone come into your life for a reason, season and/or a lifetime. Remember the good in everything, everyone and every experience and move forward.
- When you begin to have doubts and worry, **catch yourself**. What is meant to be is meant to be. It's within God's will, not yours. What you have or don't have is not as important as your faith and your belief in love.
- When you are saddened because it seems as if every time you move one step forward, you are pushed two steps backwards, **catch yourself**. Know that for every action, there is a reaction. Put another plan in place to move forward again. Sometimes you have to make changes in yourself or your situation to move forward.
- And when any situation that could possibly happen to you actually happens, **catch yourself** and always, always remember the glass is half full, positive thinking, strong faith, and love.

Love always. Love daily. 365 Love.™

Have you told someone you loved them today? I have.™

Love yesterday, today and future tomorrows,™
Torion

Message in the MUSIC
VaShawn Mitchell – Conqueror

Note the QUOTE!
"I love, therefore I am." --- Unknown

A Solid Foundation
September 2

Today's NOTE

Stability in life is based on having **a solid foundation**. Having **a solid foundation** is based on love. Love is based on faith, self-love, the love of other people and the love of other things. **A solid foundation** makes you structurally sound. It provides stability and strength through turbulent times. While certain parts of your life may change, the foundation itself keeps you standing strong. Great things are built on **a solid foundation**.

When you build a house, **a solid foundation** is required. If a short cut is taken, the house is not stable. If you leave out certain key components to building the house, it may not pass the initial inspection. Or, if it does, it eventually develops problems over time. Some of those problems become costly headaches and require repair. Some of the repairs are repetitive and others may be one time, but until the foundation of the home is repaired the correct way, the problems never go away. They are only patched temporarily.

I recall a time when the father of my children purchased a tricycle for my daughter. The instructions on putting the tricycle together the correct way were provided. However, he felt that he could do it himself. He just knew that he knew what he was doing. It took him forever to complete what appeared to be a simple task according to the instructions, but he finally got it done....without using the instructions. My daughter used her newly put together tricycle as part of the annual children parade at her daycare center. When I went to pick her up at the end of the day, her tricycle was in pieces. It fell apart during the parade. Why? Because it was not put together correctly. It was put together the way someone else wanted to put it together. Not the way the company provided instructions on how to put it together the correct way. The instructions were the basis for putting the tricycle together so that it would have **a solid foundation**. The end result was a disappointed 4 year old at the parade she was so excited to participate in.

And the lesson learned is? There are a core set of instructions to building any strong foundation. We can choose to build it our own way or the right way. If we choose our own way, it may hold up temporarily. But if it is not done the correct way, it will eventually fall apart. The only way to put it back together is to do it the right way. The way it is supposed to be done. Sometimes there is an opportunity to repair it. Other times, we have to start all over again. That may mean tearing it all down and building it back up again. You can run from learning to love, but in order to have a fulfilled life, love must be a part of it. And you have to love the right way, not your way. There is a book about it. It's called the Bible. It is your complete guide to building **a solid foundation**. It is your guide to building **a solid foundation** in love. Love always. Love daily. 365 Love.™

Have you told someone you loved them today? I have.™

Love Always. Love Daily. 365 Love.

Love yesterday, today and future tomorrows,™
Torion

Message in the MUSIC
Kirk Franklin – Love

Note the QUOTE!
"Do you wish to rise? Begin by descending. You plan a tower that will pierce the clouds? Lay first the foundation of humility." --- St. Augustine

What You Learn Along the Way
September 3

Today's NOTE
Wherever you are in your life, right now, at this specific time, it's OK. The question is, where do you need to go from here? The past is the past. When you can take what you have experienced from the past and learn from it, you are on the right track. It's not about what you did in your past, it's **what you learn along the way.**

History is an important part of growing. When you know about and learn from things that happened in the past, it establishes a foundation for how you move forward in the future. You use the things done well to repeat or expand upon, and you use the lessons learned to make changes to improve upon. This applies to your personal growth in love as well. How you loved in the past is always in the past. It's **what you learn along the way** that makes the difference. Always be open to becoming a better person. Always be open to becoming a better you. Always be open to learning more from love and about love. Always be open to loving always. Love always. Love daily. 365 Love. ™

Have you told someone you loved them today? I have. ™

Love yesterday, today and future tomorrows, ™
Torion

Message in the MUSIC
Lalah Hathaway – Learning to Swim

Note the QUOTE!
"Experience: that most brutal of teachers. But you learn, my God do you learn." -
-- C. S. Lewis

Sing a Song
September 4

Today's NOTE
What a better way to make you feel love than to **sing a song**. Music soothes the savage beast. It calms nerves. It brings joy and happiness. It is fun and exciting. When you hear some good music, you automatically feel the love from it. It makes you move, bop your head, snap your fingers, and **sing a song**. You sing out loud and you sing it like you're proud. You don't even have to know how to sing. The words just make you open your mouth and rejoice.

How many times have you been in the car riding along and your favorite song comes on the radio? What do you do? You **sing a song**. When you're in the shower all alone, you feel the urge to listen to yourself and **sing a song**. When you're just feeling good and casually listening to music, you **sing a song**. When you have your iPod in your ear and a good song comes on, you **sing a song** not having a care in the world about who is around you listening at the time. And at that particular moment, you feel good. You feel the emotion of the song. You feel like your own super star. There is magic in the music. There is love in your ability to openly and freely **sing a song**. Love always. Love daily. 365 Love.™

Have you told someone you loved them today? I have.™

Love yesterday, today and future tomorrows,™
Torion

Message in the MUSIC
Earth, Wind and Fire – **Sing a Song**

Note the QUOTE!
"A bird doesn't sing because it has an answer, it sings because it has a song." --- Maya Angelo

---

Love Always. Love Daily. 365 Love.

Live Your Life
September 5

Today's NOTE
Live your life. There is so much out there in the world for you to embrace. You are meant to love and in order to love, you must live. Go out and do something. Meet people. Have fun. Do something new. Do something different. Get up and get out. Do it now. Do it today. It's so easy to get caught up in routine. It's so easy to make excuses for doing absolutely nothing. God did not create us to just sit and exist. He created a world of wonderful, loving things. He gave His children the gift to create activities, businesses, and opportunities. He brought life into the air, the trees and nature as a whole. Open a newspaper. Search the Internet. Walk outside. Just do something. Do more and then some. You will find a life worth living. You will find love in your life. You will see that there is so much more to love on the inside and outside because you choose to **live your life**. Love always. Love daily. 365 Love.™

Have you told someone you loved them today? I have.™

Love yesterday, today and future tomorrows,™
Torion

Message in the MUSIC
Tim McGraw – **Live** Like You Were Dying

Note the QUOTE!
"Love takes off masks that we fear we cannot **live** without and know we cannot **live** within." --- James Author Baldwin

---

Love Always. Love Daily. 365 Love.

Man in the Mirror
September 6

Today's NOTE
Most relationships do not work because individuals within those relationship have self checks to do. They either realize it and do nothing about it or don't realize it, and jeopardize the relationship as a result of it. You cannot love someone else if you don't know how to love yourself first. When you don't love yourself, you put your baggage on the other person in the relationship or you accept things from others that are not good for you. You may be carrying personal burdens from past hurts or you may possess character traits such as anger, jealousy, envy, and selfishness, that need to be addressed before you can love another person the right way. With self-love comes the ability to look at the **man in the mirror** and notice if there is still work to do. It is taking a look at the **man in the mirror** and accepting who you are and what you do. It is knowing the difference between right and wrong. It is knowing the difference between good and bad. It is realizing that you have some personal healing to do. It is realizing that you need to learn more about love and how to love. It is realizing that you are a child of God and that God is in you. It is the ability to let go and let God. It is taking a look at the **man in the mirror** and knowing that you are love. Your actions are a reflection of love. You are not the judge or the victim. You are able to forgive yourself for things you have done to hurt you and others. You are able to forgive others for things they have done to you. You can look at the **man in the mirror** and be happy. Not only do you see love and happiness within you, you see love and happiness in all things around you. You feel, see, hear, and speak love. When you do your self-check, put plans in place to grow in love, and put actions in place to move forward with those plans, you will eventually look at the **man in the mirror** and see love. That is when you love yourself completely. That is when you are ready to love others. Love always. Love daily. 365 Love.™

Have you told someone you loved them today? I have.™

Love yesterday, today and future tomorrows,™
Torion

Message in the MUSIC
Michael Jackson – **Man in the Mirror**

Note the QUOTE!
"Love yourself, for if you don't, how can you expect anybody else to love you?" --- Unknown

Love Always. Love Daily. 365 Love.

It is What it Is
September 7

Today's NOTE

You can't control change in others, you can only control change in yourself. So, stop expecting others to change to who and what you want them to be. Let them live and change for who they are destined to be. You cannot force that change. You can only love them and pray for change that is within God's will for them. Love them to the point where you can realize that **it is what it is.**

In the book, The Mastery of Love by Don Miguel Ruiz, the author has an interesting analogy about accepting people for who they are and not expecting them to be something they are not.

A dog is a dog and a cat is a cat. If you want a dog, why get a cat expecting it to act like a dog (and vice versa)? A cat will never be a dog. A dog will never be a cat.

It is what it is. This concept is similar with people. When you meet people and get to know them, they are who they are. You should accept them as they are or move on to meet people who have character traits aligned with the type of people you want to be around. When you get things you don't want, you don't care of them. You neglect them or mistreat them. You sometimes throw them away or give them to someone else. You typically don't spend money on things you don't want. You typically don't proactively go out and do things you don't want to do. **It is what it is.** You either like it or you don't. You learn to like some things over time. At times, you eventually learn to like some things that you did not realize you liked. But what you learned to like was not because it changed. You just learned to like it. Love does not expect people to change for us. Love expects us to make changes in ourselves. Love expects us to love others as they are. The next time you meet someone, remember that **it is what it is.** Expect them to be who they are and accept them for that or move on. Don't expect them to change into something you want them to be when that is not who they are. Don't allow someone to change you into what they want you to be. Love does not force change. Love is a change agent that happens in a person's own time on their own personal journey. Love allows you to accept others by remembering that **it is what it is.** Love always. Love daily. 365 Love.™

Have you told someone you loved them today? I have.™

Love yesterday, today and future tomorrows,™
Torion

Message in the MUSIC
Ruben Studdard – Change Me

Note the QUOTE!
"As you become more clear about who you really are, you'll be better able to decide what is best for you - the first time around." --- Oprah Winfrey

At This Time
September 8

Today's NOTE
At this time and at this moment, I am full of love. I always have been and I always will be. I recognize that love is all I need and have discovered that it resides in me. It is in the air I breathe. It is in the sun and the moon. It is in the day and the night. It is in this time and that time. It is before and after. It is what it is. **At this time**, I have accepted who I am and know that I am good. I am growing on the inside and my light is beginning to shine. I am becoming a better person aligned with God's purpose for me each and every day. I am strength and courage. I am happiness and joy. I am full of wonderfulness. I am me. I am God's special creation and I am filled with greatness.

All these things that I am, so are you. Open your eyes and your heart to love and realize the reality of who you are and the power that true love possesses. Realize that you have everything even when you have nothing. Realize that all of your needs are taken care of even when you only have a little. Realize that you are somebody and you are always loved. You love and you are loved in return **at this time** and all times. Love always. Love daily. 365 Love.™

Have you told someone you loved them today? I have.™

Love yesterday, today and future tomorrows,™
Torion

Message in the MUSIC
Algebra – **At This Time**

Note the QUOTE!
"Do not love me because I love you. Love me for loving me." --- Unknown

The 5 W's
September 9

Today's NOTE
Think about **the 5 W's** --- Who, What, Why, Where and When --- and ask yourself the following questions:

- Who are you?
- What is your purpose in life?
- Why do you need to change?
- Where do you go from here?
- When are you going to do something about it?

Now think about everything you know about love. Remember that God is love and love is all things good. Remember all that love involves to include self-love, the love of others, inspiration and positivity. Remember that you, not others, control your own happiness. Now think about **the 5 W's** again and ask yourself those same questions as it relates to your personal growth in love. Are the answers the same or different? How are you going to get the "where" and "when" done? Act on it and do something about it. Love always. Love daily. 365 Love.™

Have you told someone you loved them today? I have.™

Love yesterday, today and future tomorrows,™
Torion

Message in the MUSIC
Casting Crowns - Who Am I

Note the QUOTE!
"I am more than I know myself to be." --- Unknown

When Will You Choose?
September 10

Today's NOTE
The past it behind you, the present is today, and tomorrow is yet to come. The choices you make today will determine how you live your life tomorrow. It's never too late to choose love. Choosing to love today automatically changes the rest of your day leading to the future of your tomorrow. So, **when will you choose?** Love always. Love daily. 365 Love.™

Have you told someone you loved them today? I have.™

Love yesterday, today and future tomorrows,™
Torion

Message in the MUSIC
Kem - When I'm Loving You

Note the QUOTE!
"The greatest power that a person possess is the power to choose." --- J. Martin Kohe

---

Love Always. Love Daily. 365 Love.

Get Back Up!
September 11

Today's NOTE

If you dropped a $100 bill on the ground, what would you do? You would pick it back up, right? And for every time you dropped it, you would pick it back up without a second thought. You wouldn't think twice about it. That bill has value and you can do something with it. It means something. And you know it. I don't know of anyone who would drop money knowingly without picking it up, regardless of its value.

If you were walking, tripped up and fell on the ground right now, you would **get back up**. When you trip, tumble and fall, you **get back up**. It's as easy and simple as that.

Now apply this same concept to life. With life comes setbacks and "falls." However, it does not have to be as hard to **get back up** as we sometimes make it. Whenever you fall, **get back up!** For every two steps you get pushed backwards, plan your next move forward. Do not give up. You are an important person. You are a child of God. You mean something to someone. Your life is important and it has purpose and meaning. While you are on your journey to fulfill your purpose in life, you may be presented with setbacks. Take those setbacks as set ups for something bigger, better and greater. Take them as lessons learned and **get back up!** Dust yourself off, and **get back up!** Pick yourself up as you would with that $100 bill...every time. You are more valuable than that bill. And for each time you fall, **get back up** again and again and again. Remember that you sometimes have to go through something to get to something better. You sometimes fall because you learn as you **get back up**. That's life. That's love. Love always. Love daily. 365 Love.™

Have you told someone you loved them today? I have.™

Love yesterday, today and future tomorrows,™
Torion

Message in the MUSIC
Donnie McClurkin - We Fall Down

Note the QUOTE!
"When real people fall down in life, they get right back up and keep walking." --- Sarah Jessica Parker

Love Always. Love Daily. 365 Love.

The Way
September 12

Today's NOTE
There are so many ways to love. We share love through gifts, acts of service, physical touch, words of affirmation, and quality time. We share romantic, charitable, brotherly and family love. Love gives and receives. **The way** you give and receive love is unique to you. **The way** others give and receive love is unique to them. Of all the many ways to love and be loved, what's important is your choice to love. **The way** you choose to love is up to you. However, **the way** you love should include love for yourself, other people and other things. Choose love. Learn to love. And love **the way** you love. Love always. Love daily. 365 Love.™

Have you told someone you loved them today? I have.™

Love yesterday, today and future tomorrows,™
Torion

Message in the MUSIC
Jill Scott - **The Way**

Note the QUOTE!
"**The way** to love anything is to realize that it might be lost." --- G. K. Chesterton

Through the Rain
September 13

Today's NOTE
Sometimes you have to go through something to get to something. You have to go **through the rain** to get out of the rain. You have to experience the bad to realize and appreciate the good. You experience life's challenges to experience love. Love builds the inner strength to help you endure. It gives you hope. It builds on your faith. When you discover what love truly means and what love truly is, you find that you can make it through anything. The hurt and the pain quickly fade away. Worries disappear. Everything that once looked down now looks up. And you begin to realize that with love, you can make it **through the rain** and the sun will shine again. Love always. Love daily. 365 Love.™

Have you told someone you loved them today? I have.™

Love yesterday, today and future tomorrows,™
Torion

Message in the MUSIC
Mariah Carey - **Through the Rain**

Note the QUOTE!
"God didn't promise days without pain, laughter without sorrow, sun without rain, but He did promise strength for the day, comfort for the tears, and light for the way." --- Unknown

Love Always. Love Daily. 365 Love.

Get to Know It Better
September 14

Today's NOTE
Part of establishing a new relationship is getting to know the other person. As you find out more about the person, you decide if you do or don't want to keep seeing them. If you really like the person, you want to spend more time with them. As your interest grows, you want to know more and more about them. You want to share in their joy. You want to give to them. You feel good thinking about them. You enjoy talking to them and about them. You wake up and go to sleep thinking about them.

I have established a new relationship with love. Once I found out how great it was, I wanted to **get to know it better**. I learned more about it and kept going. I made it a daily part of my life. And it has been a true blessing. Establish your relationship with love and make a concentrated effort to **get to know it better**. It is then that you will find what a positive difference it can make in your life. Love always. Love daily. 365 Love.™

Have you told someone you loved them today? I have.™

Love yesterday, today and future tomorrows,™
Torion

Message in the MUSIC
Mary J. Blige – **Get to Know You Better**

Note the QUOTE!
"True love comes once in a lifetime. Open your eyes and your heart and see the miracle in front of you." --- Unknown

Always Want More
September 15

Today's NOTE

We are children of God. And He wants us to do something with our lives. He also wants us to learn and grow. He wants us to **always want more** for ourselves. For every goal we accomplish, we need to set a new one. This allows us to keep growing. And in doing so we build character. We experience life. We evolve as a person and get closer to fulfilling our purpose.

There are several men and women in the Bible who fulfilled their purpose after many years. Those years were filled with good and bad life experiences. However, it was those life experiences that prepared them for who they were meant to be. They **always wanted more** because they knew there was more to accomplish. And as they traveled along their journey, they became even stronger in faith and they grew in love.

As you move along life's journey, **always want more**. Always want to be the best that you can be. Always want to be a better person. Always want to do better. Always want to accomplish more. Always want to fulfill your dreams. Always want to strive for a better life inside and out. Always want to live life to the fullest. Always want to learn. Always want to love. Love always. Love daily. 365 Love.™

Have you told someone you loved them today? I have.™

Love yesterday, today and future tomorrows,™
Torion

Message in the MUSIC
Michelle Williams – The Movement

Note the QUOTE!
"Personally, I'm always ready to learn, although I do not always like being taught." --- Winston Churchill

Motivated to Do Something Better
September 16

Today's NOTE
Have you ever felt down and heard a person speak so positively that it changed your thought process for the better? Have you ever been ready to give up and you heard a sermon from the pastor that inspired you to keep going? Have you ever been lost in not knowing what direction to go in and a friend or family member gave you some advice or guidance that changed your life for the better? Have you ever questioned your purpose in life, read the Bible or a good motivational book, and set a path that moved you forward in a more positive life changing direction? If you answered yes to any of these questions, you are not alone. You experienced a touch of love.

That's what love does. Love motivates. It motivates you to do more and be more. It provides a new level of inspiration. God spreads His love through the use of people and things. He uses creative ways to uplift and encourage us through love. Sometimes we see it coming and other times we do not. Learn more about love. Accept love. Realize it's power to change and make a difference and **get motivated to do something better**. Love always. Love daily. 365 Love.™

Have you told someone you loved them today? I have.™

Love yesterday, today and future tomorrows,™
Torion

Message in the MUSIC
Deitrick Haddon – The Greatest

Note the QUOTE!
"Really great people make you feel that you, too, can become great." --- Mark Twain

A Noun
September 17

Today's NOTE

A noun is defined in simplest form as a person, place, or thing. It can be used as the subject of a clause or the object of a verb. While love can be classified as a verb, it can also be classified as **a noun**. As **a noun**, it is defined as a feeling of warm personal attachment, passion or desire for another. Take a brief moment to read and think about the many ways of love.

- Be love
- Give love
- Share love
- Want love
- Need love
- Desire love
- Make love
- See love
- Hear love
- Taste love
- Walk in love
- Realize love
- Provide love
- Dance love
- Sing love
- Talk about love
- Believe in love
- Wish for love
- Dream love
- Ask about love
- Learn about love
- Teach love
- Glorify love
- Pray for love
- Rejoice for love
- Magnify love
- Understand love
- Have love
- Try love
- Practice love
- Embrace love
- Grow in love
- Care about love
- Show love
- Know love
- Love love

Love always. Love daily. 365 Love. TM

Have you told someone you loved them today? I have. TM

Love yesterday, today and future tomorrows, TM
Torion

Message in the MUSIC
India Aire – Ready for Love

Note the QUOTE!
"Love starts from the heart, not from the eye." --- Unknown

You Are
September 18

Today's NOTE
I wanted to take this time to remind you of how incredible **you are**. First and foremost, **you are** God's creation and **you are** meant for greatness. **You are** meant to love, be loved and share love with others. **You are** one of a kind and uniquely you. **You are** love and with that you possess the power to become something magnificent and make a difference. **You are** in control of you and your choices. **You are** the music to your own personal multiplatinum song. **You are** the roots of a strong tree of life. **You are** the foundation to a great inner monument. **You are** the wings that spread wide and strong to support the flight of a powerful bird. **You are** all that your potential allows you to be and then some. **You are** so many great and wonderful things yet to be explored. **You are**... Believe it and be it. Love always. Love daily. 365 Love.™

Have you told someone you loved them today? I have. ™

Love yesterday, today and future tomorrows,™
Torion

Message in the MUSIC
Kem – **You Are**

Note the QUOTE!
"Love is the magician that pulls man out of his own hat." --- Ben Hecht

Greatness
September 19

Today's NOTE
I always encourage my children to be the best that they can be. In doing so, I frequently remind them that they are meant for **greatness**. You can do whatever you put your heart into. And with that, your options are limitless. I know this because I know that God brought us to this world to fulfill a purpose. That purpose has significance and meaning. Not to us, but to Him. It may be small or grand, but whatever it is, it is **greatness**. It may make a difference to one person or many, but in His eyes, it is **greatness**. We should never sell ourselves short of anything but being the best that we can be. We should live each day striving to love, love better and love more. For it is in love, that we find meaning and purpose. And in that meaning and purpose is where our **greatness** resides. Love always. Love daily. 365 Love.™

Have you told someone you loved them today? I have.™

Love yesterday, today and future tomorrows,™
Torion

Message in the MUSIC
Raheem DeVaughn – **Greatness**

Note the QUOTE!
"The **greatness** of art is not to find what is common but what is unique." --- Isaac Bashevis

Love Always. Love Daily. 365 Love.

My Children
September 20

Today's NOTE

Words cannot express how much love I have for **my children**. I realize that they are a special gift from God. His love brought them life through using me as the targeted vessel. I am humbled by the thought of being blessed to experience the miracle of childbirth and being able to truly claim the title of Mother.

My children are special to me. They grew inside of me. They heard my voice. They moved with limited space. They reacted to my actions. They obtained nourishment from my womb. As my body transformed, so did theirs. From the look of a small pea, to the formation of small hands and feet, to a fully developed, healthy baby, they grew and they grew. Then, they were here. I remember the mile long smile on my face as the doctors brought them to me. Out of all the possible complications, love and faith, delivered **my children** to me as beautiful, healthy babies. And while they were born three years apart, I remember each moment as if it was yesterday. What a magnificent joy.

To see them learn to sit up, crawl, walk, talk, form sentences, play, cry and have their first boo - boo's. To the first day of school, the first crush and the first dance. To extracurricular activities, thinking they're in love, peer pressure and finding themselves. To selecting friends and finding out who the true friends really were, or were not. My daughter is a gifted singer. My son is a talented artist. Both of **my children** are very creative in their own unique way. For all that they were, who they are, and what they are destined to be, they are **my children** and I am a proud mother. As young adults, I see so much potential in them that has yet to reach its climax. They have their own purpose to fulfill and they are meant for greatness. This, I know. As they continue to experience what life presents to them, I will be there along the way. I get excited at the thought of what is yet to come. Lifting them up when they fall, and cheering them on as they continue to move forward. I am their mother and they are **my children**. They always have been and they always will be. Spoken from the heart of a mother who loves. Love always. Love daily. 365 Love.™

Have you told someone you loved them today? I have.™

Love yesterday, today and future tomorrows,™
Torion

Message in the MUSIC
Cheryl Pepsii Riley – Thanks for My Child

Note the QUOTE!
"The child must know that he is a miracle, that since the beginning of the world there hasn't been, and until the end of the world there will not be, another child like him." --- Pablo Casals

The X-Factor
September 21

Today's NOTE
Today, in 2011, was the first showing of the TV singing show, **The X-Factor**. It is a spin-off of the long running American Idol show. I listened to singers who lived for the opportunity to share their gifts with others. Singers who needed a break that would change their lives for the better. The two hour special brought lots of life stories to my living room. The testimonies provided by some of the singers who made it to the next level brought tears to my eyes. The 42 year old, single mother of two who was told that she was too old to make it in the singing business that had to bring her children with her to the audition. The 20 year old whose mother gave him two years to make it with his singing dream or he had to go the school and get a degree. This was nearing the end of his two year time period. The 14 year old who was one of 6 family members living in a small two bedroom house. The 70 day recovering drug addict and father who performed his original, uplifting, inspirational song and received a standing ovation. And the stories go on and on. God is so good. I cried tears of joy for the singers who were able to move one step closer to fulfilling their dreams. While there is only one slot for the winner, what a difference this moment made for those that moved on for the rest of their lives. Love kept them from giving up on their dreams. Love brought them to the auditions and gave them the patience to wait in line amongst thousands of others. Love gave them the gift of song. Love was shared from the resounding applause received from the thousands of people in the audience. Love filled the hearts of those who needed it. Love touched someone and gave them hope. Love was present on **The X-Factor**. Love always. Love daily. 365 Love.™

Have you told someone you loved them today? I have.™

Love yesterday, today and future tomorrows,™
Torion

Message in the MUSIC
Lauren Hill – His Eye is on the Sparrow (I Sing Because I'm Happy)

Note the QUOTE!
"When a singer truly feels and experiences what the music is all about, the words will automatically ring true." --- Monserrat Caballe

I Saw Her Cry
September 22

Today's NOTE
As I stopped at a red light on my way to work this morning, I looked in the rear view mirror of my car and **I saw her cry**. Heavy tears rolled down from her eyes. Her head dropped as she appeared to think harder about what was hurting her on the inside. Her hand covered her mouth, then her eyes. While I was not in the car with her, I heard her, and I connected with her. I could not see her tears, but felt how heavy they were. I did not know who she was, or what she was going through, but when **I saw her cry**, I immediately began to pray for her. I prayed a big prayer.

God, please watch over her and remove the hurt from her heart. Send her a sign to let her know that everything is going to be OK and that You will take care of things for her. Touch her with Your unconditional love and show her the light of the sun behind the rain in her tears. Let her see the beauty of the rainbow that is soon to appear. Show her that you are love and that Your love is all she needs. Open her heart to reveal that the best is yet to come. Remind her that she sometimes has to go through something to get to something and that "This too shall pass." Then allow her to take a deep breath, guide her eyes to the mirror, let her look at herself, and witness a beautiful smile. --- Amen

I don't know what happened to her after I drove away and we parted ways, but I believe in the power of prayer and have faith that she is OK. Say a special prayer for someone you don't know today. Do it because you know that someone is always in need of prayer. Do it to pick someone up and clear the tears from their eyes. Do it because **I saw her cry**. Love always. Love daily. 365 Love.™

Have you told someone you loved them today? I have.™

Love yesterday, today and future tomorrows,™
Torion

Message in the MUSIC
Mariah Carey – Angels Cry

Note the QUOTE!
"Happiness lies for those who cry, those who hurt, those who have searched, and those who have tried. For only they can appreciate the importance of people who have touched their lives." --- Unknown

Why?
September 23

Today's NOTE
Sometimes you feel things can get no worse than they are. You have tried and tried. You have prayed and prayed. You have done what you feel to be all of the right things to do. And you just don't understand **why** you still have to keep going through. You don't understand **why** things have not changed. You break down and ask, "**Why?**" **Why** me? **Why** now? **Why** this? **Why**....?

God hears you. He always hears you. And He will answer your prayers. He is working on you right now. He is guiding you in a direction that is within His will. He is getting you out of something to move you into something different. He is watching you grow. He is building your faith. And He is doing these things because He loves you. You are His child and He wants the best from you and for you. Sometimes bringing out the best means allowing you to experience things in order to learn from them, but He does love you. He will see you through. Have strong faith, believe and love. Love always. Love daily. 365 Love.™

Have you told someone you loved them today? I have.™

Love yesterday, today and future tomorrows,™
Torion

Message in the MUSIC
Tonex – **Why**

Note the QUOTE!
"God is at home; it is we who have gone for a walk." --- Meister Eckhart

Something Good To Say
September 24

Today's NOTE
I had the honor of attending the 2nd Annual First Lady's Lunch as a guest. It was a celebration for the first lady (pastor's wife) of Mt. Vernon Baptist Church in Atlanta, GA. The program included a group participation activity, poetry, and singing. It was also an opportunity to fellowship with one another. After lunch, the church members and other guests were allowed the opportunity to speak about the first lady. The room was filled with so much positivity and everyone had **something good to say**. While I did not know the first lady personally, I felt that the comments about her gave me an opportunity to get to know who she was, her character, and what she stood for. It was a confirmation that when you demonstrate love, your light shines. And those that do and do not know you can see it. As a result, when a person has an opportunity to speak of you and about you, they always have **something good to say**. Let love fill your heart and support your character. Let love provide the power supply to make your light shine. Let love support your thoughts and the thoughts of others so that there is always **something good to say**. Love always. Love daily. 365 Love. ™

Have you told someone you loved them today? I have. ™

Love yesterday, today and future tomorrows, ™
Torion

Message in the MUSIC
Lamar Campbell – More Than Anything

Note the QUOTE!
"Love is one of the hardest things to say and one of the easiest things to hear." --- Unknown

---

Role Model
September 25

Today's NOTE
The organization I work for required a select group of executives to take an *Executive Speak* class. The purpose was to ensure we were properly prepared to represent our organization for public speaking engagements. One of the four presentation formats required as part of the class was to select one of eight topics and speak on it. The topic I selected was...*Who is your **role model** and why?* I gravitated to this specific topic because I have learned to love and wanted to share what I shared in class as a part of 365 Love.

A **role model** is someone you look up to and learn from. It's someone you want to model your life, behaviors, and/or character traits after. Well, everyone I encounter on a daily basis has the potential to be my **role model**. I look at every encounter as a lesson learned. If I can gain one good experience from a person, they become a **role model** for that moment and for that lesson learned. I learn from both good and bad behaviors. For they teach me what to be like and what not to be like. They show me how people respond to certain behaviors. They help me grow as a person dealing with other people. And from that, I learn. I may pass someone in the hallway and see them smile. The way they smiled, may have made me and others feel good for that moment. If I liked that feeling, I may want to use that behavior so that I can make others feel that way as well. No matter how big or small the learning experience, the point is that I learned from it. If I learned anything from what another person has said or done to help me grow into a better and more loving person, they become my **role model**. Love looks for the best in others. Love allows you to learn from their best. Always look for the best, learn, grow and love. Find the love in your **role model**. Love always. Love daily. 365 Love.™

Have you told someone you loved them today? I have.™

Love yesterday, today and future tomorrows,™
Torion

Message in the MUSIC
N'Sync – Something Like You

Note the QUOTE!
"I never thought a **role model** should be negative." --- Michael Jordan

Write a Song
September 26

Today's NOTE

Sometimes I tickle myself. I may hear someone speak about a topic or have a thought running across my mind and say, "Ooh, I can **write a song** about that." A song is another way of communicating how a person feels through music. It is a form of expression. It speaks for those who cannot think of the words to say for themselves. I have written a good number of songs in my day. The same things that motive me to write 365 Love notes are the same things that motive me to write 365 Love songs - life experiences, interactions with others and of course, my favorite subject, love.

I recall listening to School House Rock as a kid. Those simple, cartoon based, singing commercials taught me about multiplication, conjunctions, nouns, verbs, the preamble, and how a bill becomes a law. When I eventually got to those subjects in school, I would sing the song in my head to play back what I learned for tests, class work, etc. Someone thought to **write a song** to teach children basic education topics. This same concept can be and is often used to teach others how to love. Whether it's a gospel song, a rhythm and blues song, a pop song, a county song, a rock song, a rap song, or a jazz song, someone decided to **write a song** to convey a message. Someone decided to **write a song** to tell you and others about love. If a message can be conveyed through the words of a song, and someone can learn from that message, then that's a good thing. The next time you hear a song that touches your heart and has purpose and meaning, think about the person who decided to **write a song**. Think about how God used them to send a message to you and so many others. Think about how the words of the song are teaching you and others how to love. Love always. Love daily. 365 Love.™

Have you told someone you loved them today? I have.™

Love yesterday, today and future tomorrows,™
Torion

Message in the MUSIC
Earth, Wind and Fire – I **Write a Song** for You

Note the QUOTE!
"You're a song written by the hands of God." --- Shakira

Forgive Many Times
September 27

Today's NOTE

I once heard someone share an interesting view point on the subject of forgiveness - "Sometimes you have to **forgive many times**." I reflected on this for a moment and had to agree with her. Some people are in your life for a reason and a season. Others are there for a lifetime. While we are all on our own personal journey to grow in love, we have to learn to forgive those that are still a "work in progress" or not as far along. We have to forgive those that know they are doing wrong and those that don't know they are doing wrong. Totally forgiving a person does not mean that the relationship will be the same or continue to exist. However, in some cases, because of the nature of the relationship, you have to continually interact with a person. And where they are on their love journey may present new situations which requires you to **forgive many times**. It may be a child, a parent, a significant other, a boss, a coworker, or a friend.

Another situation is when you think you have let things go and forgiven, but you realize you have not. If you continue to talk about a specific person or situation that hurt you, you have not forgiven. If the thought and/or presence of someone that hurt you causes a change in your demeanor, you have not forgiven. When a situation reminds you of a person that hurt you and your thoughts change for the negative, you have not forgiven. In these cases, detecting unforgiveness in your own heart is the way to begin the process of forgiving. Once detected, you have to let it go and forgive, even if it means you have to **forgive many times**. Each time you catch your thoughts, forgive. Forgive as many times as it takes until you are there. God forgives and so must you. In order for you to live a life aligned with love, you must forgive. A clean heart forgives. Love forgives. Love always. Love daily. 365 Love.™

Have you told someone you loved them today? I have. ™

Love yesterday, today and future tomorrows, ™
Torion

Message in the MUSIC
India Aire – Wings of Forgiveness

Note the QUOTE!
"There is no love without forgiveness, and there is no forgiveness without love." --
- Bryant H. McGill

Love Always. Love Daily. 365 Love.

Um Good
September 28

Today's NOTE
God is love. And when I think about how much love He gives, it makes me feel **um good**. Each day I wake to an **um good** feeling. I look in the mirror and smile because of past and present blessings. I am excited about what the day has to bring. I look outside and see the beauty is all that surrounds me. Love fills my lungs as I breathe in and out, and I am ready for whatever is about to be presented to me. I'm ready because I love and that is **um good**.

Do you know it? Can you feel it? Fill your mind and your heart with love and experience the goodness of that **um good** feeling. And the best is yet to come. Love always. Love daily. 365 Love.™

Have you told someone you loved them today? I have.™

Love yesterday, today and future tomorrows,™
Torion

Message in the MUSIC
Smokie Norful - **Um Good**

Note the QUOTE!
"People see God every day. They just don't recognize him." --- Pearl Bailey

---

Love Always. Love Daily. 365 Love.

Change Your Sad Story
September 29

Today's NOTE

I was listening to a radio talk show and heard listener after listener call or write in about relationships they were in with people who were using them, mistreating them and/or abusing them. These sad stories included cheating, adultery, physical abuse, disappearances, lack of financial contribution, stealing, laziness, lack of quality time, verbal abuse, and more. The list went on and on and on. They would point out all of the bad things done to them by others for extended periods of time and would then ask for advice on how to deal with the situation. It was one sad story after the other. Somewhere in the middle of each story was the comment, "I know s/he loves me, but..." or "I love them, but..."

I have heard these same stories from family members and friends. They stay in long term relationships with others who are not truly demonstrating love or just don't know how to love. They continue to accept abusive behaviors that cause pain and hurt. I too have been in a few similar situations in my past. So, I can honestly say that I can relate. And maybe you can too.

Are these stories similar to yours? If so, I know something that has the power to **change your sad story**. That power is within you and right now, you just don't realize it. You don't know how to use it. Or maybe you just don't know where it is or how to get it. That power is called self-love. I've said it before and I will say it again and again. When you love yourself more than you love others, you know when someone or something is not good for you. You are able to move forward and make better relationship choices. You know that you are never alone even when you are by yourself and you are fine with it. You know that God loves you and gives you the power to love yourself. He wants what is best for you and gives you what you need to be complete. He gives you the power to **change your sad story** into a story of love and happiness. And that love is all the love you need. That love comes first from within. No other person can give you the kind of love you can give yourself. Strong faith knows that God's love is the ultimate love that provides the power behind self-love. Love always. Love daily. 365 Love. ™

Have you told someone you loved them today? I have. ™

Love yesterday, today and future tomorrows, ™
Torion

Message in the MUSIC
Terra Naomi – Happy Story

Note the QUOTE!
"Love turns sad stories into testimonies that cause positive change to create happy stories for others." --- Torion

The Good, the Bad and Love
September 30

Today's NOTE

No one said that life would be easy. But what is true about life, is that love makes it worth living. In all that we experience in life, there is **the good, the bad and love**. We enjoy the good times and want them to exist in all that we do. We want to have a good time even when we are doing bad things. We want everything to go our way. We want to have it easy with no troubles, trials or tribulations. That's the good life, right? Well, good things will happen to us, especially when we make good choices and choose to do the right things, but we will experience the bad things as well. Each day we encounter experiences with different people and things. Those encounters may bring about good situations or bad situations. Additionally, our own personal choices bring about good and bad situations. It is these situations that build and mold us. We will go through them again and again. As we grow in faith and love, they become easier and easier to deal with or at times happen less often. Love helps us see the good even when bad things happen. There are lessons to be learned which help us grow in love and become better as a person. That's life. And life brings with it **the good, the bad and love**. Love always. Love daily. 365 Love.™

Have you told someone you loved them today? I have.™

Love yesterday, today and future tomorrows,™
Torion

Message in the MUSIC
Earth, Wind & Fire – Love's Holiday

Note the QUOTE!
"We cannot do great things on this Earth, only small things with great love." --- Mother Teresa

Love Always. Love Daily. 365 Love.

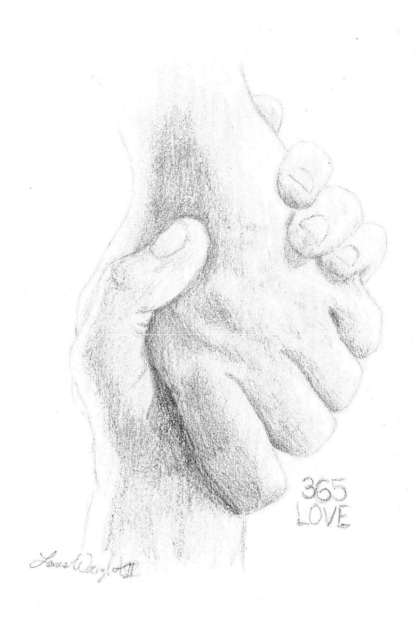

Love Always. Love Daily. 365 Love.

October

"The best exercise of the heart is reaching down and lifting someone else up."
— Tim Russert

Choices
October 1

Today's NOTE
We all make **choices**. Your **choices** determine what happens or does not happen to you and potentially others. Good **choices** usually result in good situations. Bad **choices** usually result in bad situations. Often times, people blame others for their own personal **choices** when it is their **choices** that put them in the position they are in today. Love is good and I choose to love. I choose love for good outcomes. And for all the **choices** I have to make, I will make a conscious effort to align them with love. I may not make the right **choices** all of the time, but as I make mistakes, my **choice** to love will allow me to learn from those mistakes in order to make better **choices** in the future. Love always. Love daily. 365 Love.™

Have you told someone you loved them today? I have.™

Love yesterday, today and future tomorrows,™
Torion

Message in the MUSIC
India Aire - I Choose

Note the QUOTE!
"It is our **choices** that show what we truly are, far more than our abilities." --- Joanne Kathleen Rowling

---

Love Always. Love Daily. 365 Love.

You Can't Hide Love
October 2

Today's NOTE

You can't hide love. When it surrounds you, there is nothing you can do about it. Of all the wrong things that could happen, there are just as many right things that could happen. Of all the bad things around you, there are just as many good things around you. That's because of love. When you are in a place filled with love, **you can't hide it**. It rubs off on you because it's contagious. Think about places filled with negativity – drug houses, abusive homes, etc. Now think about places filled with love – churches, charitable organizations, etc. No matter how much you try to run from the feeling of love in a place of love, it catches up with you. You can't run from it. And once it catches you, it becomes a part of you and **you can't hide it**. The more you surround yourself with love, the more you grow in it. You begin to see more love in people, places and things. Position yourself around positive people and positive things. Fill your mind and your heart with loving thoughts. Open your eyes to see the love in all things around you. Love always. Love daily. 365 Love.™

Have you told someone you loved them today? I have.™

Love yesterday, today and future tomorrows,™
Torion

Message in the MUSIC
Earth, Wind, and Fire - **Can't Hide Love**

Note the QUOTE!
"Love doesn't hide. It stays and fights. It goes the distance, that's why love is so strong. So it can carry you all the way home." --- Unknown

What is Meant for Me is Meant for Me

October 3

Today's NOTE

There are people in my organization that have had a strong influence on my career progression. There are also people that have been able to use some of my ideas to bring about new and/or improved opportunities for themselves. Each of these situations led family, friends and/or coworkers to inquire about my thoughts on them. My response each time was, **"What is meant for me is meant for me."**

If someone has the organizational authority to control my career progression and chooses not to move me forward, then I am not meant to move forward under their authority at that time. I am meant to learn more where I am at that time. I am meant to grow more where I am or in some other way. It could also be that they are meant to learn something from their experience with me. As I do my job and do the right things, I will move forward in time. Moving forward may not always be what or when others anticipate. It may not even be in that particular job or career. Love will move me forward at the right time and to a position that is right for me. **What is meant for me is meant for me**.

The same applies with ideas. No one can take an idea from me that is meant for me to prosper from. If someone else benefits from my idea, then I accomplished something. I made a positive difference in their life. I learned from the experience. It was an acknowledgement of something good I contributed to, directly or indirectly. My idea caused a positive change for someone. There was a purpose behind it and the person was meant to prosper from it at that time. If their gain was based on a wrong doing, then they will eventually have to deal with a lesson learned from that situation. Love allows you to help others. And helping others may not always be in a way we think it is. No one can take an idea from me that was truly meant for me. **What is meant for me is meant for me**.

No one can hold you back or keep you from progressing but you. Whenever you stop, you are giving up. Love does not give up. Whatever you are meant to accomplish will be accomplished as long as you continue to love and have strong faith. If you continue to move forward, you are doing fine. We all have a purpose in life. And that purpose is different for each of us. We all meet people who are in different places on their journey to love. For everyone we meet, we have an impact on their lives and help them move further along on their journey. And they in turn have an impact on our lives as well. When it is your time to shine, you will shine. What is meant for you is meant for you. **What is meant for me is meant for me.** And no one can ever take that away. Love always. Love daily. 365 Love.™

Have you told someone you loved them today? I have.™

Love Always. Love Daily. 365 Love.

Love yesterday, today and future tomorrows,™
Torion

Message in the MUSIC
VaShawn Mitchell - Can't Take My Joy Away

Note the QUOTE!
"True love cannot be found where it does not exist, nor can it be denied where it does." --- Unknown

Talk to People
October 4

Today's NOTE

Communication is an important part of love. Verbal communication is one of many ways to express thoughts, ideas, and beliefs. It is a way to share and let others know you care. It is a way to tell someone how you feel. Some people are good with talking to others. Some are a work in progress. Others have not yet realized their need for development in this area. Effective verbal communication is based on how you talk to a person. You should **talk to people** the way you want to be talked to.

- How do you talk to people when you are angry?
- How do you talk to people when you don't like something they said or did?
- Are you calm?
- Are you overly excited?
- Do you think about what you say before you say it?
- Do you raise your voice, yell and/or call a person out of their name?

I have met people who were not used to a person expressing themselves or responding out of anger without yelling. Talking to express how you feel about a certain situation was not the norm for them, but their experience in communicating with me by just talking changed them and helped them realize that you can still get your point across without yelling or calling a person out of their name. It has a more positive outcome. You listen more. You begin to think differently about what to say and what not to say. Often times, things are easier to resolve. There is a better response and/or end result. You realize that how you **talk to people** truly does make a difference. You realize that how you **talk to people** represents how you love. Love always. Love daily. 365 Love.™

Have you told someone you loved them today? I have.™

Love yesterday, today and future tomorrows,™
Torion

Message in the MUSIC
India Aire - **Talk to Her**

Note the QUOTE!

"Fear less, hope more; Eat less, chew more; Wine less, breathe more; Talk less, say more; Love more, and all good things will be yours." --- Swedish Proverb

---

Love Always. Love Daily. 365 Love.

I Am Love
October 5

Today's NOTE
I am love. I have an inner spirit that glows and allows my light to shine. I am special and unique. I speak good things, think good thoughts, see good things, and hear good sounds. I look for positive ways to make a positive difference in my life and the life of others. I smile at the thought of love, loving me, loving you, and loving others. I act on my positive thoughts in positive ways. I always do my best and believe in a continuous learning process. **I am love**. I am growing, knowing that there is more love in me for me to give. I recharge so that I can do more and be more for a purpose. I am continuing the work to gain new spiritual highs. **I am love**. Love always. Love daily. 365 Love.™

Have you told someone you loved them today? I have.™

Love yesterday, today and future tomorrows,™
Torion

Message in the MUSIC
Jennifer Holiday – **I Am Love**

Note the QUOTE!
"Love is above all, the gift of oneself" --- Jean Anouilh

Love Always. Love Daily. 365 Love.

I Can Do Bad All By Myself
October 6

Today's NOTE
I can do bad all by myself. So, I don't need any negative energy around me. I don't need a "so called" friend who is full of envy or jealousy. I don't need a "nay sayer" always pouring negative thoughts in my head. I don't need a person around me bringing the "junk still in their trunk" to pull me down. I don't need anyone who is unhappy with themselves, trying to make me unhappy too. I don't need physical or mental abuse. I don't need someone trying to change me. I don't need discouragement.

As I have said before, **I can do bad all by myself.** What I need is love and those who love around me. I need positive energy. I need "true" friends who are encouraging and uplifting. I need positive friends who pour positive thoughts in my head. I need a person with a trunk of good things that contribute and lift me up. I need people who are happy with themselves that want me to be happy too. I need physical and mental respect. I need someone who will accept me for me. And changes in me will be because I see the need for a positive change in me. I need encouragement. I need love. Love always. Love daily. 365 Love.™

Have you told someone you loved them today? I have. ™

Love yesterday, today and future tomorrows, ™
Torion

Message in the MUSIC
Mary J. Blige - **I Can Do Bad All By Myself**

Note the QUOTE!
"Happiness is the spiritual experience of living every minute with love, grace, and gratitude." --- Denis Waitley

Another Day to Live My Life
October 7

Today's NOTE

On this day in 1968, I was born the fourth child of the Harden family. It was the first day of my journey to live, learn, grow and love. From the little girl who loved to dance in the clothes basket, twirl her baton in the middle of the yard, and roller skate 5 out of 7 days a week, to the college graduate, executive, mother of two, who has found love and continues to grow spiritually in love. Since my birth, I have been in and out of situations. I have experienced joy and pain. I have been a leader and a follower. I have met good people and bad people. I have had good times and bad times. I have loved and been loved in return. I have been happy and sad. I have been up and down. I have experienced life. And the life I experienced has led me to become who I am today.

I often times reflect on where I have been, what I have experienced in life, and how it has made me who I am today. But my birthday is typically a day of deeper reflection for me. I wake with a great level of thankfulness in my heart. For I have awakened to **another day to live my life**. And what a good life it is. I am excited to see the sun shine through the window. I am alive, healthy, and well. I have my sanity and am able to do and see things that so many others do not have the opportunity to. Another year has passed and I am still here. I have another opportunity to make a difference. I have another day to fulfill my purpose in life. I have another day to love. What a joy that brings to my heart. I look forward to what is in store for me today, tomorrow, through the remainder of this year and the next. I look forward to growing more in love and sharing love with others. I have love to give and love is always all around me. I do not take this or any other day for granted as I am grateful for and appreciate knowing that each day is **another day to live my life**. For today is the present, which is always a gift in itself and tomorrow is never promised. Love always. Love daily. 365 Love.™

Have you told someone you loved them today? I have.™

Love yesterday, today and future tomorrows,™
Torion

Message in the MUSIC
Earth, Wind & Fire – All About Love

Note the QUOTE!
"Love means to commit oneself without guarantee, to give oneself completely in the hope that our love will produce love in the loved person. Love is an act of faith, and whoever is of little faith is also of little love." --- Erich Fromm

I Am Changing
October 8

Today's NOTE

Sometimes change is good, especially when it is for the better. Take a look at your life from time to time and do a personal assessment. Does anything need to change to make you a better person? Do you need to change some behaviors to help you move forward? Do you need to evolve spiritually? You can keep doing the same thing over and over, or you can do something different. And with that difference comes change.

Successful businesses continue to find ways to reinvent themselves. They introduce new and improved services and/or products as times and people change. They come up with new ways to market their products. They research and study their market and customers to make sure they are doing the right things, the right way, and for the right reasons to evolve. As markets change and business issues are presented, they work to maintain, grow and remain profitable. They are always looking for ways to improve and become better and better. One year's success does not guarantee another. Continuous improvement is a must.

You can apply this same principle to your personal growth in love. Just because you have accomplished one milestone, does not guarantee you will not be presented with challenges that you will have to overcome. You have to continue to learn. You have to continue to grow. You have to continue to experience. And with every experience, you have to find the lessons learned and grow from them. You have to change for the better. You have to change for love. And that change is something good.

I know **I am changing**. **I am changing** daily as I continue my journey in love. That change is good. I can feel it. **I am changing** to become a better me in order to make a more positive difference to others. **I am changing** in the way I show, share and give love. **I am changing** in the way I study and embrace love. **I am changing** spiritually. I realize that I am still a work in progress and more work needs to be done, but what I also realize is that I am making the effort and I can see and feel the difference. **I am changing**. What about you? Love always. Love daily. 365 Love.™

Have you told someone you loved them today? I have. ™

Love yesterday, today and future tomorrows,™
Torion

Message in the MUSIC
Jennifer Holiday – **I Am Changing**

Note the QUOTE!
"Change is the essence of life. Be willing to surrender what you are for what you could become." --- Unknown

Don't You Worry 'Bout a Thing
October 9

Today's NOTE

Don't you worry 'bout a thing. It's going to be alright. While you have control of some things, God has the ultimate control of all things. It's up to you to do what you can with what you have. It's up to you to try your best. It's up to you to give it your all. And once you have done all you can do, leave the rest to Him. If it is meant to be, it is meant to be. If it is meant for you to have, it is meant for you to have. As long as you have done all that you can, you are going to be fine regardless of the outcome. Your desired outcome may or may not be within God's will, but the actual outcome will be the best one for you at this time and at this moment. The outcome may be a temporary setback to put you on a path to move forward. Or, it may just be a step forward. So, **don't you worry 'bout a thing**. It is taken care of. It's already done. Leave your stresses outside the door. Hold your head up high. Clear the sad tears from your eye and replace them with tears of joy. Rejoice and smile a grand smile. Get ready for what is in store for you. Look for the goodness in it and know that love is always with you and in you. Have strong faith and believe. Love always. Love daily. 365 Love.™

Have you told someone you loved them today? I have. ™

Love yesterday, today and future tomorrows, ™
Torion

Message in the MUSIC
Stevie Wonder - **Don't You Worry 'Bout a Thing**

Note the QUOTE!
"Trust in the Lord with all your heart; do not depend on your own understanding. Seek His will in all you do and He will show you which path to take." --- Proverbs 3:5-6

Love Always. Love Daily. 365 Love.

The Question Is...
October 10

Today's NOTE

With life comes **questions**. We question what is and what is not. We **question** who, what, why, where, when, and how. It's natural. That's how we learn. I want you to stop and think for a moment. Think of any **question** that could come to mind. Now respond to that question with the word, "love." Next, find a way to make that response a true statement. Depending on where you are on your journey to love, this may be easy to do or difficult to do. However, it is possible. I've tried it and it works every time. Here are few examples:

Who is going to love me? Love
God is love and He loves you always. When you learn to love God, you learn to love yourself. When you learn to love yourself, you learn to love others. When you love others, the right person comes into your life to love you in return.

What is going to happen to me next? Love
Whether it's today, tomorrow, next week, next month, next year or longer, you will live and experience life. And until you find love, you will continue to be presented with situations that attempt to draw you closer and closer. The more you fight it, the tougher things will get. When you finally release your heart to accept and know love, you will see things change for the positive.

Why did this happen to me? Love
God loves you and wants the best for you. He wants to bring about positive change in you. Sometimes things happen to you to position you for something greater. It builds your character. It builds on your faith. Sometimes things have to be taken away to humble you or to make you realize that a change is needed for the better whether it is within you or someone else.

Where am I going to get the money from? Love
If it is meant for you to get out of the financial situation, love will make a way. The money will come from the right place at the right time. Sometimes you may put yourself in financial situations that you are not meant to be pulled out of. Love maintains those situations to teach you a lesson in hopes that the previous experiences help you become a better steward of your money in the future. Sometimes whatever you need (or want) the money for is not meant for you to have. It was what was best for you because of love. Love allows you to not put yourself in a position which causes financial stress.

When will the pain go away? Love
You have to have strong faith, let go, and let God handle your situation. God's love takes the pain away. You may suffer physically or mentally, but with faith, the pain will go away. It's in His time. You have to believe.

How am I going to get out of this situation? Love

Love Always. Love Daily. 365 Love.

Sometimes you are put in situations to make you love more and build on your faith. Whether you remain in the situation or come out for the better, or what you feel is the worst, there is a purpose for it. You are meant to learn from it and cause positive change as a result of it. Love will change the situation for whatever it is meant to be. Love allows you to do the best you can with the situation.

Now, try it again. Think of any and every **question** you could ask. Think about the outcome as the glass being half full vs. half empty. Think about every response as a lesson learned resulting of your knowledge of love. Think positive thoughts about every situation. See the good result out of every **question**. It's there. That's how love works. It's always there. It's everywhere. It always has been. Love always. Love daily. 365 Love.™

Have you told someone you loved them today? I have.™

Love yesterday, today and future tomorrows,™
Torion

Message in the MUSIC
The Winans – **The Question Is**

Note the QUOTE!
"A loving heart is the beginning of all knowledge." --- Thomas Carlyle

---

Love Always. Love Daily. 365 Love.

Your Time
October 11

Today's NOTE
We are born to exist here on earth for a certain period of time. The specific time period is unknown. You have **your time** and I have mine. Some of us are meant to be here for a short period of time and others for a longer period. The reality is that we are born, we live and we die. What have you done with **your time**? What are you doing with **your time**? What will you do with **your time**?

Your life should be one of love. And what you do with **your time** should make a positive difference to one person or many. You should live to continually spread love to others so that it can keep going and going. In order to do that, you have to continue to work on loving yourself and demonstrating love to others. That love shows itself in the things you say and the things you do. You still have **your time**. It's right here, right now. Use it wisely. Use it to love. Love always. Love daily. 365 Love.™

Have you told someone you loved them today? I have.™

Love yesterday, today and future tomorrows,™
Torion

Message in the MUSIC
Eric Benet – Love, Patience and **Time**

Note the QUOTE!
"The **time** is always right to do what is right." --- Martin Luther King, Jr.

Love Always. Love Daily. 365 Love.

The Worst Brings the Best
October 12

Today's NOTE
The news media is filled with stories of bad events such as car accidents, murders, fires, natural disasters, wars and other misfortune. No one with a conscious likes to see or hear about bad things happening to other people. And no one personally wants to experience anything bad. But for every bad event, there is something good that can and does come from it. That good is a strong demonstration of love in the form of people coming together to help those in need and positive change. After a natural disaster, people volunteer their time and money to save lives and rebuild communities. In times of death, people come together to pray for the families and friends of those who lost their loved ones. In personal relationships, those we did not know or realize cared, show their love and support. People change their lives realizing that they lived through a situation that could have potentially ended their life. They grow in faith and change for the better. They begin to realize the value of love and life. And the list goes on and on. You see, **the worst brings the best**. You have to be able to look at the situation as the glass being half full vs. half empty. Everything happens for a reason. For every bad situation, you can find something good that came out of it. You can learn from it. When you love, it makes the lesson learned easier and easier to see. We are all meant to learn from life, whether it's through our own personal experience or the experiences of others. And life is meant to help us learn. It is meant to humble us. It is meant to drive us to love. And the best is yet to come. Love always. Love daily. 365 Love. ™

Have you told someone you loved them today? I have. ™

Love yesterday, today and future tomorrows, ™
Torion

Message in the MUSIC
Vashawn Mitchell – His Blood Still Works

Note the QUOTE!
"Love is the beginning, the middle, and the end of everything." --- Jean B. H. Lacordaire

Another Blessing
October 13

Today's NOTE

God is good. Just when you think things could get no worse, He steps in and proves once again how much He loves. What an amazing God He is. Even when things are going well and looking up, God steps in and makes everything even better. Each and every moment of each and every day, He provides yet **another blessing**. There is so much to be grateful for. Every part of my body that is functional and other parts He is working to heal is **another blessing**. Everything I have, don't have and am yet to receive is **another blessing**. Everyone He allows the opportunity to cross my path for a reason, season and/or a lifetime is **another blessing**. All that I endure to help me grow in love is **another blessing**.

Strong faith proves itself again and again that God's love is the ultimate love. This past month has provided great testimony to this.

- A close friend lost both of her jobs. Just when things were beginning to get rough, God gave her **another blessing** by providing the funds needed to pursue her own business and an opportunity to move that much closer to fulfilling her dreams.

- My 95 year old grandmother was given one week to 2 months to live. She has made it through the first two weeks in good spirits with a constant smile on her face, laughter in her heart, continual gratefulness and a family full of love. God has provided her and our family with **another blessing**.

- Family emergency situations presented tight financial binds. God provided **another blessing** by eliminating the financial bind just when it was needed most.

Isn't God good! I am always excited to see what His love has in store for me and others as He provides yet **another blessing** again, and again, and again. Love always. Love daily. 365 Love.™

Have you told someone you loved them today? I have. ™

Love yesterday, today and future tomorrows, ™
Torion

Message in the MUSIC
Williams Brothers – **Another Blessing**

Note the QUOTE!
"Because we love, God is present." --- Thomas Merton

Exercise Your Heart
October 14

Today's NOTE
Exercise is an important part of remaining healthy. It can be accomplished by walking, jogging, running, playing sports, dancing, bicycling or a number of other active activities. Some of us are good at exercising on a regular basis to maintain our health. Some have accepted a challenge to exercise in an effort to become healthier. Others are still trying to get started. Out of all the body parts and conditions you work to improve through exercise, you should also include a concentrated effort to **exercise your heart**. **Exercise your heart** not just from a physical perspective, but from a love perspective. Just as you would dedicate time and energy to exercising for your personal health, you should dedicate time and energy to **exercise your heart** for love. Love in an effort to continually love. Love to become more loving. Practice strong faith. Believe. Love yourself and others. Be charitable and give of your time and talents. Do the right things and treat people right. Share with others in an effort to help them grow in love. Be the best that you can be with your abilities and practice love in all that you say and do. Act on love frequently to continually **exercise your heart**. A healthy heart leads to a healthy life. A heart filled with love, leads to a loving life. Love always. Love daily. 365 Love.™

Have you told someone you loved them today? I have.™

Love yesterday, today and future tomorrows,™
Torion

Message in the MUSIC
Debra Killings – Do Right

Note the QUOTE!
"The best **exercise of the heart** is reaching down and lifting someone else up."
--- Tim Russert

Total Praise
October 15

Today's NOTE
Sometimes you need to take out a little time to give praise. Not just some praise or a little bit of praise, but **total praise**. Give **total praise** for the many blessings bestowed upon you. Give **total praise** for God's love, for His love is merciful. Give **total praise** for your life and your love. Give **total praise** for love yesterday, today and future tomorrows. Rejoice and be happy about all that is. Give the complete package. Give it your all. Love always. Love daily. 365 Love.™

Have you told someone you loved them today? I have.™

Love yesterday, today and future tomorrows,™
Torion

Message in the MUSIC
Fantasia – **Total Praise**

Note the QUOTE!
"Give thanks to the Lord, for He is good! His faithful love endures forever." --- Psalm 106:1

Love Always. Love Daily. 365 Love.

Hold My Hand
October 16

Today's NOTE

If you have lived, there has been at least one or more times in your life when you just wanted someone to be there for you. You wanted to feel that you had support for what you were trying to do or accomplish at that particular moment in your life. You wanted to feel loved by someone; by a person. You wanted someone to give you that extra encouragement to push you forward. You needed additional inspiration or confirmation. You needed a helping hand. You needed a friend to lift you up. You needed a reminder that your personal love for yourself can help you do it. You may even need that right now at this particular moment. Or, you may need it tomorrow, the day after that, or sometime in the near future.

Well, wherever you are at this moment or in a future point in time, I would like to let you know that I am here for you. You can **hold my hand**. And while I may not be there with you physically, know that I am reaching out to you. My hand is extended. And as I grab yours, I hold it gently and squeeze it just enough for you to feel the love that I have for you. **Hold my hand** and know that you can do anything you put your heart into. You are love and you are loved. And with the power of love that is in you, you can accomplish great things. I support you. I encourage you. I lift you up to see all that is meant for you. You can do it. I know you can. And when you begin to have doubts, you can reach out and **hold my hand**. When you fall down, you can reach up and **hold my hand**. I will help pull you up again and again. For I love and have faith that when you are unable to encourage yourself, God will use me to support you. That is what He does. That is one of the ways in which He loves. He will give me what I need to give you what you need when you **hold my hand**. That's love. Love always. Love daily. 365 Love.™

Have you told someone you loved them today? I have.™

Love yesterday, today and future tomorrows,™
Torion

Message in the MUSIC
Michael Jackson - **Hold My Hand**

Note the QUOTE!
"Love should run out and meet love with open arms." --- Robert Lewis Stevenson

---

Love Always. Love Daily. 365 Love.

Enough
October 17

Today's NOTE

Whatever you have right now, at this point in time in your life, is **enough**. It's just **enough**, just for you. It's **enough** to help you get by. It's **enough** to force you to make a choice to do what's right, to do something different, or to do something a different way. It's **enough** to make a difference. You may not realize it, but it is. You may be doing well or at a low point in your life, but you have **enough**. You have a little or a lot because of who you are and what we are destined to be. You have **enough** to push you forward. You have **enough** to make you humble and appreciative. You have **enough** to cause a positive change in you. You have **enough** to push you closer and closer to love. When you realize that what you have is **enough** for you, you will make choices, plan, act, progress and see positive change. That change will be driven by a renewed faith in love. Love always. Love daily. 365 Love.™

Have you told someone you loved them today? I have.™

Love yesterday, today and future tomorrows,™
Torion

Message in the MUSIC
Tonex – Real With You

Note the QUOTE!
"If you have love in your life, it can make up for a great many things that are missing. If you don't have love in your life, no matter what else there is, it is not **enough**." --- Ann Landers

Who Says
October 18

Today's NOTE
Never, ever allow anyone tell you that you cannot accomplish your goals. Never, ever allow anyone to define who you are. You are uniquely you. You were created for a greater purpose. **Who says** someone else has the right to make you believe you are less than who you are. You have value beyond any "nay-sayer's" imagination. Have confidence in yourself and always believe. Love always. Love daily. 365 Love.™

Have you told someone you loved them today? I have.™

Love yesterday, today and future tomorrows,™
Torion

Message in the MUSIC
Elena Gomez - **Who Says**

Note the QUOTE!
"One must learn to love... and the journey is always toward the other soul." --- D. H. Lawrence

---

Love Always. Love Daily. 365 Love.

Remove the Barriers
October 19

Today's NOTE

Love is waiting for you. But before you can truly receive it, you must **remove the barriers** you have put up against it. Remove the concrete walls, bridges and doors you have built over time. Forgive those who have hurt your heart and turned you against it. Throw away the pride and ego that are additional road blocks. Recognize and eliminate the shield covering your eyes so that you can see its existence or non-existence in those who are a part of your inner circle. Kick the lazy spirit to the side and stop waiting for something to happen so that you can do something to make things happen. Get rid of those bad habits that hold you back, prevent your progression, and cause you to lose out in life. Let go of your personal guilt for something you did or didn't do in the past. Regain your faith in knowing that love is here for you and will never leave you alone.

Once you **remove the barriers**, clear your eyes, open them wide, look ahead of you, move forward and greet love. Smile at it. Say, "hello" and have a personal conversation with it. Get to know it better. See the beauty in it. Notice how it makes you better. Recognize the knowledge you can gain from it. Learn from it. See how it motivates and inspires. Watch it create happiness. Feel its healing power. Want it. Desire it. Receive it. Share it and watch it grow. Love always. Love daily. 365 Love.™

Have you told someone you loved them today? I have.™

Love yesterday, today and future tomorrows,™
Torion

Message in the MUSIC
LeToya – Not Anymore

Note the QUOTE!
"Your task is not to seek love, but merely to seek and find all **the barriers** within yourself that you have built against love." ---- Rumi

It's Not in Vain
October 20

Today's NOTE
Past and present events that have taken place in your life were **not in vain**. No matter how good or bad it has been, or may seem to be, it all has a purpose. And everything from this point on has a purpose. The key is for you to eventually get it. You may not be able to at this time. It may come now or later. But until you get it, never give up. Always reach for something better. For every fall, pick yourself back up. Try a new direction. Change something. Keep going. Keep growing. The only way to move forward is to actually move. Love is the driving force for making it all worthwhile. You will be surprised at what you can do once you begin to move in a direction that is closer to love. And when you become one with love, you will realize what has been, and what used to be, was **not in vain**. Love always. Love daily. 365 Love.™

Have you told someone you loved them today? I have.™

Love yesterday, today and future tomorrows,™
Torion

Message in the MUSIC
Xscape – Is My Living **in Vain**

Note the QUOTE!
"One word frees us from all the weight and pain of life; that word is love." --- Sophocles

Inside of You
October 21

Today's NOTE

You've been searching for love for a long time. You've searched all over the place. You searched for it in the night club, the church, the work place, the gym, the grocery store, your home, and other cities, states, and/or countries. There were times when you felt you found it, but were disappointed when the truth eventually revealed itself. There were times when you felt you would never get to experience it. There were times when you would continually ask yourself various forms of the 5W questions again and again.

- Who is going to love me?
- What is love?
- Why can't I find love?
- Where is love?
- When will love find me?

Well you can stop searching. Love is **inside of you**. It's been with you all of the time. You had it with you and you didn't even know it. You have been preventing it from revealing itself to you. You have been hiding it and did not even realize it. You have been blocking it because of your limited knowledge of its power and capabilities to change yourself, people and things for the good. You have yet to discover it's true capabilities. The love **inside of you** has to grow first. It has to learn about itself. It has to understand itself. It has to shape you and make you a better person. It has to fill your heart with self acceptance. It has to evolve you to a more giving, caring and forgiving person. It has to rejuvenate your spiritual faith. And when the love **inside of you** is ready for you, it is ready for anyone and anything. The love you seek from other people, places and things will not be of a concern to you. For it is then you will see that love is truly with you everywhere. And all of the answers to your questions will reveal themselves in time. Love always. Love daily. 365 Love.™

Have you told someone you loved them today? I have.™

Love yesterday, today and future tomorrows,™
Torion

Message in the MUSIC
Mary J. Blige – Deep **Inside**

Note the QUOTE!
"True love doesn't come to you, it has to be **inside you**." - Julia Roberts

Love Always. Love Daily. 365 Love.

Road to Perfection
October 22

Today's NOTE
You are on the **road to perfection**. Your life is meant to make you new and improved on the inside and out. It's journey is one of love. Your **road to perfection** has bumps and traffic jams. It has construction workers coming out from time to time to make road repairs. It has red lights to make you stop, yellow lights to slow you down, and green lights that allow you to keep going. It has traffic cops to pull you over when you break the law. Depending on the severity, you get a warning, you pay a fine, or you spend a small amount of time in jail. But your **road to perfection** is working to perfect you. You may have a small fender bender that allows you to dust yourself off and keep going. There may be a major wreck that causes you to stop for a moment in order to have the collision repairs completed. You may have to do a trade-in for something more dependable, reliable, and/or new and improved in order to move forward in your journey. Then there are times when you have the road to yourself. It is smooth sailing and there are no issues. You go through highways, streets and country roads with a breeze. Your **road to perfection** is yours. You learn and you grow in love. Drive safely. Love always. Love daily. 365 Love.™

Have you told someone you loved them today? I have.™

Love yesterday, today and future tomorrows,™
Torion

Message in the MUSIC
Mary J. Blige – We Ride

Note the QUOTE!
"The best thing about loving and being hurt is that you get to know what true love really is. For as gold is tested in fire, and so will love be perfected in pain." --- Marvin Torres

Gospel Music
October 23

Today's NOTE
I love me some good **gospel music**. There's something about waking up in the morning and turning on the inspirational sounds of those who give the highest praise. I also look forward to hearing the praise team, deacon board and choirs sing at church every Sunday. And then to hear the vibrant sounds of gospel choirs at concerts and other social events is an added bonus. The one thing about **gospel music** that is different than all other music is that when the lead singer can really sing, you are touched and moved by the spirit. And when the lead singer can't sing, it doesn't even matter, because the message is usually so powerful that you find the spirit in the overall effort. **Gospel music** is the one type of music that is guaranteed to inspire and uplift regardless of who wrote the lyrics, who is singing the song, who is listening and how it is being delivered. No matter what situation you have been through or are currently going through, **gospel music** has a way of touching you. It knows just the right song, just for you. There is always a message in the music that reaches your inner spirit. You see tears of joy fall down the faces of listeners because of how much they can relate. You hear shouts of joy and thankfulness as the message resonates with personal experiences. You see dances of praise when the spirit flows through the bodies of those who are touched by its power. That's because **gospel music** is filled with faith and love. And the power of love always has a way of touching the depth of the soul. That's love and **gospel music**. Love always. Love daily. 365 Love.™

Have you told someone you loved them today? I have.™

Love yesterday, today and future tomorrows,™
Torion

Message in the MUSIC
Debra Killings – **Message in the Music**

Note the QUOTE!
"Music takes us out of the actual and whispers to us dim secrets that startle our wonder as to who we are, and for what, whence and where to." --- Ralph Waldo Emerson

19 with 14
October 24

Today's NOTE

I was listening to a radio talk show and heard about a woman who wrote in asking for advice on how to handle 14 grandchildren. After listening further, it was revealed that her son is **19 with 14** children by different women, all born within a 2 year period. Paternity tests confirmed that all 14 children were his. The explanation the son gave his mother was that it was his goal to conquer women. Little does he realize that his decision has had an impact on the lives of many. His lack of knowledge of what love is and how to love has impacted his life, his mother's life, his children's lives, their mother's lives, and the lives of so many others. I'm sure you can think of a number of other issues and concerns with this situation. I can think of several myself. However, that is not my purpose for writing about this.

Today, I would like to ask you to pray for this boy and so many other boys and girls who are lost and have yet to find love. Pray big. Pray to break a cycle of children bringing more children into the world at a time when they are still growing themselves. Pray for the lives they touch and those they have an influence over. Pray that they discover the love inside of them and the power it has to make positive change. Pray that they are watched over and cared for in a way that uplifts and allows them to grow spiritually. Pray for positive pulls forward at times when they may feel pushed back. Pray for awareness. Pray for hope. Pray for a desire for self improvement. Pray for all that is love. Even though you may not know them, your prayers will definitely be heard and will help someone, somewhere, in some way. Love always. Love daily. 365 Love.™

Have you told someone you loved them today? I have.™

Love yesterday, today and future tomorrows,™
Torion

Message in the MUSIC
Mariah Carey – I Want to Know Where Love Is

Note the QUOTE!
"To love another you have to undertake some fragment of their destiny." --- Quentin Crisp

Your Thoughts (Revisited)
October 25

The life you live and the joy it brings to you depends on your way of thinking. It's based on **your thoughts**. It's what you decide to keep on your mind. When you think positive thoughts, you look at life optimistically. When you think negative thoughts, you look at life pessimistically. The glass is either half full (positive) or half empty (negative). **Your thoughts** allow you to accept life experiences as lessons learned for future growth (positive) or fear, burden, shame, and/or worry (negative). **Your thoughts** make you feel good or bad. **Your thoughts** help you move forward of hold you back. You control **your thoughts**. You choose what you place in **your thoughts**. They are yours and yours alone.

When you take the time to think about positive things, good experiences, things you like and happy times, you are the one who actually forms those specific thoughts in your mind. Positive thoughts always make you feel good. You make yourself feel the way you feel based on **your thoughts**. And **your thoughts** can make you feel good all of the time. **Your thoughts** can control your outlook on life. **Your thoughts** can make you happy each and every day. They are **your thoughts**. And when you learn to love, it becomes that much easier to do because love promotes positivity. Love brings on a natural ability to see the world from a different perspective. Love brings a more positive perspective. Love brings a happier perspective.

I keep love in my thoughts. It's always there. It bleeds positivity in how I view each day. Try it daily and watch what a difference it makes. Love always. Love daily. 365 Love.™

Have you told someone you loved them today? I have.™

Love yesterday, today and future tomorrows,™
Torion

Message in the MUSIC
Mary J. Blige – Can't Get You Off My Mind

Note the QUOTE!
"What we think, we become." --- Budda

Forever Young
October 26

Today's NOTE
Children are a joy. When they are little, they don't have a worry in the world. They don't think about it and don't realize it, but as they grow older, they begin to want to grow up faster. When they actually get older, they long for the days when they were young again. The older they get, comes an emphasis on things to make them look and feel younger. This ranges anywhere from surgeries, diets, and fitness, to clothing, cosmetics and other material items. Some are superficial and some are beneficial. Out of all the things one can try, I happen to know the ultimate secret to staying **forever young**. And I am willing to share it with you. It's easy to obtain. It includes patience and kindness. It involves giving and sharing. It doesn't cost a thing, just your willingness to open your heart and mind to receive it. Once you receive it, learn about it, and get to know it, you will see and feel the difference. It's power is impactful. Are you ready? Here it is....the secret is <u>love</u>. That's right, love. Try it. Make it a part of your daily routine and notice how youthful you become on the inside and out. For it is love that keeps you **forever young**. Love always. Love daily. 365 Love.™

Have you told someone you loved them today? I have.™

Love yesterday, today and future tomorrows,™
Torion

Message in the MUSIC
Josh Krajcik (from The X-Factor) - **Forever Young**
(Original Song by Rod Stewart)

Note the QUOTE!
"The heart that loves is always young." --- Greek Proverb

Forever, For Always, For Love
October 27

Today's NOTE
God is good. And all that He does for us is **forever, for always, for love**. Love is His greatest gift to us. It is also the greatest gift we can give to ourselves and others. He wants us to love ourselves and others as He loves us. He is forgiving and wants us to love with forgiving hearts. He wants us to love more. He wants our love to shine a bright light, a magnificent glow. He wants our love to resonate with smiles, happy thoughts and happy moments. In all that we say and all that we do, it should be done **forever, for always, for love**. Love always. Love daily. 365 Love.™

Have you told someone you loved them today? I have.™

Love yesterday, today and future tomorrows,™
Torion

Message in the MUSIC
Luther Vandross -- **Forever, For Always, For Love**

Note the QUOTE!
"If you would be loved, love and be loveable." --- Benjamin Franklin

---

Love Always. Love Daily. 365 Love.

Just Do It
October 28

Today's NOTE

I had a conversation with one of my staff members about the spiritual goals we have for the future. He is close to retirement and wants to do missionary work on a regular basis. He and his wife travel to other countries every year to do it now and have developed lesson plans to use as part of their ministry work. It is wonderful to hear about the work he does for others and his plans to spread love. His greatest fear is that he is not good enough or not qualified. He speaks in the presence of ministers that have more experience than he does and he is sometimes intimidated by what they have accomplished vs. where he is. He asked his spiritual mentor for advice on next steps and the response was, "**Just do it.**"

My point exactly. If you have already gotten started, why not **just do it**? If it is meant for you, it is meant for you. Your qualifications are given to you by God. And when He wants to use you as a vessel to deliver a message and make a difference, your experience does not matter. Love will guide you every step of the way. Everyone has to start somewhere. Some of the greatest ministers had to experience their first sermon and go out to do missionary work for the first time. In order to accomplish anything you must take the first step. You can't get anywhere if you don't take some type of action. And when you are reaching for a specific goal, you have to start by doing. And so, I say to you, "**Just do it!**" Take that leap of faith and **just do it**. For whatever it is you want to accomplish, change or become, believe that you can and **just do it**. You cannot learn if you don't try. You will not succeed if you don't begin. For every action, there is a reaction. And to get a reaction you have to **just do it**. To be all that you can be you have to **just do it**. To grow in love you have to **just do it**. To share love with others you have to **just do it**. Love always. Love daily. 365 Love.™

Have you told someone you loved them today? I have.™

Love yesterday, today and future tomorrows,™
Torion

Message in the MUSIC
Lamar Campbell - Use Me

Note the QUOTE!
"Love accomplishes all things." --- Petrarch

Remember
October 29

Today's NOTE

We live in a world that allows us the opportunity to get things fast and quick. There are fast food restaurants, ready-made microwaveable meals, the Internet, cable with on demand, automated teller machines, check cards, e-mail, instant messaging, text messaging, and a number of other things to allow us to get what we want fast and quick. Sometimes we get so used to getting things fast and quick, that we forget where we came from and what it took to get to where we are. We lose sight of the evolution process, become impatient and have the expectation that everything is supposed to come fast and quick. We want it now, at this moment, at this instant. One extra minute is not good enough. Even when it comes to love, we want it now, in a hurry, fast and quick.

What we have to **remember** is that some of the most precious and valuable things in life take time and come in time. When you speed up the process, it is not the same. It lacks what is needed to make it whole, complete or valuable. It is of poor quality and/or is not fully developed. It may even require extra work or care. **Remember** that wine is at its best with time. **Remember** how a caterpillar transforms into a butterfly with time. **Remember** that people become great leaders in time. **Remember** that a baby is born from a mother's womb with time. Most importantly, **remember** that love is patient. Patience involves time. As the world around you continues to move fast and quick, always **remember** that the best things in life sometimes take time. Love takes time. Love involves quality time. Love is a learning process that takes place over time. Love gives to others with time and in time. Love cannot be rushed by time. And as you take the time to **remember** love, think of all that it is and all that it does. Think of the greatness it possess and the greatness in you as a result of it. Don't get stuck into getting things so fast and quick that you forget to **remember** how good love is with patience and time. Love always. Love daily. 365 Love.™

Have you told someone you loved them today? I have.™

Love yesterday, today and future tomorrows,™
Torion

Message in the MUSIC
Jill Scott – Do You **Remember**

Note the QUOTE!
"Always **remember** to slow down in life; live, breathe and learn; take a look around you whenever you have time and never forget everything and every person that has the least place within your heart." --- Unknown

Wake Up!
October 30

Today's NOTE

Wake up! Wake up! You are asleep and you don't even realize it. You are in a dream that has a hold on you. It is preventing you from moving forward because you won't **wake up!** And while you are sleeping, you are missing out on all that love is. Open your eyes and see what it has to offer. **Wake up** out of the dream you created so that you can see how magnificent you are. **Wake up** so that you can finally let go of anger, ego, pride, worry, depression, shame, jealousy, judgment and/or any other negative energy keeping you from love. **Wake up** so that you can feel love's positive energy flow through you and all around you. Be encouraged, inspired, motivated, happy, joyful, wonderful, giving, caring, and sharing. **Wake up** and know that with love, you can let go, move forward and move on. See how much you have been missing. Experience the power love has and all the daily blessings it has for you. If need be, take a big stretch, yawn, and wipe your eyes a few times. Just **wake up!** While you are sleeping, anything is possible. But when you awaken in a place of love, everything is possible. **Wake up! Wake up!** Love always. Love daily. 365 Love.™

Have you told someone you loved them today? I have.™

Love yesterday, today and future tomorrows,™
Torion

Message in the MUSIC
Jill Scott - When I **Wake Up**

Note the QUOTE!
"If you want to make your dreams come true, the first thing you have to do is **wake up**." --- J.M Power

---

Everlasting
October 31

Today's NOTE
Not many things last a lifetime. People and things grow older and eventually lose some of their abilities or functionality. Some things become outdated and obsolete. Some things break. Some things lose their color or become worn out. Others things are thrown away or uncared for because they no longer matter or have meaning to a person. People grow old and eventually pass on.

One thing that is guaranteed to last for a lifetime is love. Love is **everlasting**. It never fades and it never goes away. It may be hidden, shut out, refused, denied, or yet to be discovered, but love is there always and forever. The material items you possess mean nothing when you leave this earth. They are thrown away or shared among a select few individuals. One thing that remains **everlasting** in the heart of all those you've touched is love. With love, you provide a foundation for more love. It's contagious, so it spreads and keeps spreading. That foundation is the catalyst for helping love to grow. It is a piece of you that attaches itself to someone and helps them grow in love. It may remain dormant for a short or extended period of time, or it may spread immediately. But in time, it will eventually become active and release itself. It's there because of you. Because you loved and shared love with others. The love you shared is and will always be **everlasting**. Love always. Love daily. 365 Love. ™

Have you told someone you loved them today? I have. ™

Love yesterday, today and future tomorrows, ™
Torion

Message in the MUSIC
Natalie Cole – This Will Be (An **Everlasting** Love)

Note the QUOTE!
"True love is hard to find but when found, it's **everlasting**." --- Unknown

---

Love Always. Love Daily. 365 Love.

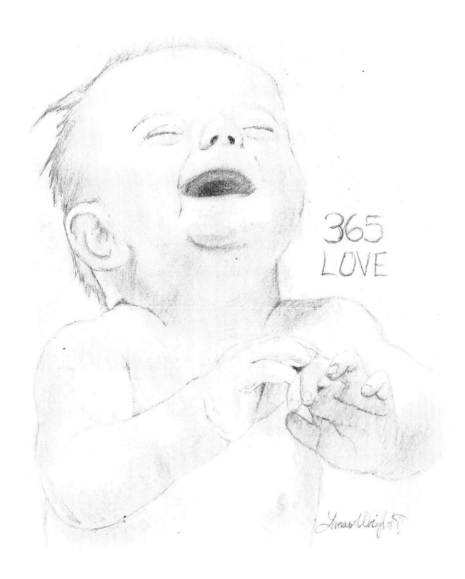

Love Always. Love Daily. 365 Love.

November

*"Joy is not in things.
It is in us."*
— *Richard Wagner*

911
November 1

Today's NOTE
911! Help! Please, help! This is an emergency! **911**! Send the paramedics, the fire department and the police. Make use of the surrounding neighbors who are witnesses to this emergency situation. Call family and friends who are dear and near. **911**!

Bring the paramedics in to stabilize the situation. Let them read the vital signs to determine what needs to be done to get the blood pressure back to normal and the heart beating again. Get the fire department to put out the fire and find the source of the problem to prevent another outbreak. Give them room to rescue anyone still trapped inside the danger zone. Allow the police to direct the crowd so that no one else gets hurt. Use them to control the distractions that may interfere with the other servicemen's ability to do their work. Ask the neighbors to watch out for one another to make sure it does not spread. Take care of those that are burned out until they are able to obtain the support needed to move forward. Let family and friends provide additional comfort by being there. Share in the responsibility of providing what is needed until they are able to rebuild and stand on their own. Everyone's support is needed. This cannot be done without you. **911**! This is a real emergency. I need you, s/he needs you, we need you, they need you because there is a need to rescue love. And with everyone's support, strong faith and prayers, no matter how small or how large, love will survive. Love always. Love daily. 365 Love.™

Have you told someone you loved them today? I have.™

Love yesterday, today and future tomorrows,™
Torion

Message in the MUSIC
Kirk Franklin - **911**

Note the QUOTE!
"Love and compassion are necessities, not luxuries. Without them, humanity cannot survive." --- Tenzin Gyatso

LOL
November 2

Today's NOTE
LOL (Laugh Out Loud)! **LOL** because sometimes that's just what you need to do or have to do. **LOL**! Love does not always have to be so serious. You can have fun with it too. Laughter is infectious, just like love, because it is filled with love. And love allows you to **LOL**. Love and **LOL**....

- Seeing a good comedy show
- Hearing the laughter of a child
- Seeing your grandmother laugh
- Watching yourself dance and sing in the mirror when you know you are not good with either
- Enjoying the company of a friend
- Telling childhood stories that your mom never knew about until now
- Thinking about things you did as a child and not understanding why you did them in the first place
- Watching children learn how to do things on their own
- Being tickled
- Hearing children say something you said when you least expected it or did not think they heard you say in the first place
- Because someone else is laughing too
- Just because you want to

Laughter is good for the soul. Even when you have to **LOL** at yourself. It is a strong medicine for the mind and body. It relaxes, boosts, releases, and protects. It makes your heart feel happy on the inside and out. It takes the pain away. It heals. And most importantly, it loves. And that's a good kind of love. So go ahead and **LOL**. Share your laughter with someone else so that they can **LOL** too. Love always. Love daily. 365 Love. ™

Have you told someone you loved them today? I have. ™

Love yesterday, today and future tomorrows, ™
Torion

Message in the MUSIC
Brandy – Happy

Note the QUOTE!
"Laughter is the way to true love." --- Unknown

Love Always. Love Daily. 365 Love.

Messages of Love
November 3

Today's NOTE

Love works in mysterious ways. It is sometimes presented to us when we least expect it and most often at times when we need it most. It comes to us directly, or in the form of messages from different people and different things. Once it catches us, it spreads and becomes contagious.

- One of my family members had a really bad evening and was feeling a little blue about a series of events that took place. I listened to the hurt in her voice as she explained these and the related events from the past weighing on her heart. While I provided words of encouragement at the time, shortly after our discussion, I decided to send a **message of love** wishing her a day filled with joy, reminding her that she was loved and appreciated. It indeed brightened her day.

- When I arrived to work, I received **messages of love** from my staff members in the form of greeting cards with words of encouragement for some personal things going on in my life. I in turn visited each of them one-by-one to return the **message of love** with a personal "thank you" and hug of appreciation.

- I volunteered to be in the church Christmas play for the first time ever. As soon as I walked in the room for rehearsal, I was assigned the role of Mary. The director had never seen me act, she had not heard me read the script, nor did she know me personally. She had only observed me in church. I've never even been in a play before. When I asked why she felt I should play this role, she replied that she prayed for God to send her a "Mary" the day I volunteered to be in the play. So, when I told her I was joining the drama ministry, she knew it was me. She received her **message of love**.

- For this particular play, Mary is one of the main characters and has several lines. After reading the script, the choice of words Mary has to say are aligned with personal thoughts I have expressed in previous 365 Love messages. Again, another **message of love** intended to contribute to my continuous journey of growth in love.

Messages of love are all around you. They sometimes go unnoticed, but they are there. And when you least expect it, they come to your awareness. As you grow in love, you begin to notice them more and appreciate their value to yourself and to others. Your love spreads and you become a catalyst by proactively sharing **messages of love** with others. Love always. Love daily. 365 Love.™

Have you told someone you loved them today? I have.™

Love Always. Love Daily. 365 Love.

Love yesterday, today and future tomorrows, ™
Torion

Message in the MUSIC
Trin-I-Tee 5:7 – Love

Note the QUOTE!
"Love is the best friend of humankind, the helper and the healer of all ills that stand in the way of human happiness." --- Plato

Best of Joy
November 4

Today's NOTE
The **best of joy** is in a place close and dear to you. That place is so close that you can hear it, see it and touch it when you actually realize where it is. The **best of joy** is inside of you. God gave it to you. Listen to it. Watch what it can do. Feel its power. It's the gift of love that so often goes unrealized. People look for the **best of joy** in others and in material things. However, the **best of joy** comes from within. It has always been around. It was there then. It is here now. And it will be here forever more. Look inside of you. Know that the **best of joy** comes from what God has given you. Stop looking for it in other places. No one or nothing can give it to you. Stop carrying the weight of the world on your shoulders, looking for something or someone to remove it. You have the power within you. You have love within you. And love is all you need to have the **best of joy**. Have strong faith and believe. Love always. Love daily. 365 Love.™

Have you told someone you loved them today? I have.™

Love yesterday, today and future tomorrows,™
Torion

Message in the MUSIC
Michael Jackson - **Best of Joy**

Note the QUOTE!
"**Joy** is not in things, it is in us." --- Richard Wagner

A Friendly Reminder
November 5

Today's NOTE
This is just a **friendly reminder** to let you know that you are loved. You know this, but sometimes you just need to hear it to be reassured. You have grown in love and know that love is within you. You know that God loves you and that you have the power to control your happiness, but sometimes you just need a **friendly reminder**. Sometimes you just need to hear it from someone else. Just when life starts to pull you backwards, you need a **friendly reminder** to bring you forward. Mission accomplished. Love always. Love daily. 365 Love.™

Have you told someone you loved them today? I have.™

Love yesterday, today and future tomorrows,™
Torion

Message in the MUSIC
Brian McKnight – I Remember You

Note the QUOTE!
"Love remembers everything." --- Ovid

Plans for You
November 6

Today's NOTE
There are **plans for you**. These plans existed before you were even born. You have purpose and meaning. You are meant to love. No matter how long it takes, and no matter what it takes to get you there, you are meant to love. These **plans for you** include trials and tribulations. They include ups and downs. They include joy and happiness. Everything is a part of the **plans for you**. Everything is meant to help you grow in love. When you try to change the **plans for you** into something you think it should be, you are derailed and put back on track again. When you try to ignore the **plans for you**, they continue to draw you near to them. God wants you to love. No ifs, ands or buts about it. Love is in His **plans for you**. Go ahead and actively participate. Love always. Love daily. 365 Love.™

Have you told someone you loved them today? I have.™

Love yesterday, today and future tomorrows,™
Torion

Message in the MUSIC
Deitrick Haddon – Trusting God

Note the QUOTE!
"For I know the **plans** I have **for you**." --- Jeremiah 29:11

Love Always. Love Daily. 365 Love.

Who I Was, Who I Am and Who I Am Yet to Be
November 7

Today's NOTE

Who I was is history. I was **who I was** at that time in my life. The past is behind me and must not hold me hostage from progress. I have to leave it where it is, in the past. It was one of the many learning phases of my life. **Who I am** is different than **who I was**. You may see me now and not even know me. I have grown in love and there is a difference in the light that shines from me. People may judge me for **who I was** or **who I am**, but I am only accountable to love. And love is the only one that knows and sees the real me, the progress I have made, and the direction I am headed in to become that much better. I am and always have been able to make choices that can change **who I am**. Those choices will determine **who I am yet to be**. I experience more of life each day. And it is those life experiences that teach me more about love. They guide me on the journey to become **who I am yet to be**. **Who I am** will become **who I was** as I move forward to **who I am yet to be**. And as I grow to become **who I am yet to be**, love will always be there to guide me. Love always. Love daily. 365 Love.™

Have you told someone you loved them today? I have.™

Love yesterday, today and future tomorrows,™
Torion

Message in the MUSIC
Rhema Marvanne - Just As **I Am**

Note the QUOTE!
"A person can be so changed by love as to be unrecognizable as the same person."
--- Terrence

Love Always. Love Daily. 365 Love.

Stay Covered
November 8

Today's NOTE
Just when things are looking good, feeling good, and seem to be at their best.... here they comes. Here come issues. Here come problems. Here come...... It makes you feel like once you finally get yourself out of the storm, you're getting ready to go through yet another one. It is during these times when it is important for you to **stay covered**. **Stay covered** in your faith and belief in love. When you love, you know that God will take care of things for you. When you love, nothing is as bad as it seems. Love is a strong, sturdy shelter, protecting you from harm. Love propels itself around you to prevent damage. Love blocks out those things that are not good to you and for you. Love covers you completely. Keep love close and know that it helps you **stay covered**. Love always. Love daily. 365 Love.™

Have you told someone you loved them today? I have.™

Love yesterday, today and future tomorrows,™
Torion

Message in the MUSIC
Ramiyah – **Covered**

Note the QUOTE!
"There is no fear in love. But perfect love drives out fear." --- I John 4:18

Your Walk
November 9

Today's NOTE
It's easy to talk. You can tell people all the great things you want them to know about you, your life, your accomplishments, and your possessions. You can tell them anything to make them "think" you have a certain character, or are a certain type of person. But the truth is not in your talk, it's in **your walk**. Action speaks louder than words. And **your walk** speaks loudly. What do others really hear and see? What does **your walk** tell others about you? Does **your walk** demonstrate love? Does **your walk** shine a light for others to see their way out of dark situations? Does your walk represent things that are good? Take note of **your walk** as you move along your personal journey to love. Position yourself to make choices aligned with love and watch a notable difference in **your walk**. Love always. Love daily. 365 Love.™

Have you told someone you loved them today? I have.™

Love yesterday, today and future tomorrows,™
Torion

Message in the MUSIC
Aly & AJ – **Walking** on Sunshine

Note the QUOTE!
"Spread your love everywhere you go." --- Mother Teresa

Stand
November 10

Today's NOTE
It is always good to hear about good things and see good things happen. Love is the source behind it all. In a life filled with so many distractions, love keeps you focused and sets you on the right path. I am a living testimony to the greatness that comes from its power. I am a strong believer of what it is capable of. I have witnessed how it brings about positive change.

We build strong beliefs for certain causes. We fight for those causes. We **stand** for those causes. We have internal character traits that define who we are. We believe in who we are. We **stand** for what we believe in. I believe in love. I believe in its purpose. I believe in the cause. I am passionate about its movement. I promote its growth for I know of the goodness it brings. I know the positive difference it makes. I know it is pleasing to God and is aligned with His purpose for all. I **stand** for it. I **stand** for love. I **stand** with confidence. I **stand** proudly. What do you **stand** for? Love always. Love daily. 365 Love.™

Have you told someone you loved them today? I have.™

Love yesterday, today and future tomorrows,™
Torion

Message in the MUSIC
Victory in Praise & Arts Mass Choir – **Stand**

Note the QUOTE!
"If you don't **stand** for something, you will fall for anything." --- Peter Marshall

---

Love Always. Love Daily. 365 Love.

We Would Not Exist Without It
November 11

Today's NOTE
There are many things in life that we need in order to live and survive. Food, clothing and shelter are the three things most commonly thought of in response to basic, everyday needs. But there are a number of other things we need that we at times overlook or take for granted. We need oxygen from the air to breathe. We need water to replenish the water loss in our body and prevent dehydration. We also need water for the plants to grow. We need bees and other insects to pollinate so that certain plants can grow to provide us with food. Plants go through photosynthesis to contribute to the oxygen we breathe. We need the sun as a source of energy for almost every manifestation of life on earth. And the list goes on and on. Life would be a challenge and/or will cease to exist if some or all of these things were not here. However, none of these things would exist without love. God is love. And love is the creator of all things. It creates life and all that is needed to support its continued existence. It provides an ongoing means for our survival. **We would not exist without it**. We have everything we need when we have it. The next time you think about what you don't have, think about how love provides you with daily blessings and the gift of life. Love provides a means for your existence. And give thanks for all that is. Love always. Love daily. 365 Love.™

Have you told someone you loved them today? I have.™

Love yesterday, today and future tomorrows,™
Torion

Message in the MUSIC
Usher - **Without You**

Note the QUOTE!
"True love is what humanity needs to keep hope alive and to make life worth living." --- Unknown

Stand Up, Scream, Shout and Cheer
November 12

Today's NOTE
My pastor once presented an interesting analogy as part of his sermon on how people **stand up, scream, shout and cheer** during major sporting events. At the same time, some of those same people are afraid to **stand up, scream, shout and cheer** when it comes to giving praises to love. He also pointed out how much people give to support sporting events and gain nothing in return whether their team wins or loses. You receive love regardless of how big or small the contribution. You receive love even when there is no contribution at all. And love wins every time.

When you think about it, that's pretty mixed up. God is love. And with love, there is so much to gain. It costs nothing, but with it, the rewards are great. So why not **stand up, scream, shout and cheer** about it? When you give praises to love, when you give your life to love, love makes you rich. Rich in oneself. Rich in peace and happiness. Rich in self realization that what you have and are yet to receive are and will be everything you need. One would think that if you can give for the love of sports, you can give to the one who provides for you, supports you, and gives you life. You can give to love. You have an unselfish desire to give love freely. You are excited about it. You are proud to know it, share it and talk about it. You naturally want to **stand up, scream, shout and cheer** about it. What makes you **stand up, scream, shout and cheer**? Hopefully, your response included love. If not, keep living. Your journey to grow in love will get you there. Love always. Love daily. 365 Love. ™

Have you told someone you loved them today? I have. ™

Love yesterday, today and future tomorrows, ™
Torion

Message in the MUSIC
Marvin Sapp – Praise You Forever

Note the QUOTE!
"When you love someone, telling them you love them isn't enough. You must make them feel the love that you have for them." --- David Lisiecki

Superman
November 13

Today's NOTE

My favorite fictional super hero is **Superman**. I've seen all of the movies and the various TV series. I've seen the cartoons and read the comic books. **Superman** is from another planet. His special powers come from the energy of the sun. He was raised by earthly parents who taught him strong moral values. It is those moral values that drive him to protect the innocent from those who want to cause them harm. Meteor rocks from the planet, Krypton, have a negative impact on his powers. Green kryptonite makes **Superman** weak and can cause his death if he is exposed to it for an extended period of time. Red kryptonite gives **Superman** strong desires to do bad things and cause harm to others.

There is a **Superman** inside of each of us. It is in the form of love. We have the power to do great things. We have the power to be great. We get our power from a greater love who is the source of our energy (like the sun). And the closer we get to love, the greater our power becomes. The more we love, the more we share love with others. We become caring. We become giving. We provide protection to others in loving ways.

Life presents situations (meteors) we have to overcome to maintain our energy, our power, our love. Lack of self-love (green kryptonite) drains our energy. It takes away our power by allowing us to accept anything from anyone. It pulls us into a place of nothingness. It makes us forget where the source of our energy comes from. It blocks it from us. When we are able to realize the love inside of us, accept ourselves and appreciate our uniqueness, we are able to reconnect with the source of our energy. We reconnect with love. With the power of love from self-love, we become **Superman** again.

Other non-loving feelings (red kryptonite) such as greed, envy, anger, unforgiveness and jealousy, give us negative energy. While we may feel we are moving forward, we are really moving backwards. We lose focus on all the good that our power possesses, and spend it on the negative. We take away all we can have by using negative energy on these non-loving feelings. These feelings give the desire to cause harm to others or want to see others suffer or fail in some way. These feelings are not aligned with love at all. When we realize that what we have is good enough, we gain that energy back. When we stop interjecting negative energies from non-loving feelings and realize love is the ultimate source of all energy, we have a life filled with great things. When we remove or let go of any and all barriers (red and green kryptonite) and align ourselves with love, we are **Superman** once again.

Live a life full of love. Realize the power you carry with you every day. Energize yourself from the energy source and bring forth your **Superman**. Love always. Love daily. 365 Love.™

Have you told someone you loved them today? I have. ™

Love yesterday, today and future tomorrows, ™
Torion

Message in the MUSIC
Monica – **Superman**

Note the QUOTE!
"I'm not prophet or a stone aged man, just a mortal with potential of a **Superman**. I'm living on." --- David Bowie

---

Love Always. Love Daily. 365 Love.

Hakuna Matata
November 14

Today's NOTE

Hakuna matata is a Swahili phrase that means "no worries." It's about leaving the past behind and living for today. It's about being stress free and moving forward to a better tomorrow. It's about letting go. When you love, you experience the true meaning of **hakuna matata**. For love has no worries. Love leaves those worries in the hands of God. Loves allows you to realize that there is no need to worry, because you have strong faith. The next time you feel those worries coming along, take a deep breath and say to yourself, "**hakuna matata.**" The next time you feel stress coming on, think to yourself, **hakuna matata**. The next time you are in a tough situation that is draining your personal energy, **hakuna matata. Hakuna matata** because it is all in the hands of love. And love will take care of it for you. Love always. Love daily. 365 Love.™

Have you told someone you loved them today? I have.™

Love yesterday, today and future tomorrows,™
Torion

Message in the MUSIC

Timone and Pumba – **Hakuna Matata**
(from the movie, *The Lion King*)

Note the QUOTE!

"Every evening I turn my worries over to God. He's going to be up all night anyway." --- Mary C. Crowley

Be Used
November 15

Today's NOTE
Position yourself to **be used**. Not in the way that allows you to be taken advantage of by others, but in a way that allows you to be taken advantage of by love. True, real, spiritual love. Self-love and the love of others. Position yourself to **be used** by love to support its cause. Participate in how contagious it can be. Spread it and contribute to its growth. **Be used** by love to share, give, teach, console, motivate and inspire. **Be used** by love to make a difference in your life and the lives of others. **Be used** for the good of love and all that it has to offer. If you must **be used**, **be used** for love, by love, and with love. Love always. Love daily. 365 Love.™

Have you told someone you loved them today? I have.™

Love yesterday, today and future tomorrows,™
Torion

Message in the MUSIC
Bill Withers – Use Me

Note the QUOTE!
"One of the deepest secrets of life is that all that is really worth doing is what we do for others." --- Lewis Carroll

Sad Occasion, Happy Ending
November 16

Today's NOTE
As family gathered at the hospital in preparation for his passing, tears were shed, prayers were said and love was shared. Memories of childhood days were reflected upon. As time to pull the plug drew nearer and nearer, more tears were shed. Heartfelt words expressed not wanting to let go, while at the same time realizing it was time. Looking into the eyes of loved ones, giving kisses on the cheek, long, extended hugs, rubbing of the hands, caressing the feet, family touched his body for the last and final time. I felt their pain. I felt their sorrow. We connected. And for that moment, no matter if you were family or a friend of the family, we were one. When the time to disconnect the machines finally came, there was complete silence. Family stared as they watched the flat line appear within 10 minutes. Then, he was gone. It was a **sad occasion**, but a **happy ending**.

Someone close and dear to me lost their father today. And while death is typically considered a **sad occasion**, it is also a part of a **happy ending**. Love teaches us that we are here to fulfill a purpose. And life on earth is only temporary. When we pass on, we move to another place. And when you love, that place is one of continuous love, peace and serenity. The suffering that took place during the time before passing is no more. Healing for family and friends begins. Worrying for what is or is not going to happen is eliminated. Fellowship of happy times takes place. Family members and friends learn to move on. Love takes control and continues on with life for those who remain and the one who has passed. Love takes control of the **sad occasion** and creates a **happy ending**. Love always. Love daily. 365 Love.™

Have you told someone you loved them today? I have.™

Love yesterday, today and future tomorrows,™
Torion

Message in the MUSIC
Smokie Norful – Same Sad Song

Note the QUOTE!
"Love takes control of the **sad occasion** and creates a **happy ending**." --- Torion

---

Love Always. Love Daily. 365 Love.

The Cure
November 17

Today's NOTE
Love possess the power to cure so many things. We fail to realize that **the cure** is right in front of us and surrounds us every day in many different ways. What some of us envision is needed for **the cure** may not actually be **the cure**. Love uses us and others for **the cure**. And the ultimate outcome of **the cure** is because of love. Love can, will and does heal. And healing comes with belief and action based on that belief. Having and not having, living here or there, staying or going, is still a part of **the cure**. Love and **the cure** will always bring about positive change.

Love is the Cure

Love is **the cure** for an unhappy heart.
It cleanses the veins, and provides a new start.
It molds, it shapes, it bends and turns,
It helps, it heals, it grows, it learns.

Love is **the cure** for the hurt and the pain.
It brings a new view of the sun after rain.
It clears, it hears, it brightens, it shines,
It sees, it speaks, it opens the mind.

Love is **the cure** for the downs and the lows.
The remedy to revive what was lost in one's soul.
It removes, it erases, it absorbs, it embraces,
It pushes and reveals a new beauty inside and on faces.

Love is **the cure** for the least and the lost.
In times of destruction, in times of lost thoughts.
It builds, it gives, it helps, it lives,
It knows, it provides, it shows, it survives.

Love is **the cure** for the failures and the falls.
It gives new heights and strength to stand tall.
It lifts, it rises, it removes the disguises,
It inspires, it achieves, it conquers, it believes.

Love is **the cure** for everything.
The provider of new life, deliverer of good things,
From the waters, to the trees, from the ants to the doves,
Love always. Love daily. 365 Love.
© 2011

Love Always. Love Daily. 365 Love.

Love always. Love daily. 365 Love.™

Have you told someone you loved them today? I have.™

Love yesterday, today and future tomorrows,™
Torion

Message in the MUSIC
Ben Tankard – You Will Know

Note the QUOTE!
"Love **cures** people - both the ones who give it and the ones who receive it." ---
Karl Menninger

143
November 18

Today's NOTE

I just want to tell you, "I love you." If you can't understand this in English, then I'll try a different language like Spanish. "Te amo." What about French? "Je t'aime." Will Swahili work? "Naku penda." Maybe the language is not the problem. I've put the words on paper, but I'm not sure you've received the message yet. If there is a chance that it will come across better when expressed with numbers, then I say to you, "**143**." Ah! Looks like I have your attention now. That's right, **143** ---1 (I), 4 (love), 3 (you). **143** because you are who you are. **143** because of who you are yet to be. **143** because of your laugh and your smile. **143** because it's a part of my life's purpose. **143** just because I want to. **143** because you are my sister, brother, parent, child or friend. **143** because you crossed my path for a reason. **143** because love created you to be. **143** because I love. Love always. Love daily. 365 Love.™

Have you told someone you loved them today? I have.™

Love yesterday, today and future tomorrows,™
Torion

Message in the MUSIC
Musiq Soulchild – **143**

Note the QUOTE!
"To love and to be loved is the greatest happiness of existence." --- Sydney Smith

One Word
November 19

Today's NOTE
Today I just wanted to sit back, relax and love. I took a deep breath, inhaled, exhaled and felt.....ahhhh! What a blessing it is to have love in my life. What a joy it is knowing what it is. What an incredible gift to receive it daily. As I thought about love, all that it is, and all that it means, I concentrated on the many ways to describe this **one word** using just **one word**. The number is limitless, and so is love itself. I was able to come up with a few.

- God
- holy
- spiritual
- joy
- happiness
- good
- patient
- kind
- peace
- giving
- caring
- fun
- laughter
- forgiving
- bright
- motivating
- uplifting
- inspiring
- life
- music
- art
- you
- me
- family
- friends
- sunlight
- rain
- rainbows
- food
- clothing
- shelter
- gifts
- talents
- sanity
- healing
- protection
- balance
- great
- powerful

How many **one word** words can you think of to describe love? Love always. Love daily. 365 Love.™

Have you told someone you loved them today? I have.™

Love yesterday, today and future tomorrows,™
Torion

Message in the MUSIC
Chrisette Michele – Love is You

Note the QUOTE!
"Love is all we have, the only way that each can help the other." --- Euripides

Encourage Yourself
November 20

Today's NOTE
Sometimes you have to just **encourage yourself**. When no one else is around and you are in the midst of making choices, **encourage yourself**. Love will speak to you and through you to give you what you need to **encourage yourself**. You know that God is love. Through Him all things are possible. And all of the possibilities from His love bring about positive change. So, when you know what love is and where love comes from, you are able to **encourage yourself**. You can **encourage yourself** to be the best that you can be. You can **encourage yourself** to let go. You can **encourage yourself** to get up and take action. You can **encourage yourself** to do something. You can **encourage yourself** to make a change. That's what love is and that's the power it has inside of you. When you discover its full potential, you discover your true abilities. You live, you learn, and you move forward as you **encourage yourself**. Love always. Love daily. 365 Love.™

Have you told someone you loved them today? I have.™

Love yesterday, today and future tomorrows,™
Torion

Message in the MUSIC
Donald Lawrence & The Tri-City Singers - **Encourage Yourself**

Note the QUOTE!
"Correction does much, but encouragement does more." --- John Wolfgang von Goethe

---

There's an Angel Among Us
November 21

Today's NOTE

My grandmother passed away on November 21, 2011 at the age of 95. As I thought of creative ways to express her life for the funeral program, I asked family and friends to tell me in just a few words what they would say to or about my grandmother at that particular moment. Their responses made me think about angels. Angels are messengers from God. They protect and guide human beings and carry out God's tasks. That's what my grandmother did. She helped so many people. Her home was a place you could always come. This included family, friends and strangers. She helped those in need when they could not help themselves. She transformed lives.

There's An Angel Among Us

There's an angel among us.
Her spirit is in the air. She's been with us for some time.
You just didn't realize she was there
She watched most of us grow.
Helped us out when in need.
Always forgave when you did something wrong
Always smiled and asked for your knees.

There's an angel among us.
I can sit and reflect. Of the many good things about her.
I will never forget
Her unconditional love,
Her unselfish ways, Her giving spirit,
Her love for each day.

There's an angel among us.
Close your eyes, stop and breathe. Reflect on who it is.
Reflect on what it means.
For you never really, really know,
who an angel could be. For God uses each and every one of us,
That includes you, her, him and me
But this one, this particular angel,
Has touched so many lives. She lived as an example.
She fed your soul and your mind.

There's an angel among us.
I think you know who she is.
While we may no longer be able to touch her directly,
In our memories she will always live.

Love Always. Love Daily. 365 Love.

Her wings were invisible to human eye,
But they grew day by day. When it was time for her to fly,
God took her away.
To a most glorious place,
full of love, happiness and peace. For her purpose here was done
And her love was left to keep.
© 2011

People come and go in our lives. God places them there for a certain timeframe and for a specific reason. He uses them to make a difference and to teach us lessons. He uses them to help us grow and become better people. He uses them as a demonstration of love. They are angels in disguise. Who are the angels in your life? Are you an angel to someone else? Open your eyes and take notice of those who are truly messengers attempting to make a positive difference in your life. Appreciate them while you have the opportunity to do so. Live a life of love so that you can demonstrate love to others. Love like an angel. Love always. Love daily. 365 Love.™

Have you told someone you loved them today? I have.™

Love yesterday, today and future tomorrows,™
Torion

Message in the MUSIC
Anita Baker – **Angel**

Note the QUOTE!
"When angels visit us, we do not hear the rustle of wings, nor feel the feathery touch of the breast of a dove; but we know their presence by the love they create in our hearts." --- Unknown

---

Love Always. Love Daily. 365 Love.

Every Time
November 22

Today's NOTE

Love is there for me all of the time, **every time**. When I turn left, when I turn right, it's right there. When I'm up, when I'm down, it's right there. When I sit, when I stand, there it is. When I'm high, when I'm low, it's there. When the sun is shining, when it's rainy and wet, there it is again. When I smile, when I cry, you know it's there. **Every time** I turn around, love is there. I claim it and it is so. I don't have to try too hard, I just believe and it is so. What a wonderful blessing to have love by your side all of the time, **every time**. It's there for you too. Open your heart, your mind and your soul to receive it and it is yours. **Every time** you need it, love is there. Love always. Love daily. 365 Love.™

Have you told someone you loved them today? I have.™

Love yesterday, today and future tomorrows,™
Torion

Message in the MUSIC

LTD - (**Every time** I Turn Around) Back in Love Again

Note the QUOTE!

"**Every time** you smile at someone, it is an action of love, a gift to that person, a beautiful thing." --- Mother Teresa

What I've Been Waiting For
November 23

Today's NOTE
How are you feeling today? Fine I hope. Isn't today a good day? Correction, isn't today a great day? Of course it is. It is great because today and every day is a blessing. Today is the opportunity for a new beginning. Today is the opportunity to do something different. You know this, right? You know this because you know what love is and what love can do, right? You know this because you know that each day is filled with love, right? Awesome! That's just **what I've been waiting for**. I've been waiting for you to grow in love. I have been working on you through love. I have been used to share the love I have with you, especially for you. And to know that you have grown in love is exactly **what I've been waiting for**. Thank you. Now, keep it going and keep growing. Love always. Love daily. 365 Love.™

Have you told someone you loved them today? I have.™

Love yesterday, today and future tomorrows,™
Torion

Message in the MUSIC
Brian McKnight - **What I've Been Waiting For**

Note the QUOTE!
"Love is missing someone whenever you're apart, but somehow feeling warm inside because you're close in heart." --- Kay Knudsen

Overjoyed
November 24

Today's NOTE
Love makes me feel **overjoyed**. It is a feeling of greatness. I am **overjoyed** with extreme happiness. That's right. I am elated. Love brings that type of joy in your life. Speak it into existence and believe in it. Try it out. Be consistent with it. Be **overjoyed** with great delight. Be **overjoyed** with life. Be **overjoyed** with love. Love always. Love daily. 365 Love. ™

Have you told someone you loved them today? I have. ™

Love yesterday, today and future tomorrows, ™
Torion

Message in the MUSIC
Stevie Wonder - **Overjoyed**

Note the QUOTE!
"True love is when you touch another's soul just by being yourself." --- Unknown

It's Me Again
November 25

Today's NOTE
It's me again, reminding you to share love. Share love in your words and your actions. **It's me again** encouraging you to learn more about love. Read about it. Talk about it. Listen to it. **It's me again** praying for your personal growth in love. Growth in loving yourself and loving others. Spiritual growth. **It's me again**, just providing you with a quick, direct and to the point note to love. Love always. Love daily. 365 Love.™

Have you told someone you loved them today? I have.™

Love yesterday, today and future tomorrows,™
Torion

Message in the MUSIC
J. Moss – It's Me Again

Note the QUOTE!
"Love is life. And if you miss love, you miss life." --- Leo Buscaglia

---

Strength
November 26

Today's NOTE

The more you move forward, achieve, accomplish, and grow, the greater the probability of life testing your **strength**. It tests your **strength** as a measure of how much love you have inside of you. Your **strength** is determined by your faith, what you believe in and how much you believe. You obtain that **strength** from love. Love is the power that fuels your **strength**. It is your source of energy. It is your Die-Hard battery. It is your guiding light. The more you grow in love, the stronger you become. The more you love, the stronger you are. Develop your **strength** in love. Learn about love. Share love. Grow in love. For when you need it most, your energy is there to endure. As time passes, and passes, your Die-Hard battery lives up to its warranty. It's dependable and keeps you fully charged. When things get dark, your inner light shines and allows you to see the way. When the weight of the world is thrown at you, your **strength** will prevail through love. Love always. Love daily. 365 Love.™

Have you told someone you loved them today? I have.™

Love yesterday, today and future tomorrows,™
Torion

Message in the MUSIC
India Aire – **Strength**, Courage and Wisdom

Note the QUOTE!
"Love knows no limits to its endurance, no end to its trust, no fading of its hope. It can outlast anything. Love still stands when all else has fallen." --- Unknown

---

Love Always. Love Daily. 365 Love.

Blessed and Highly Favored
November 27

Today's NOTE
So often we get caught up in day to day activities that we forget to recognize how much we are loved. Our mere existence is a testimony to that. We are truly **blessed and highly favored**. We are given the opportunity to make our own choices. And regardless of those choices, we are still loved. We have so much that is taken for granted. We have so much that we fail to be humbled about. We often times linger on the have-nots vs. the haves. Life is a blessing. Each day is a blessing. Love is a blessing. Take note, step back, and accept the reality that regardless of what is or what is not, you are **blessed and highly favored**. Your life is yours. Your path is set just for you. What you have is just for you. Your gifts and talents are yours. Everything about you, for you, with you and around you is just for you. Everything that has been, is and yet to come is just for you. So appreciate it and show love for it. Be **blessed and highly favored**. Love always. Love daily. 365 Love.™

Have you told someone you loved them today? I have.™

Love yesterday, today and future tomorrows,™
Torion

Message in the MUSIC
Clark Sisters - **Blessed and Highly Favored**

Note the QUOTE!
"For today and its blessings, I owe the world an attitude of gratitude." --- Unknown

---

Love Always. Love Daily. 365 Love.

For You
November 28

Today's NOTE

This day is **for you**. It is **for you** to make your own choices. It is **for you** to give and receive. It is **for you** to accept. It is **for you** to make a difference. It is **for you** to change. It is **for you** to live. It is **for you** to create whatever you can imagine. It is **for you** to start something fresh and new. It is **for you** to begin something or end something. It is **for you** to continue moving forward. It is **for you** to learn from. It is the present. And the present is a gift uniquely designed **for you**. This day is yours. It is just **for you**. What are you going to do with it? Love always. Love daily. 365 Love.™

Have you told someone you loved them today? I have.™

Love yesterday, today and future tomorrows,™
Torion

Message in the MUSIC
Kenny Lattimore - **For You**

Note the QUOTE!
"No gift compares to the gift of love." --- Unknown

Love Always. Love Daily. 365 Love.

Abundantly
November 29

Today's NOTE
Love is given to us **abundantly**. It is provided in large quantities. It is extreme. It is a part of everything and it is infinite. It is powerful. It is great. Because of love, life can be lived **abundantly**. Life can be lived to the fullest. Go for a walk. Talk. Go get something to eat. Drive somewhere. Pick up the phone and call somebody. Pull $1.00 out of your pocket. Access your bank account. Go lay in your bed. Turn on the TV. Go get a snack out of the kitchen. Search the Internet on your computer. Take a photo. Read a book. If you were able to do some of all of those things, you are loved **abundantly**. You have those things and abilities regardless of how small or large. You have it. Now, think about your age and your ability to do those things and so many other things on a daily basis. All that you have and all that you are able to do are gifts of love. They are daily blessings provided to you **abundantly**. Love always. Love daily. 365 Love.™

Have you told someone you loved them today? I have.™

Love yesterday, today and future tomorrows,™
Torion

Message in the MUSIC
J. Moss – **Abundantly**

Note the QUOTE!
"To love **abundantly** is to live **abundantly**, and to love forever is to live forever." --- Henry Drummond

---

Love Always. Love Daily. 365 Love.

Get Positioned
November 30

Today's NOTE
It's so easy to get caught up depending on others for things we should be able to do for ourselves. However, when you do this on a consistent basis, the people you depend on become a crutch, stunting your personal growth. We depend on others for comfort. We depend on others for finances. We depend on others for food, clothing and shelter. We depend on others for love. What we sometimes forget is that we should not place emphasis on the dependence of others. If we must depend on anything or anyone, we should depend on love. Love allows us to **get positioned** to support ourselves. Love allows us to **get positioned** to become self-reliant. Love allows us to **get positioned** to realize the power we have through self-love. Love allows us to **get positioned** to grow, prosper, take action, achieve and accomplish. As you continue your journey through life, be prepared to **get positioned** to do more and become more. **Get positioned** for love. Love always. Love daily. 365 Love.™

Have you told someone you loved them today? I have. ™

Love yesterday, today and future tomorrows,™
Torion

Message in the MUSIC
Eric Benet – Be Myself Again

Note the QUOTE!
"Do all things with love." --- Og Mandino

Love Always. Love Daily. 365 Love.

December

"The greatest gift that you can give to others is the gift of unconditional love and acceptance."
— Brian Tracy

Your Five Senses
December 1

Today's NOTE
Open your hands. Touch something. Look at your hands and what they have touched. Take a deep breath, in and out. Smell the fragrance of the air. Listen to the sounds in the air. Listen to the sound of your breathing. Smack your lips. Taste the freshness.

If you were able to do any or all of those things, you are blessed. Blessings come from love. You were able to use **your five senses**. You were able to see, hear, smell, touch and taste. These are gifts of life that we use every day. **Your five senses** are another reason to be grateful. They are another reason to be thankful. They are another reason to appreciate life and love. They are gifts that are sometimes taken for granted. However, if they were taken away, you would definitely notice a difference and have a greater appreciation for them. So, why not appreciate them now? Love all that you are, all that you have and all that you are able to do with **your five senses**. Love always. Love daily. 365 Love.™

Have you told someone you loved them today? I have. ™

Love yesterday, today and future tomorrows, ™
Torion

Message in the MUSIC
Jill Scott – He Loves Me

Note the QUOTE!
"Love is not blind; it is an extra eye which shows us what is most worthy of regard." --- James Matthew Barrie

---

Love Always. Love Daily. 365 Love.

For Life
December 2

Today's NOTE
For life... That's a long time. Or is it? Life is not promised. The time we have to live life is not known. Life can be as little as a few days, hours, minutes or seconds. Life can be as long as a century plus. It's the time between birth and death. It has a limit. It has a max. Whatever time it is, it is **for life**. The time you have **for life** and what you do **for life** is based on your specific life's timeline. You can waste life or preserve life. You can throw away life or enjoy life. You can choose life. And in choosing life, you can live **for life**. In living **for life**, you can live to love **for life**. **For life** is meant to love. Love is one of our life's purpose. Love is something that we will always have **for life**. Love is something we have to give **for life**. It is plentiful. It is abundant. It is forever. It is **for life**. Use it wisely. Live in it. Love for it. Love always. Love daily. 365 Love. ™

Have you told someone you loved them today? I have. ™

Love yesterday, today and future tomorrows, ™
Torion

Message in the MUSIC
Jodeci - Love You **For Life**

Note the QUOTE!
"One day your **life** will flash before your eyes. Make sure it's worth watching." --- Unknown

---

Love Always. Love Daily. 365 Love.

Loves You Anyway
December 3

Today's NOTE

You are born and you experience life. Life includes the ups and downs, the good and bad. It also includes lots of mistakes. Those mistakes are a result of the choices you make. And through those mistakes, you live and you learn. For all that you go through, and all that you do, good or bad, there is always someone who is going to **love you anyway**. They will love you even when you don't deserve it. That's what love does. When a person truly loves, they will love you regardless. It does not mean that they will continue to tolerate bad behaviors or mistreatment from you, but their love will remain with you whether you remain within their inner circle or outside of it.

God is love. He loves you regardless. He knows all you are going to do even before you do it. And because He is a forgiving God, He **loves you anyway**. Loving parents and grandparents will **love you anyway**. Through your teenage years, attitudes, poor choices in friends, bad grades, acting out, mid life crisis, changing behaviors, bad finances, your good and your bad, they **love you anyway**. Your best friend, who truly knows what love and friendship truly is, will tough it out with you through thick and thin. They will love you through the good times and the bad times, when you like them and when you don't, when you need them and when you don't, and when you forget about them all together. A true friend will **love you anyway**. Your pet dog will **love you anyway**. They will be there when you are good to them, when you are angry with them, and when you sometimes forget they exist. They have unconditional love for you. So, never think that you are not loved. Someone always loves you. And someone will always **love you anyway**. Love **loves you anyway**. Love always. Love daily. 365 Love.™

Have you told someone you loved them today? I have.™

Love yesterday, today and future tomorrows,™
Torion

Message in the MUSIC
Mr. Jonz - You **Loved Me Anyway**

Note the QUOTE!
"The greatest gift that you can give to others is the gift of unconditional love and acceptance." --- Brian Tracy

Amen
December 4

Today's NOTE

Amen is typically a word used during worship following prayers and hymns. It is defined as "so be it" or "truly." It is also used to express strong agreement with something. Today, I would like to encourage you to give love an " **Amen.**" For all that you know about love, where it comes from, where it lives, who provides it, the power it provides, what it does, what it means, how it works, who possesses it, how it touches lives, how it transforms, and then some, give love a great big, enormous, "**Amen.**" Say, **Amen**, because you believe in love. Say, **Amen**, because you are in strong agreement with love. Say, **Amen**, because you know that it is the truth and that it truly does exist. For all that love provides, **Amen**. For all that love gives, **Amen**. For all that love is and is not, **Amen**, **Amen**, **Amen**. Love always. Love daily. 365 Love. ™

Have you told someone you loved them today? I have. ™

Love yesterday, today and future tomorrows, ™
Torion

Message in the MUSIC
Andrae Crouch – Let the Church Say **Amen**

Note the QUOTE!
"Dear God, Please send to me the spirit of Your peace. Then send, dear Lord, the spirit of peace from me to all the world. **Amen**." --- Marianne Williamson

Sweet Love
December 5

Today's NOTE

Most people I know like sweets. It can be a sweet taste, as sweet look, a sweet behavior, or a sweet smell. It can be a little sweet, moderately sweet, or very sweet, but they like it sweet. It could be a dessert, a drink, a natural fruit, a fragrance, an appealing look, or a character trait. It's just sweet. If you like sweets, you know what you what, when you want it and how you want it. The sweetness is sometimes hard to resist. The scent increases your craving for it. The sight of it makes you want it or want more of it. If it's free, you take as much as you can. You may consume it in large quantities or small, depending on your habits, but you have to have something sweet. While some can say that sweets are not good for you, there are some sweets that are. Sweetness is built into some of the most healthiest foods we eat naturally. Sweet behaviors that demonstrate kindness, caring and sharing are good character traits to have. Sweet fragrances can provide aromas that are calming and relaxing. Then there's **sweet love**. That's the love that is oh, so good. It bottles up all that is good about the other sweets into one. **Sweet love** is patient and kind. **Sweet love** does not envy or is not jealous. **Sweet love** shares and cares. **Sweet love** gives. **Sweet love** is a smile, a laugh and a "hello." **Sweet love** is saying, "I love you," because I really do. **Sweet love** is yesterday, today, and future tomorrows. **Sweet love** is all good and then some. The next time you go to the store, see something passing by, or meet someone and notice something sweet, add a little **sweet love** to it in the process. Love always. Love daily. 365 Love.™

Have you told someone you loved them today? I have.™

Love yesterday, today and future tomorrows,™
Torion

Message in the MUSIC
Anita Baker – **Sweet Love**

Note the QUOTE!
"You never lose by loving. You always lose by holding back." --- Barbara DeAngelis

For All We Know
December 6

Today's NOTE
You never know what a person is going through. Some people carry the weight of the world on their shoulders and look absolutely normal. They speak, they smile, they have a regular conversation as if their life is OK. Others show their struggles in their body language and their actions. As you walk down the hall, down the street, around your home, in the mall, in the store, there is no set give away to let you know that someone is in need of love. Not just love from a romantic relationship perspective, but the love that lets you know someone cares. That someone is listening. That someone understands you. That someone can relate to you. That someone has an inspiring spirit. Sometimes it is those moments of love that make the biggest difference. Because each person has the ability to "keep things inside," let's not take for granted that because someone "looks" OK, they are actually OK. **For all we know** about love, demonstrate it in all that we do. Demonstrate love in every contact you have with a person. Say, "Hello." Exchange a friendly smile. Say, "Thank You." Tell a person you appreciate their support or help. Be kind to everyone you encounter. Ask a person how they are doing today. Say something positive in your interaction with others. Say something good about the day or night that reminds a person about other good things going on around them. **For all we know** about love, we know that love is contagious. So, the things we do to demonstrate love, regardless of how small they may appear to be, go a long way. They make a difference. Love makes a difference. Love always. Love daily. 365 Love.™

Have you told someone you loved them today? I have.™

Love yesterday, today and future tomorrows,™
Torion

Message in the MUSIC
Donnie Hathaway - **For All We Know**

Note the QUOTE!
"Never underestimate the power, because love can do miracles which you never thought possible." --- Unknown

If You Really Love Me
December 7

Today's NOTE

If you really love me, then tell me. Go ahead, say it. It's not that difficult. I'm not asking you to be in love with me, but if you love me in any way just say it. Say those three words that come together and have a positive, powerful meaning. Say them, because you know what love is and how to love. Say them because you really mean it. Open your mouth, form your lips and say, "I Love You." See, now wasn't that easy? Now, **if you really love me**, say it again. This time just let it go and let it flow. Now tell someone else.

It's easy to take for granted that people near and dear to us know how we feel about them. Whether its family, a friend, or a spouse. Sometimes we get so used to others being around that we neglect to express ourselves to them. We neglect to let them know that we care. It's OK to let someone know you love them. It's something that should be done on a regular, consistent, daily basis. Then no one ever has to wonder. Love wants you to love. Love wants you to feel love. Love wants you to know love. Love wants you to say, "I love you." Love always. Love daily. 365 Love.™

Have you told someone you loved them today? I have.™

Love yesterday, today and future tomorrows,™
Torion

Message in the MUSIC
Stevie Wonder - **If You Really Love Me**

Note the QUOTE!
"True love doesn't consist of holding hands, it consists of holding hearts." --- Unknown

One Thing About You
December 8

Today's NOTE

As the year draws close to an end and the holiday season is upon us, family, friends, and businesses host holiday festivities and year end celebrations. There are prayers, meals, kind words of thanks and appreciation, gifts, awards and/or bonuses. Let's not leave out the fact that fun and fellowship take place.

I had the pleasure of attending a year end appreciation / holiday luncheon with some of my staff members. As we waited on our meals, one of my employees made the following request-- "Tell **one thing about you** that you feel others do not know and share one of your dreams." It's interesting how that **one thing about you** can provide enlightening insight into who a person really is and what they believe in. There was so much positive energy in the room. Many of the things shared were pure love. People were doing things out of love. People had dreams aligned with love. People gave of themselves out of love. People loved.

One staff member's daughter adopts children with medical disabilities and provides them with the means to receive the medical attention they need. The same staff member does missionary work and wants to do this full time upon retiring. Another staff member's sister is the founder of schools that provide an education to children in poor countries. Another staff member has a passion for helping people and is working to obtain a degree in HR. Another found out about some 30+ homeless children attending a certain school and found the means, with the support of some other friends, to provide for those children and their families for Christmas and some period after that. Another staff member has a passion for helping the elderly and would like to continue to work with them on a more consistent, long term basis. I, in turn, was able to share my current and future plans for 365 Love.

These are testimonies that love still exists. These are testimonies that people love. These are testimonies that people who love, think loving thoughts and want to share love with others. These are testimonies that love gives. These are testimonies that love is contagious, love brings change and love makes a difference. These are testimonies that the **one thing about you** that is most important is love. Love always. Love daily. 365 Love.TM

Have you told someone you loved them today? I have.TM

Love yesterday, today and future tomorrows,TM
Torion

Message in the MUSIC
The Clark Sisters – Jesus is A Love Song

Note the QUOTE!
"Intense love does not measure. It just gives." --- Mother Teresa

Try a Little Tenderness
December 9

Today's NOTE
Sometimes it's good to just **try a little tenderness**. Everybody can't take the hard core, loud, screaming, tell it like it is in order to get your point across way of handling things. Love is kind. And in an effort to demonstrate kindness you can **try a little tenderness**. All of the yelling, screaming and harsh words is not good. It does not always have a positive impact and can leave a lifetime of scars. Sometimes, what needs to be said, or what needs to be done, should be said or done with **a little tenderness**. While this may not work for all, it definitely works for love. There is a saying that goes, "You can kill a person with kindness." I have seen this work too often and could give several personal experiences as testimonies that it works. So many people expect strong reactions to certain actions. **A little tenderness** can have just as powerful of an impact if and when it is not expected. It can have just as powerful of an impact even if it is expected. Sometimes **a little tenderness** is saying "no," holding firm, preventing, teaching, and letting go. Sometimes it is just letting someone know you care. Sometimes it allows a person to truly hear things differently. It does not mean that you have to allow a person to run you over or take advantage of you. It just means that you don't have to demonstrate loudness, anger or frustration. It means that you are handling things with love. So, the next time you are in a situation where you need to really get through to someone, make a difference to someone, or have an impact on someone that could be life changing for them or for you, **try a little tenderness**. Try love. Love always. Love daily. 365 Love.™

Have you told someone you loved them today? I have.™

Love yesterday, today and future tomorrows,™
Torion

Message in the MUSIC
Otis Redding – **Try a Little Tenderness**

Note the QUOTE!
"The most powerful symptom of love is **tenderness** which becomes at times almost insupportable." --- Victor Hugo

---

Love Always. Love Daily. 365 Love.

Define Yourself
December 10

Today's NOTE

The word "define" is used to state the meaning of something. It is used to explain, specify, set boundaries for, or determine. It is also used to describe or identify qualities. Now that clarity on the meaning of the word "define" has been provided, **define yourself**.

- What is your meaning or purpose?
- Who are you?
- What boundaries have you set in your life?
- How would you describe yourself?
- What qualities do you have?
- What specific character traits do you demonstrate?

Did you answer those questions based on your own thoughts of who you truly are? Or were they based on what someone told you they wanted you to be? Or were they based on someone you want to be like? Now, ask yourself this final question. Are your responses aligned with love and a person who loves?

Your purpose in life is to love. Love God, love yourself, love other people, and love other things. Who you are is enough. Regardless of whether you are aligned with love, you are and always will be a work in progress. No one is perfect and everyone's journey is different. You were created from love. Your journey to love is yours. Not Mary's. Not Bob's. Not your mom's. Not your best friends'. It is yours. When you **define yourself**, it should be about you, and only you. It should be the true you that knows you. God is love and love is in all things that are good. And when you go back and reflect on the responses to the questions asked to **define yourself**, you will see where you are and how much more work you need to do. Loving yourself involves always doing your best. That includes doing your best when it comes to love. Love always. Love daily. 365 Love.™

Have you told someone you loved them today? I have.™

Love yesterday, today and future tomorrows,™
Torion

Message in the MUSIC
Brandy – The Definition

Note the QUOTE!
"Do you want to know who you are? Don't ask. Act! Action will delineate and **define you**." --- Thomas Jefferson

Peace
December 11

Today's NOTE

Peace is a state of mutual harmony with oneself and with others. **Peace** comes from within. Inner **peace** is a state of being mentally and physically at **peace**. It allows you to deal with conflict. It is a stress eliminator. This same **peace** drives resolution to conflict from wars, among groups, with family situations, etc. But before all of this is able to take place, love must be in place. And with love in place, **peace** will reign. With love in place, **peace** brings joy and happiness. With love in place, no one person or thing can define or change the **peace** within you. Your **peace** is in your hands. Your **peace** is in your control. Your **peace** is your decision. Your **peace** comes from love. Love helps you find the inner **peace** to let go and let God. Inner **peace** results from self-love. **Peace** results from love. Love always. Love daily. 365 Love.™

Have you told someone you loved them today? I have.™

Love yesterday, today and future tomorrows,™
Torion

Message in the MUSIC
Mary J Blige – No More Drama

Note the QUOTE!
"When you find **peace** within yourself, you become the kind of person who can live at **peace** with others." --- Peace Pilgrim

---

Open Door
December 12

Today's NOTE

There is a door open for you. Can you see it? It's right there. Right in front of you. It is the door of opportunity. It is the door of positive change. It is the door of self-improvement. It is the door of peace, happiness, and freedom. It is the door that leaves the past in the past and brings forth a new and improved present. It is the door of love. It's always there. And it welcomes your entry. Why are you not walking through it? What are you afraid of?

Love is present always, at all times. There are times when it is not realized. And there are times when there are conscious choices not to embrace it or demonstrate it. We remain stagnant and satisfied. We choose not to walk through the door because of excuses such as laziness, procrastination, lack of confidence, fear, insecurities and worry. We won't go through the door because we are carrying the weight of jealousy, envy, anger, and vengeance. These things give false impressions that they are heavier than they really are and falsely restrict our movement. We remain in a constant place visualizing the **open door**, dreaming about the **open door**, talking about the **open door**, ignoring the **open door**, and we fail to walk through. We fail to act. We know about the **open door**. We know what's behind the **open door**, but……

Today, I challenge you to make a move and walk through that **open door**. Go to love. Realize its full potential and all that it has to offer you. Know who it is and what it is. Feel its power and live life to the fullest. Know that is the greatest gift you could receive or give. Go for it. Be energized. Have confidence. You can do it. I know you can. It all begins with that **open door**, that **open door** called love. Love always. Love daily. 365 Love.™

Have you told someone you loved them today? I have.™

Love yesterday, today and future tomorrows,™
Torion

Message in the MUSIC
The Clark Sisters – I'm Going On

Note the QUOTE!
"God is **open**ing the **door** for you. Why don't you walk through?" --- Unknown

The Best That You've Got
December 13

Today's NOTE
When you love and love yourself, you always do your best. Not someone else's best, your best. You give it **the best that you've got**. And only you know when that is accomplished. You are satisfied with the end results as long as you know you put all you could into it. Regardless of the outcome. Did you give it **the best that you've got** today? Did you put all that you could into whatever it was you were attempting to accomplish? Did you demonstrate that you loved and loved yourself by the quality, time and effort you put into what you did today? If not, rethink, refocus, and try again. Not later, now. With whatever it is you are doing. Reading with focus, cleaning, studying, working, planning, playing, giving, sharing, etc. Whatever it is, give it **the best that you've got** now. Repetition through practice develops habits. Make demonstrating **the best that you've got** a habit. A good habit. A habit of love. Love always. Love daily. 365 Love.™

Have you told someone you loved them today? I have.™

Love yesterday, today and future tomorrows,™
Torion

Message in the MUSIC
Anita Baker – Giving You **the Best That I've Got**

Note the QUOTE!
"God makes three requests of his children; do the best you can, where you can, with what you have, now." --- African-American Proverb

The Center of My Joy
December 14

Today's NOTE

I have joy in my life. I smile a grand smile because of this joy. I am happy with all that is and is not because of this joy. I shine my light each day in hopes that it will guide others along their way. And it's all because of love. With love in my life, I know that all things are possible.

The center of my joy is the core of my existence. **The center of my joy** feeds the potential in me and brings forth great things. **The center of my joy** keeps my head up, when life attempts to pull it down. **The center of my joy** allows me to live, to give, to care, and to share. **The center of my joy** humbles me and completes me. **The center of my joy** builds my faith. I believe, and it is so. **The center of my joy** is love. Love always. Love daily. 365 Love.™

Have you told someone you loved them today? I have.™

Love yesterday, today and future tomorrows,™
Torion

Message in the MUSIC
Richard Smallwood – **Center of My Joy**

Note the QUOTE!
"A joy shared is a joy doubled." --- Unknown

Love Always. Love Daily. 365 Love.

Who's Loving You
December 15

Today's NOTE
Everybody exists because of love. Everybody wants to be loved. Everybody needs to be loved. So, **who's loving you**? I'm sure that a number of different responses came to mind. And the responses depend on where you are on your journey to love. If you were thinking about love and relationships, you may have mentioned a boyfriend, girlfriend or spouse. If you were thinking about brotherly love, you probably thought about a close friend, a pastor or mentor. If you were thinking about family love, you probably thought about your parents, siblings, grandparents or other relatives. If you were thinking about charitable love, you thought about God. Regardless of what you thought of, you should have come up with at least one response to **who's loving you**. That's because there is always someone who loves you. God loves you first and foremost. God is love. And love loves you more than anything or anyone. And when you know that love loves you, there is love inside of you that brings forth self-love and realization that love comes from many things. You always know **who's loving you** because your eyes are open to love, your heart is open to love, and you have a connection with love. Love always. Love daily. 365 Love.™

Have you told someone you loved them today? I have.™

Love yesterday, today and future tomorrows,™
Torion

Message in the MUSIC
The Jackson 5 – **Who's Loving You**

Note the QUOTE!
"True love is out there along with someone who cares." --- Unknown

---

Love Always. Love Daily. 365 Love.

Love on Top
December 16

Today's NOTE
Write a list of some things you want. It can be a list of all the things you want to accomplish. It can be a list of things you want to do in life. It can be a list of places you would like to travel. It can be a list of things you want to change. It can be a list of gifts. Whatever it is, put it down on that list. Now, think real hard for a moment. What's the one thing that will help you obtain or reap the benefits of anything on that list? The answer is simple. The answer is love. Love takes care of all your needs and wants. As you grow in love, you will find that your list will change. For some of the things you want, you will begin to realize you already have them, or you just don't really want them anymore. They have less significance. Some things are that much easier to obtain or reach for. So, if love will take care of the list, then put **love on top**. Make it #1 on your list. And with **love on top**, everything else will fall into place. With **love on top**, you realize its importance. You take care of it first. It is "Numero Uno." You are able to accomplish your goals. You are able to achieve. You are able to gain rewards. You receive. Now that **love** is **on top**, you must strive to achieve it first. You must learn to love, give love, and receive love. You love love (God), yourself, others and other things. With that accomplished, you've got it made from there. Love always. Love daily. 365 Love.™

Have you told someone you loved them today? I have.™

Love yesterday, today and future tomorrows,™
Torion

Message in the MUSIC
Beyonce – **Love on Top**

Note the QUOTE!
"Put love first. Entertain thoughts that give life. And when a thought of resentment, or hurt, or fear comes your way, have another thought that is more powerful--a thought that is love." --- Mary Manin Morrissey

A Special Prayer for My Daughter
December 17

Today's NOTE

A full year has almost passed. Love continued to grow inside of me and around me. And with that growth, came life events to strengthen my faith and cause positive change. My daughter is on her personal journey. She has been up and down. She is being molded by the potter's hands. She is being drawn to God's love. He is sitting her still for a moment so that she can find her way home. To Him. To love. While I understand that everything happens for a reason and within God's will, as a mother, that journey for your child can sometimes be difficult to bear, but with love, we have to put it all in God's hands, because we know that He always has a plan. With love, we can turn all of the worries over to Him. All of God's children are meant for greatness. My daughter is included. He has blessed her with gifts that are yet to reach their fullest potential based on the plan He has for her life. He is still working on her. For she, and all of us are still a work in progress.

Today I cried. I cried for my daughter. I cried for her as a mother. I cried for her situation. I cried because I miss her. I cried when I heard someone sing a song. I cried because I know that something great will come out of her situation. I cried because I know that God has it all under control. And as I cried, I said **a special prayer for my daughter**.

Father, you are such an awesome God. You are the ultimate love and only you know what is best for each of your children. Place your hands on my daughter so that she may feel your presence. Show her that she is being positioned to do great things. Let past and present experiences humble her and open her heart to receive you. Send her a sign to confirm that you are the greatest love of all. God, show her that you are the light when things are dark. Give her strength when she is weak. Show her the way when she is lost. Give her sight when she cannot see. Wrap your arms around her when she has a need to be comforted. Lift her up when she falls down. Turn her frown upside down. Guide her. Direct her. Position her to do your will. Lord, I know that you have a plan for her and what she is going through is part of that plan to get her to where you want her to be. Her life will be a testimony to uplift so many people. Use her, use her life, and use her voice and other gifts to do great things. And Lord, I thank you in advance for the implementation of your master plan. I leave it all in your hands, because I know that it is all under your control. I have strong faith and believe in the power of your love. In your name I do pray. Amen.

I then took a deep breath, wiped the tears from my eyes, smiled and said, "Thank you, God." Love always. Love daily. 365 Love.™

Have you told someone you loved them today? I have.™

Love yesterday, today and future tomorrows,™
Torion

Message in the MUSIC
Usher – **Prayer for You** (Interlude)

Note the QUOTE!
"Pray and let God worry." --- Martin Luther King, Jr.

Open My Heart
December 18

Today's NOTE
I have had my share of heart breaks. However, I never gave up on love. I always believed in love and believed that there are other people who knew love. And in knowing love, other people loved themselves and were able to love others. While my experiences may have led me to be more careful with my heart, I always went into a new relationship with an open heart. I prayed for love to **open my heart** to grow in love, know love and receive love. I knew that love would not come to me or be recognized by me unless I **opened my heart**.

A closed door prevents things from coming in. A closed door does not invite opportunity. The same applies to a closed heart. In order to grow in love, you must **open your heart** to receive it. It does not mean that all things will be perfect in doing so, but in your journey you will learn what love is and what love is not. You will become more aware. You will grow spiritually and in self-love. And at that time, you will find love all around you. Love always. Love daily. 365 Love.™

Have you told someone you loved them today? I have.™

Love yesterday, today and future tomorrows,™
Torion

Message in the MUSIC
Yolanda Adams – **Open My Heart**

Note the QUOTE!
"Have a heart that never hardens, a temper that never tires, and a touch that never hurts." --- Charles Dickens

Love Always. Love Daily. 365 Love.

Teacher
December 19

Today's NOTE

Did you know that you were a **teacher**? Well, you are. Someone, somewhere is learning from you. They may have learned from you in the past. They may be learning from you right now. They will definitely learn from you in the future. You are a **teacher** based on your actions and your failure to act; what you say and what you don't say. Most often, we think of a **teacher** as someone who has completed the required college curricula that qualifies one to teach students in grade school or college. We may also consider a **teacher** as being a subject matter expert. Everyone is a **teacher**. This includes the young, the old, the rich, the poor, the leader and the follower. Life in itself qualifies you and everyone else to be a **teacher**. While you may not specialize in a specific subject matter as required by the Board of Education or the University System, you do specialize in living your own unique life. And in living, you share your life experiences with others. They learn from you and you from them. Whether you want to or not, you make a difference with every encounter you have with another person. You teach and they learn. You have an impact on their life whether it is positive or negative. So, what have you been teaching lately? What are others learning from you and about you? How are you helping others to become better people? What actions and behaviors do you demonstrate that motivate, uplift and inspire? How do your actions and behaviors align with those of love? Love is the ultimate **teacher**. Love is good. And love shares good things. The more you love, the more love you spread, the more positive impact you have on others. As you go through your day, each day, think about who you are and how you as a person have an impact on others. Think about love, how you love, and your role as a **teacher**. Love always. Love daily. 365 Love. ™

Have you told someone you loved them today? I have. ™

Love yesterday, today and future tomorrows, ™
Torion

Message in the MUSIC
Musiq Soulchild – **Teach Me**

Note the QUOTE!
"A good teacher is like a candle. It consumes itself to light the way for others." --- Unknown

---

Love Always. Love Daily. 365 Love.

A Hug
December 20

Today's NOTE
Sometimes it's good to just give someone a great, big, fat, juicy **hug**. **A hug** is a way of showing concern, care, affection, sympathy, happiness, and forgiveness. **A hug** is applicable during the happy times and the sad times. **A hug** is a form of love. It's good for the soul. It brings about a smile. It's "just because." **A hug** gives and can silently lift the spirits of a troubled heart. You never really know the full impact it has on another. Just know that it does indeed have an impact. If you haven't hugged someone today, go ahead and do it now. And while you're at it, give yourself **a hug** too. Love always. Love daily. 365 Love.™

Have you told someone you loved them today? I have.™

Love yesterday, today and future tomorrows,™
Torion

Message in the MUSIC
Kirk Franklin – **Lovely Day**

Note the QUOTE!
"**A hug** is the perfect gift; one size fits all, and nobody minds if you exchange it." --- Unknown

The Perfect Gift
December 21

Today's NOTE

December is the month we celebrate Christmas. People spend hours and hours in the stores in search of **the perfect gift**. They wait outside in long lines for the super sale store opening. They spend extended hours searching the Internet. They think of creative ways to create a uniquely designed item. All for the purpose of finding or creating **the perfect gift**.

The perfect gift cannot be found in a material item, because **the perfect gift** is love. While material items may be given out of love, they are no substitute for love itself. And love is unlike any material item you can find. It does not require long lines or hours of walking, looking, and searching. It cannot be purchased. It cannot be wrapped. It does not cost, but provides a great return on investment. It's memory lasts a lifetime. It does not break. It does not require a warranty. It does not need batteries. It can be given regardless of your income, budget or funds availability. It does not require an accessory item in order for it to be operable or complete. There are no temperature controls required. There are no age limitations or restrictions. It is available to anyone and everyone. There is enough to meet all demands. It is worldwide and can be found everywhere. It does not run out. It does not become outdated over time. It can transform, change, convert, create and multiply. It does not rust, tarnish, tear or dissolve. It is durable and is functional in water, heat, sunlight, and extreme weather conditions. It is dependable and always works. It comes in all shapes and sizes. It does not have a negative impact if consumed in large quantities.

The perfect gift of love comes from the heart. Love is actions, words, expressions and thoughts. Love speaks, hears, touches and feels. It gives of one's self and one's time. It is the reason for the season; the birth of Jesus Christ. The gift of love. Love perfected. **The perfect gift**. Give love. Love always. Love daily. 365 Love.™

Have you told someone you loved them today? I have.™

Love yesterday, today and future tomorrows,™
Torion

Message in the MUSIC
Kirk Franklin & The Family – Silver and Gold

Note the QUOTE!
"The greatest gift you can give to others is **the gift** of unconditional love and acceptance." --- Brian Tracy

I Understand
December 22

Today's NOTE

I understand what you are going through. **I understand** what you have been through. **I understand** why you feel the way you feel about moving forward. **I understand** that you are experiencing life. And in my understanding, I want you to know that everything will be OK. Everything is going to be alright. Because love is in control. It may not feel like it sometimes, but it is. It's all a part of the plan. Love will bring the sun after the rain. Love will make a way when there seems to be no way. Love will. You must believe that it will and it is so. **I understand** it all. I feel you. I know the resolution. The resolution is love. I know love. And love knows you. Seek it, find it, get to know it, and show it. Love understands. Understand love and let love love you. Love always. Love daily. 365 Love.™

Have you told someone you loved them today? I have.™

Love yesterday, today and future tomorrows,™
Torion

Message in the MUSIC
Smokie Norful - **I Understand**

Note the QUOTE!
"I hear and I forget. I see and I remember. I do and **I understand**." --- Confucius

Not About You, For You
December 23

Today's NOTE

Love is about giving. And giving is not always in the form of a material item. Giving can be in the form of your time, your words of encouragement, your participation, your prayers, or your support. Giving includes sharing and caring. Giving out of love includes doing the right things at the right time for the right reasons. The right thing is love. The right time is now. The right reason is because it's part of your purpose in life.

Everyone needs love. However, sometimes we get more caught up in the "me" side of love, and what love can do for us personally. We lose sight of the true meaning and purpose of love. When we live a life that is driven by love, we don't have to worry about love coming to us in return. Love and more love is a natural reward for giving love. Love is the return on investment for love itself. **Love is not about you. Love is for you.** Love uses you to fulfill a purpose. It is for you to give. And in turn, you shall receive. When you love yourself, you are giving love to yourself. In turn, you are able to give love to others. When you give love to others, you receive love in return. That return may not always come from the person or thing you gave love to, but there will be a return. Don't forget about the true meaning of love. Let go of looking for what will come to you. Give and watch what it can and will do for you. Love always. Love daily. 365 Love.™

Have you told someone you loved them today? I have.™

Love yesterday, today and future tomorrows,™
Torion

Message in the MUSIC
James Fortune – I Need Your Glory

Note the QUOTE!
"If you have much, give of your wealth. If you have little, give of your heart." --- Arab Proverb

Love Always. Love Daily. 365 Love.

A Positive Difference
December 24

Today's NOTE

Each day is an opportunity for you to make **a positive difference**. And that **positive difference** is one of love. What **difference** did you make today?

- Who did you talk to? What did you say?
- Who did you smile at? What was the response?
- Who did you share a story with? What story did you share?
- Who did you say kind words to? What words were spoken?
- Who did you "give" to? What did you give?

Love is a choice. Love gives us the opportunity to make **a positive difference**. Love allows the impact of that difference to be one that further promotes love. Because, love is contagious, that **difference** spreads. The more it spreads, the more love takes over. And with love, life is so much more fulfilling. And with a fulfilled life, there is peace, joy and happiness. Wow! What **a difference** you could make. Choose love and make **a difference** that actually makes **a positive difference**. Love always. Love daily. 365 Love.™

Have you told someone you loved them today? I have.™

Love yesterday, today and future tomorrows,™
Torion

Message in the MUSIC
Boyz II Men – Do They Know

Note the QUOTE!
"People don't understand that not only can they make **a difference**, it's their responsibility to do so." --- Florence Robinson

Love Always. Love Daily. 365 Love.

Did You Know?
December 25

Today's NOTE

Did you know that love was born today? On this day, we celebrate the birth of the most magnificent love of all, Jesus Christ. And while we should glorify Him each day, it is on this day that we remember and give added glory for the gift of His love and our gift of love to Him.

Did you know that this child and every child are born to love? A child is a gift in itself. It is a gift of love. Of all the miracles imaginable, the gift of life should be towards the top of the list. To know that a child develops from within a woman's womb and to witness its birth; a birth that brings new life, renewed life, and new opportunities to love and for love. Love provided a star to guide the shepherds and the wise men. Love provides a plan to guide a child as well.

Did you know that a child changes things? A child changes your circumstances, your time, your views on life, your actions, your situation, your finances and then some. The incredible birth that took place on this day was for the purpose of change. This child was born from love, out of love, for love. Born for you and for me. What an incredible love. Change is good, especially when love is involved. Every child is meant to bring about change. Realize the love that is intended to evolve from the birth of every child in your life.

Know the reason for the season. Know the reason for the birth of a child. Know love. Love always. Love daily. 365 Love.™

Have you told someone you loved them today? I have.™

Love yesterday, today and future tomorrows,™
Torion

Message in the MUSIC
Helen Baylor – Mary **Did You Know**
(As performed by Trinity Entertainment Group's Black Nativity)

Note the QUOTE!
"God sends children to enlarge our hearts, and to make us unselfish and full of kindly sympathies and affections." --- Mary Howitt

Speak It Into Existence

December 26

Today's NOTE

I had the privilege of participating in my church Christmas play as Mary. At the time the part was assigned to me, I made the assumption that the role only had a few lines. Once I reviewed the script, I discovered that Mary was the leading role, participating in 6 of the 9 scenes of the play. This would be my first time acting ever in my life. Because I had already committed to doing the role, I accepted the responsibility. I took it as another part of my personal journey to grow in love. I told myself that I could do this. I told the play director that I could do this. I **spoke it into existence.**

We had four weeks to prepare for the play. During this four week time frame, there were a number of personal situations preventing me from being able to focus on learning my lines. My grandmother passed, there was tension among the family due to certain actions that had or had not taken place during this time frame, I got a speeding ticket, my son got a speeding ticket, I had to have an emergency root canal, and three of my close family members were in some type of legal trouble, all for totally different reasons. Boy was the negative energy pulling away at me. It was trying its best to pull me away from doing something good. It was testing my faith. It was trying to pull me backwards as I continue to move forward in love. I am proud to say that I never gave up. Each day, I would tell myself, "I am going to get it done. I can do this." At each rehearsal, I would tell the play director that I was going to do this and that she and the members of the drama ministry would not be disappointed. It took me up to the day before the play to learn all of my lines. Even up until that time, I would continue to talk to myself and encourage myself. I never once doubted myself, even though I was struggling focusing on my lines. Everyone in the drama ministry was very supportive and encouraging as well. Not once did anyone ever doubt that it would be done. Not once did anyone give an appearance that they doubted success. It was always totally positive reinforcement. I prayed for focus so that I could memorize my lines with the emotion, energy and feeling needed to share this specific love story. **I spoke it into existence** and I did it.

The 1st show went very well. I remembered all of my lines except one in which another actress added a part to her line to help me remember mine. I in turn was able to help out another actor who forgot one of his lines in a similar way. The audience could not tell the difference. I received several favorable comments from the audience. Some asked if I was a professional or inquired about how long I had been acting. They were amazed to know that this was my first time, ever. The 2nd show was even better. I received similar comments and questions from the audience. My family and friends were amazed at my acting ability. I felt super wonderful inside. The first reason was for my ability to get into the character and be used to tell the story of the birth of love (Jesus). The second reason was knowing that regardless of what was presented to me and the challenges I faced, I

Love Always. Love Daily. 365 Love.

never gave up. **I spoke it into existence** and was able to accomplish my goal. The third reason was just knowing that love was the driving force behind it all.

This example is a real life testimony to the power of love. Love did not allow me to give up. Love allowed me to continue thinking positive. Love heard my prayers and answered them. Love allowed me to accomplish my goal. My faith in love allowed me to **speak it into existence**. Love chose me and used me in this role to share love with others. Love magnified my love and the love of others. It did it for me. It can do it for you. Love always. Love daily. 365 Love.™

Have you told someone you loved them today? I have.™

Love yesterday, today and future tomorrows,™
Torion

Message in the MUSIC
Mary Mary – **Speak** to Me

Note the QUOTE!
"The only way to **speak** the truth is the **speak** lovingly." --- Henry David Thereau

---

Love Always. Love Daily. 365 Love.

Mirror of the Mind
December 27

Today's NOTE

The most common use of a mirror is to see a reflection. The reflection allows you to see what you look like. It is a replica of you. You can see your face and your overall physical appearance. It is you seen through your eyes as a reflection of you.

There is another mirror that goes beyond a physical reflection of oneself. It is the **mirror of the mind**. It is what you think and how you act. How you act is a reflection of your thoughts, your character, and your behaviors. When you think positive thoughts, those positive thoughts are reflected in your actions. They reflect on what you say, how you say it, what you do, and how you do it. They are a reflection from the **mirror of the mind**. It's what others see in your mirror. And if you are true to yourself and who you are, you see that reflection in your mirror as well. When you love, your actions are one of love. Your thoughts are one of love. And love becomes a reflection in the **mirror of the mind**. Your love is reflected so that other see it in your mirror as well.

Take a moment to really look at yourself in the mirror. Look at your physical appearance. Look at your reflection. Now close your eyes and visualize looking through the **mirror of the mind**. Think about your actions and your behaviors. Think about what those actions and behaviors reflect about you. Try to actually see yourself through those actions and behaviors. Don't just think about today. Think about yesterday, this past month, and this past year. Now open your eyes. What do you see? Is it the same person you saw when you looked at your physical reflection? Or is it a different person? Beauty is in the eye of the beholder. However, beauty is not only defined from the physical, it also comes from within. And love creates beauty within. When you love, it reflects on the **mirror of the mind**. Is love a part of your reflection? Whatever your response is, know that there is always room to grow in love. Love is always here. It is waiting on you to embrace it, grow in it and share it. Love brings positive change. It creates a reflection that allows you to see self-love, spiritual love, brotherly love, and romantic love. It allows you to see a new you. It becomes a positive reflection in the **mirror of the mind**. Love always. Love daily. 365 Love.™

Have you told someone you loved them today? I have.™

Love yesterday, today and future tomorrows,™
Torion

Message in the MUSIC
Monica – **Mirror**

Note the QUOTE!
"How we think shows through how we act. Attitudes are **mirrors of the mind**. They reflect thinking." --- David Joseph Schwartz

Love Always. Love Daily. 365 Love.

Still Standing
December 28

Today's NOTE

We can always be more, do more, be better and do better. Life is designed for us to learn. And it is through learning that we improve. For every step backwards, there is another opportunity to step forward. Never allow the bad things in your life to hold you down. Take them as lessons learned, fuel to the fire, or negative motivators that encourage you and give you a strong desire to move forward and move on. Nothing happens when you sit still. Something always happens when you move and start motion. You may have experienced what you feel no one else has ever gone through, or no one could ever understand. Well, I can almost guarantee that someone, somewhere has gone through something similar to what you have. The key thing to remember is that you are **still standing**.

There is something about standing. When you place your feet on the floor, you put strength in your legs, you lift yourself up, and you stand tall. You can see in front of you. You can look up. That in itself is powerful. You got up. You lifted yourself up. That's what love does. Love gives you the strength to stand. And once you stand, you keep going from there. You put one foot in front of the other, and you move. You are a step closer to change. You are a step closer to creating a new day for yourself. When things get down, know that love is always there to lift you up and help you stand. And each day that you wake, breathe and stand, remind yourself that regardless of what you have been through, regardless of what you are about to go through, you are **still standing**. And that strength, that positive force will guide you along your way. Know that love gives you the strength to stand. Love always. Love daily. 365 Love.™

Have you told someone you loved them today? I have.™

Love yesterday, today and future tomorrows,™
Torion

Message in the MUSIC
Monica – **Still Standing**

Note the QUOTE!
"It don't matter what you tried to do, you couldn't destroy me! I'm **still standing**! I'm still strong! And I always will be." --- Antwone Fisher

Music
December 29

Today's NOTE
Today I just wanted to listen to some good **music**. The sounds of R&B, Pop, Jazz, and Gospel. **Music** that relaxed me. **Music** that reminded me of love. **Music** that brought back good memories. **Music** that put a smile on my face and joy in my heart. **Music** that traveled and took me to another place. **Music** I could relate to. **Music** that told me a story. **Music** that made me laugh because I thought about someone or something. **Music** that made me reflect. **Music** that made me understand love and life. I wanted to hear some **music** that soothed my soul. **Music** that provided an explanation. **Music** that gave me an experience. **Music** that brought about positive change in me. **Music** that lifted my spirits and made me want to get up and dance, dance, dance. **Music** that allowed me to be creative and imaginative. **Music** that made me want to sing. Music that allowed me to hear every individual instrument playing their part of the song. Music that was slow, moderate and fast in tempo. **Music** that made me want to release some tension and be free. **Music** that reminded me how far I have come, where I am and where I am going. **Music** that gave me hope. **Music** that cared and shared. **Music** that taught a lesson. **Music** that showed personal growth. **Music** of forgiveness. **Music** of lessons learned. **Music** that confirmed my faith. **Music** that provided a testimony. **Music, music, music**.... I just wanted to hear some good **music**, because where there is **music**, there is love. I went to my computer, open my iTunes application, shuffled over 20,000 songs, and listened my **music**. I heard everything I wanted to hear and then some. I love **music** and **music** loves me. Love always. Love daily. 365 Love.™

Have you told someone you loved them today? I have.™

Love yesterday, today and future tomorrows,™
Torion

Message in the MUSIC
Leigh Jones – **Music** (In My Soul)

Note the QUOTE!
"**Music** is what feelings sound like." --- Unknown

Sunshine
December 30

Today's NOTE
Have you ever taken a moment to think about the **sunshine**? It is warm. It is bright. It provides light. It allows you the ability to see things in front of you and around you. It dries out the rain. It produces a rainbow following the rain. It provides nourishment for growth. It gives off energy.

That sounds so much like love. And things are looking so bright right about now. Can you see it? Can you feel it? Love brings out the **sunshine**. Things may be cloudy and may seem cold, but love is all around and I see nothing but **sunshine**. It's not only on the outside, it's on the inside as well. It's a personal characteristic that is seen by others when you love. It is a radiant glow that comes from love. It's a source of energy that generates from your love. I see the **sunshine** in your smile. I feel it in your actions. I hear it in your words. Through your love, I see your **sunshine**. That's simply amazing. That's love. Love always. Love daily. 365 Love.™

Have you told someone you loved them today? I have.™

Love yesterday, today and future tomorrows,™
Torion

Message in the MUSIC
Michelle Williams – Sun Will Shine Again

Note the QUOTE!
"Love, whether newly born, or aroused from a deathlike slumber, must always create **sunshine**, filling the heart so full of radiance, that it overflows upon the outward world." --- Nathaniel Hawthorne.

The Best is Yet to Come
December 31

Today's NOTE
This is the last day of the year, but it is the beginning of something so much more. It is a time to reflect on what is and what is not. It is a time to assess where you have been, where you are and where you are going. It is a time to put a plan in place to move that much closer to love. Never stop reaching. Never give up. There is always something more in store. And when you get there, reach for more. Always strive to be the best that you can be. Always strive to do your best. Love brings out the best. When that takes place, great things are in store for you. Leave the past behind. Reflect on it and move forward. Love was present in your life all day, every day, for 365 days. Love is here today and love will be waiting for you tomorrow. Tomorrow is a new day and so is every day after that. With that in mind, **the best is yet to come.**

LOVE ALWAYS. LOVE DAILY.

365 LOVE™

Have you told someone you loved them today? I have.™

Love yesterday, today and future tomorrows,™
Torion

Message in the MUSIC
Kelly Price – I Know Who Holds Tomorrow

Note the QUOTE!
"Love, in short, makes us better." --- Fiona

Love Always. Love Daily. 365 Love.

365lovedaily.com
365lovedaily.blogspot.com

Receive ongoing inspiration and motivation to support your personal growth in love.

Visit our website to learn more.
- Join our mailing list
- Purchase products
- Find upcoming events
- Explore related references
- Share your stories
- Access the blog for more Notes, Music and Quotes

Companion Products

Love Always. Love Daily. 365 Love.™ has several companion products to reinforce the promotion of personal growth in love. Help spread love as you travel along your personal journey. Remember, love is contagious and it brings about positive change.

Live love. Give love. Share love. Wear love.

365 LOVE

   Book   Gift Cards   T-Shirts

ORDER ONLINE NOW!

Find all 365 LOVE products at

www.365lovedaily.com